Is the Pope Catholic?

Is the Pope Catholic?

A Woman Confronts Her Church

Joanna Manning

MALCOLM LESTER BOOKS

Canadian Cataloguing in Publication Data

Manning, Joanna, 1943–
    Is the Pope Catholic?: a woman confronts her church

Includes bibliographical references and index.
ISBN 1-894121-20-1

1. Feminism—Religious aspects—Catholic Church. 2. Sexism in religion. 3. Women in the Catholic Church. I. Title.

BX2347.8.W6M36 1999   282'.082   C99-930399-6

Quotations from the Bible are taken from the *Good News Bible: Today's English Version* © 1992 American Bible Society. Imprimatur: Canadian Conference of Catholic Bishops, 1994.

Editor: Meg Taylor
Text Design: Laura Brady
Cover Design: Jessica Reid

Malcolm Lester Books
25 Isabella Street, Toronto, Ontario M4Y 1M7

Printed and bound in Canada
99 00 01   5 4 3 2

A prayer for Pentecost Sunday, 1992

Come Holy Spirit
wine that gladdens, oil that glistens
and love
blazing into fire
ecstatic wisdom
playful
windswept
lover

come

Contents

Acknowledgments

This book is dedicated first and foremost to my two sons, Nicholas and Andrew. They have struggled with and supported their feminist mother through all of our sometimes turbulent years together, and grown into young men of whom I am deeply proud.

Ched Myers, who wrote the Foreword to this book, has been a constant source of encouragement and support. Author of several books, including *Binding the Strong Man: A Political Reading of Mark's Story of Jesus*, and an activist for peace and justice, Ched has inspired me to stay committed to the writing of this book and to a belief in the possibility of living the Good News in the contemporary world.

I owe a debt of gratitude to Joe Abbey-Colborne, Karen Shepherd, Rory Crath, Steve Martin, Greg Paul, Margaret Rao, and Carole Thompson at Sanctuary and the Centre for Justice, Peace and Creation, who have provided me with a safe place to work, talk, pray, and weep over the past three years, as well as given me continuing hope and energy to live out a new but also very ancient model of a Church of the Poor on the streets of downtown Toronto.

I thank the small community, past and present, at Anne Frank House, where I live, especially Hernan Astudillo, Rene Cea Avalos, Vera Bratuz, Andre Liss, Aya Kiden Oryem, Assumpta Mureman Yundo, Domenic Raco, and Kabuiko Zobeto, who have sustained me with bread, wine, music, soup, and love.

Also, I would like to pay tribute to many wonderful and courageous colleagues in or associated with the Ontario English Catholic Teachers' Association, especially Paul Cavalluzzo, Mary-Eileen Donovan, Kathleen Gardiner, Marshall Jarvis, Steve Kirby, Tim Lee, Nick Nolan, Aleda O'Connor, Maria Pereira, Angela Piscitelli, Marilies Rettig, Claire Ross, Don Schmidt, and John Ware, as well as many others who have publicly and privately defended me. They continue, against all odds, to provide a zone of freedom within the contemporary Catholic Church where adults can talk seriously about issues of faith and life.

Special thanks to those who read and critiqued my original draft: Vera Bratuz, Rory Crath, Rosemary Ganley, Linda McGlade, and Carole Thompson.

And last but not least, to Daphne Hart of the Helen Heller Agency, who first believed that it was possible to publish this book, and to my editor, Meg Taylor, and publisher, Malcolm Lester, who shepherded it through to publication.

Foreword

There is an old Bible story about King Josiah of Judah, who is told of a "book of the law" that has been discovered in the temple. The king summons all his advisors to interpret the meaning of this book, but these luminaries turn immediately to Huldah, the prophet, and it is *she* who interprets the meaning of the lost book to the king. Her reading is a condemnation of the community's apostasy, yet promises renewal if the leadership has the courage and vision to repent. In this way the Josianic reform was launched, a major turning point in the history of Israel.

Joanna Manning is a modern Huldah figure. Her rereading of Church tradition offers both judgment and hope for reform. It is long past time for our clerical aristocracies to again turn to the wisdom, truth-telling, and passion of women prophets.

Developments during the past year demonstrate the timeliness and urgency of this book. At the end of June 1998, the Pope announced new Church laws to punish those who disagree with the Vatican's interpretation of definitive teachings, including the ban on women's ordination. In late July the Vatican ruled that one bishop's dissenting vote can prevent an action by a national bishops' conference *until reviewed by the Vatican*. And in late December, as I write this Foreword, Father Jim Callan of Corpus Christi parish in Rochester, New York, has been suspended from the priesthood due to pressure from the Vatican.

Jim Callan has been the sole priest in an inner-city parish for more than twenty years and has embodied the meaning of renewal. Having inherited a dying congregation, a huge, crumbling infrastructure and a financial disaster, he has presided over a remarkable renaissance. Today Corpus Christi has eight major ministries operated for—and in many cases by—ex-prisoners, the homeless, recovering addicts, children, and hospice patients. The parish is a hive of community activity, staffed by dozens of laypeople. Callan's title was Administrator, while church bulletins and letterhead state simply that the pastor of the church is Jesus Christ. Each of the five weekend Masses (including a Spanish *Misa* and a black gospel Mass) is attended by as many as a thousand parishioners; on Thursdays, there is also a Folk Mass at the church and a Workers Mass at a downtown office building. Parishioners include the mentally and physically disabled, gays and lesbians, and not a few Protestants. But perhaps most impressive—and most troubling to the Vatican—is the fact that co-presiding at the altar, in full vestment, is Corpus Christi's associate pastor, Mary Ramerman, a laywoman. Mary and six of the lay staff were fired by Bishop Matthem Clark in November 1998.

I see Jim and Mary, along with their many collaborators at Corpus Christi, as exemplars of the contemporary struggle for the future of the Church. As an ecumenical theologian and activist committed to building a faith-based peace and justice movement, I travel around North America a great deal, conducting teaching missions with parishes, small groups, communities, and organizations. Nowhere have I been more deeply impressed by the spirit of the gospel reflected in real life than at Corpus Christi. So while as a Protestant I may find it hard to get overly excited about Vatican *pronuncimientos*, the news of Jim and Mary's silencing hits me hard. I am furious that the animators of such a true sign of ecclesial hope and compassion are being targeted by distant clerics in a desperate attempt to control the winds of the Spirit that are blowing through our churches. The losers in this punitive action are overwhelmingly the poor and women. And these groups, as Joanna Manning rightly argues in the final chapter of this book, represent the core constituency upon which the renewal of the Church depends.

The frustrating scenario of Corpus Christi, so regrettably familiar under the pontificate of John Paul II, contributes to the growing crisis facing the Roman Catholic Church. It is this crisis that is directly addressed in this book. I met Joanna in 1992 at a retreat I led for a Catholic mission agency in Toronto on the Columbus Quincentenary. She and I, though from very different backgrounds, immediately sensed that we were kindred spirits: sold on the gospel vision of justice, committed to discovering faith through solidarity with the poor, equally committed to laughing and dancing, and loyally critical of our respective Church traditions. We have crossed paths many times since then, always encouraging one another in our work. I have a keen sense of how much the writing of this book has (and will) cost her, both personally and professionally.

Joanna's fascinating spiritual pilgrimage (outlined in Chapter 1) makes it clear that she is a true daughter of the Roman Church. A true prophet loves her people enough to speak difficult and controversial truth, and Joanna's love for her tradition is manifested by the labor of this book. To be sure, it has an "edge"—what prophetic discourse doesn't? Joanna speaks frankly of a "delusional system," of the duplicity of a Church that would champion human rights in the world but not in its own institutional life.

The integrity of her polemic is anchored by three characteristics. First, these pages are grounded in serious theological reflection: Joanna has picked a philosophical fight with the Vatican, pleading for fidelity to what she argues are the true traditions of the Church. Second, her position is rooted in historical literacy: she contends that the active and committed laity of the Church have always managed, over time, to prevail over clerical error. Third, her writing is authenticated by genuine experience and praxis.

What drives Joanna Manning is the suffering and indignity of real women and other marginalized people and groups, many of whose stories have been woven into the tapestry of this book. Joanna embodies the Church she dreams of: she has opened her home and her life to the poor at Anne Frank House; she advocates for the vulnerable in society as well as within the Church, as demonstrated by her recent engagements with the Ontario provincial government; she listens as passionately as she teaches, whether it is to students or street people; and she always takes time out for prayer, or for a party.

For all these reasons, Joanna is a treasure of the Canadian Church. I pray especially that those whose stations are directly challenged by this book can find the grace to receive it as the gift it is. Moreover, it is my hope that this book will be read by men as well as women, by non-Catholics as well as Catholics, by contemplatives as well as activists. I believe that the only future open to any of our churches is one characterized by ecumenicism, lay leadership, and equality. This future is already being realized, however tentatively, all over the world among people of faith who work for peace and justice. Joanna, good prophet that she is, invites us to have "eyes to see" that future now. May we also have "ears to hear."

Ched Myers
January 1999

Introduction

In the summer of 1997, my day always began with an early morning walk, accompanied by our new puppy, around the Chinatown neighborhood in Toronto where I live. The little dog loved to run in the park, scampering between stately dancers who moved to the ancient rhythms of Tai Chi, the recording of temple bells putting me in a meditative mood. Our path home took us past a women's shelter, where a few of the women often sat outside on the steps. One day I watched as my puppy clambered up those steps to lick a bruised face, coaxing a smile from the woman's lips. My decision to write this book was sealed at that moment.

I believe that there is a direct link between the teachings of the Catholic Church on the nature and role of women and the continuing, and in some parts of the world, increasing violence against women. Furthermore, I believe that the papacy of John Paul II has harbored a concerted effort to use the authority of the papal office to keep women in a second-class position within the Church. In the last decades of the twentieth century, the Vatican has been desperately attempting to isolate the Catholic Church from the course of history.

If John Paul II had been some unknown reactionary scholar writing in the bowels of a university library, no one would have bothered much about his views on women. But we are referring to a world leader, a man who speaks in glowing terms of the revival of Christendom in the year 2000. This world leader has promoted sexism to the level of a cult in the Church. As a result, the Catholic Church remains today one of the few institutions in the world whose policies and procedures provide a sanction for the discrimination against and oppression of women. Even after John Paul II dies, it will be difficult for a successor to undo or circumvent his legacy of canonical obstacles to the ordination of women.

Although since 1989 my public comments on women and the Church have made me a controversial figure in the Canadian Catholic Church, by 1994 I thought I had achieved a *modus vivendi* with the state of the issue. Then, on the anniversary of the burning of Joan of Arc, May 30, 1994, the news broke that Pope John Paul II had come out with another definitive statement against the ordination of women to the priesthood.[1]

John Paul II stated that Jesus had not wanted women to be priests in his own day, and that Jesus had been so clear and insistent on this matter that, as Pope, he was now raising the level of the teaching that women could never represent God at the altar to a central tenet of the Catholic faith. John Paul insisted that he knew that the "mind of Christ" was eternally made up on this issue, and that it is beyond the power of the Catholic Church, and himself as the successor to St. Peter, the first pope to whom Christ bequeathed the keys of the kingdom of heaven, to ever open the door of seminaries and sacristies to women.

This papal edict was by no means the first time the Catholic Church has given a negative response to the question of women priests, but this particular statement, widely interpreted within the Catholic Church as invested with the aura of papal infallibility, dramatically increased the level and intensity of the debate. In 1998 it was placed within canon law as a teaching that cannot be denied or opposed, and one subject to the ultimate penalty of excommunication from the Catholic Church.[2]

Pope John Paul II stated in so many words that it is the eternal and abiding will of God, taught from the time of Christ onward, that there should never be women priests at the altars of Catholic churches. Patriarchy, or male dominance, is now as definitive of Catholicism as the seven sacraments or the Apostles' Creed—it has become an article of faith for Catholics.

No sooner had the 1994 edict on women priests been issued than the full force of Vatican diplomacy was deployed against the global advancement of women's rights at the UN Conference on Population and Development, held in Cairo in the fall of 1994, and later at the Conference on Women, held the following year in Beijing. This sudden resurgence in the Vatican's concern over the global advancement of women's rights was directly linked to the Pope's statement on women priests. This topic will be explored in Chapter 5.

I have never felt personally called to the priesthood, but I realized several years ago that what are often regarded as the "churchy" issues of women's ordination and the gender of God are deeply connected to the perpetuation of male dominance in every aspect of life: in politics, economics, and social structures as well as within churches and other religious institutions. The present backlash against the gains made by the women's movement, a backlash fueled by contemporary fundamentalist movements in Catholicism, Islam, and Judaism, is the desperate last gasp of a moribund patriarchal system in church and state.

The ferocity of John Paul II's 1994 pronouncement against women's ordination left me stunned; I even contemplated leaving the Catholic Church. How could I remain within an institution whose leaders had twisted the teachings of Jesus and betrayed the message of the gospel? How could they not see that their male-only version of God could be used to justify the oppression of women?

Soon after the 1994 edict, Mary Malone, a good friend and mentor in feminist theology, announced that she no longer saw a future for Christianity because she believed it to be intrinsically patriarchal. She made it public that she had decided to leave the Catholic Church in order to seek God. Mary had been for years the only Catholic feminist theologian in

English-speaking Canada. Her prolific writing, and her wit and wisdom, firmly rooted in scholarly knowledge of Church history, had been an inspiration for me and for many other Catholic women to stay in the feminist movement within the Church. Mary's departure left me feeling alone and isolated. Throughout 1995, I meditated on my own future in prayer and in deliberation with close friends.

Then in the summer of 1996, my sister Rosemary was diagnosed with intestinal cancer and rushed to hospital for emergency surgery. For a couple of weeks, her life hung in the balance. Until then, she had been a healthy and active woman. I talked to her on the phone almost every day, and she would tell me about her determination to stay alive to see her youngest son, Adrian, get married and settle down. Her brush with death and her resilient spirit sparked an urgency within my own search for direction, and I began to wonder what I would regret not having done in my life were I to suddenly face the prospect of a terminal illness.

My spiritual life was formed from an early age by the Spiritual Exercises,[3] the legacy to the Church of St. Ignatius of Loyola, the founder of the Jesuit order. In the sixteenth century, Ignatius began to guide lay people through what later became a classic way of following the gospel, one that combines mysticism and action. Through a thirty-day or thirty-week discipline of contemplative prayer, structured around four "weeks," each with a different theme, the seeker comes closer to Jesus Christ through a cycle of imaginative and deeply affective meditations.

As a teenager in a convent boarding school, I had made annual retreats under the guidance of Jesuit priests. After I entered the Society of the Holy Child Jesus as a nun, I found that the structure of the religious life we followed was based on the Jesuit Rule of Life. In the 1980s when I was in my early forties, I returned to the Spiritual Exercises of St. Ignatius, and this marked a major turning point in my life. It was then that I encountered Sister Charmaine Grilliot, a former Superior General of the Precious Blood sisters of Ohio and a gifted spiritual guide. Light-years ahead of me in her thinking, she helped me focus the psychological, emotional, and spiritual upheavals of the transition to middle age into a powerful life force which I have drawn on ever since. It is this experience which, despite years of struggle between feminist convictions on the one hand and an intransigent Church on the other, has kept me clinging to the core of the Christian message.

One of the meditations in the cycle of prayer that forms the first week of the Spiritual Exercises is an introduction to "discernment," or making choices. This involves imagining oneself on one's deathbed and understanding how this final passage from life to death will involve a surrender of all one's life choices into the hands of God. Death will place the final seal on all the small choices made over the span of a lifetime. This particular meditation involves imagining how you would consider a particular choice you are wrestling with now as viewed at the moment of your imminent death. You ask your dying self a series of questions: Do I have any regrets about my life? Are there things I could have done but put off? How does this particular decision I have to make look from the vantage point of death? This is not mere speculation, but a profound moment of prayer which focuses the mind in a searingly honest way around the real issues.

When I thought about the suddenness of my sister's unforeseen illness in that summer of 1996, this meditation came to mind. I realized that were I to face death at this moment in my own life, the one thing I would really regret would be not having written a book, more specifically, a book that would express my thoughts about women and the Catholic Church.

My sister died in October 1998. A few weeks before her death, I visited her and took a copy of the final draft of this book. She read it, and gave it her blessing.

John Paul II and those Catholics who follow and uphold his views on women, curtailing the women's movement within and outside the Church, have risked leading the whole Church into error. In fact, as I will discuss in this book, the Pope's pronouncements on women have placed some of the Church's central teachings on creation, redemption, and resurrection in jeopardy.

Is the current Vatican teaching on women's ordination heretical according to traditional Catholic theology? I believe it is. Why? Because the male leaders of the Catholic Church now publicly preach and promote a novel twist in the Catholic interpretation of both Scripture and tradition by defining God as intrinsically male. On that basis, the patriarchal structure of the Church is justified as the eternal will of God. I believe that John Paul's recent declarations against women's ordination amounts to a denial that the history of the Church and the world is evolving under the guiding influence of the Spirit of God. That is why the central question raised by the title of this book, *Is the Pope Catholic?* is one that should be considered with the utmost seriousness.

From the ban on women at the altar to the interventions of the Vatican at the UN conferences on population at Cairo and on women at Beijing, John Paul and his supporters have attempted to halt the progress of women toward full equality, both personal and political. They have done so by attempting to constrict the vast range of evolving relationships between women and men, women and the Church, and between women and God within the confines of an outdated, dualistic, and discredited approach to anthropology and theology. This has bitterly divided the Catholic Church and undermined its ability to witness to the gospel in the contemporary world.

As a teacher of some thirty years, the last fourteen in Catholic schools in the province of Ontario, I have also experienced firsthand how the long arm of Vatican policies on women can reach right into the classroom, snuffing out little sparks of enlightenment that would awaken the girls to their own strength. Sexual harassment in and out of the classroom, dating violence on and off campus, the lingering patriarchal attitudes of teachers and administrators—all of these obstacles to the equality of young girls can be magnified in Catholic schools by the teaching that the inequality of men and women in the Church reflects the eternal will of God.

This book tells a story. It is a story that is both personal and political. It is a story that has to be told right now, on the cusp of the new millennium. The choice to write this book is one that, come what may, I will confidently place in the hands of my God when I die. I have written this book in the name of global sisterhood, and in the hope of a more peaceful and loving world for all of our children. All the way from the steps of the women's shelter in Toronto to the ripples extending around the globe from the conferences at Cairo and Beijing, I am ready to cast my bread upon the waters of world history.

Chapter One

A Spiritual Journey

"Joanna, why do you even bother about the Vatican? Don't you know that nobody takes it seriously any more?" I'm often asked these questions when I introduce myself as a Catholic feminist.

The Catholic Church, through its patriarchal and hierarchical structures, has created relationships of dependency and passivity that are in fact dangerous to the well-being of women and children. And while the struggle for women's equality extends far beyond the confines of the Church, the tentacles of this particular institution reach into women's lives around the globe. That is why I still "bother about" the Catholic Church's teachings on women.

This book incorporates insights from feminism, from history, and from theology. One of the great contributions made by feminist theory in this century has been to break down the artificial barriers dividing the personal from the political spheres of activity, the rational from the emotional in the human psyche, and academic discourse from human experience. This book seeks to meld theory and practice, scholarship and experience, and to draw on stories from my own life as well as what I have learned from other women to demonstrate the personal and political impact of the Church's teaching. It is neither purely anecdotal nor purely analytical but, like life, falls into that gray area which is a mixture of both.

The narrative will unfold as a series of positive and negative answers to the question of why I remain actively involved in the contemporary struggle over the role of women within the Catholic Church. I know from the study of history that all institutional change is the product of events and energies which come both from within and from outside the particular institution in question. At certain moments in time a collective synergy forms, fueled by movements from outside and aided by a critical mass working for change from within. It is at the juncture of these two that major change takes place. The fall of the Berlin Wall in 1989 is a recent case in point. While many dissidents left the Soviet Bloc and lived in exile to fight for change from outside the system, many stayed and suffered imprisonment, even death, to struggle for change from within. The two forces converged at a certain moment in history, breaking down what had seemed to be a permanent wall between political enemies.

Catholics such as myself have chosen to remain "behind the wall" of patriarchal control in the Church in order to struggle for change from within. Catholics who leave the Church of their own choice as opposed to being exiled by excommunication are all too easily written off as malcontents and dismissed as lapsed Catholics by the powers that be within the Church. I have put my hand to this plough, and I intend to follow the furrow unless I too end up being tossed out of the fold.

On balance, though, there are more positive than negative reasons why I choose to stay within the Catholic Church. I am deeply rooted in a Catholicism shaped and colored by my earliest memories of childhood in postwar England. And it is through the mystical tradition of the Church that I have come to know Jesus Christ and to drink deeply of that liberating life poured out on the world through his death and resurrection. This new spirit of liberation has, paradoxically, also nourished the roots of feminism, which has flowered later in my life through prayer, study, and experience.

The intensity of contemplation and commitment forged through my spirituality and prayer life has led me deeper into the life of God, revealed anew in our own time in all the beauty and diversity of its feminine dimension. I feel as comfortable in prayer being held on the generous lap of the Mother of Life as I do carried on the broad shoulders of the Father of Life. I experience the Trinity as a profound and exuberant expression of teeming energy and immeasurable diversity. All of this rich understanding of God's revelation has been latent within the Catholic tradition and is only now coming to light. As Jesus said, "There are many more things I have to say to you, but they are too much for you to bear: the Spirit who is the Advocate will come and lead you into the fullness of truth."[1]

Although I was born Catholic, I was not raised as a cultural Catholic in the same way as, say, many an Italian or Polish believer. In fact, my British cultural background has sometimes come into conflict with my religious affiliation. My mother's ethnic origin was a combination of Welsh, Irish, and English, and my father, who became a Catholic after he married my mother, claimed that his ancestors had come over with the Viking raiding parties who settled in Northumberland in pre-medieval England. My personal commitment to social transformation has its origins within all of these influences.

THE FORMATIVE INFLUENCE OF THE SECOND WORLD WAR

Within this heritage of Viking, Druid, and Celt lie my earliest childhood memories of postwar Britain in the late forties and early fifties: triumphant in the glow of victory, but deprived of many material things. My parents, both of whom were born in 1899, had met halfway across the world in Singapore and married in 1930. My mother, Josephine, was an accomplished singer and pianist, as was her older sister, my aunt Ethel. Both had graduated from the Royal Academy of Music in London, my mother with the silver medal for performance. The two sisters then decided to seek their fortune in the British colony of Malaya. My father, Reginald, was already there, working with the General Electric Company (GEC) on setting up one of the first radio connections for the BBC World Service.

In the twilight of the British Empire, their life was a social whirl of exclusive clubs and cocktail parties. My older sisters, Barbara and Rosemary, and my brother, Anthony, were all born into a world of colonial privilege, which included live-in servants and nursemaids. This comfortable life was to be rudely shattered in the late thirties with the march of Japanese armies through Asia. My father, with great reluctance, decided that the time had come to take the family back to England, and he secured passage on one of the last boats out of Singapore.

The family arrived back to a Britain still reeling from the results of the Great Depression, which had hitherto hardly touched their existence. Soon Britain would be plunged into blackouts, a beleaguered island threatened by Nazi bombing and invasion from across the English Channel. I was born as what my mother called "a surprising afterthought" (both she and my father were then in their mid-forties), at the mid-point of the Second World War. I later learned that the circumstances of my actual birth were deeply marked by the wartime context.

It was June 1943, and my father was working in London on the last stages of the development of radar for use in the North Atlantic. He would commute for days at a time from the village of Tring in Hertfordshire, where the family was living. Because petrol rationing was then in effect, ambulances were not available to take women in labor to hospital at short notice, so my mother had been deposited in the hospital some days before her due date. I delayed my appearance, and she became restless and began to miss my sisters and brother, who were unable to get transportation to the hospital to visit her. Breaking hospital rules, my mother arranged with one of the nurses to take her home for the day.

In the early afternoon of that same day, she went into labor. The District Nurse was dispatched in her tiny Austin A40 to collect my mother. Because this was an unexpected call, she exceeded the limit of her petrol ration. Halfway up a hill, the small car ran out of gas and ground to a stop.

The nurse's frantic efforts to prevent it from rolling backward caused it to roll onto its side into a ditch instead. My mother, well advanced in her contractions, was forced to crawl out through a small sun roof. The nearest house turned out to be that of the Anglican vicar. My mother was heaved into a chair in the front parlor and offered sherry while the ambulance was summoned. Her valiant efforts to keep the proverbial stiff upper lip from turning into a grimace of pain became the stuff of family legend. She was rushed to the delivery room just as my mop of dark hair was beginning to crown.

Her chief concern was that my father should remain in ignorance about her act of rebellion. In my father's world, order, whether of class, conduct, or convention, reigned supreme. To break hospital rules for the sake of a spontaneous visit home would, to him, have been both unimaginable and inexcusable. Thanks to a conspiracy of silence among the hospital staff, he only learned the true story later. Thus did an act of female transgression mark my entry into this world.

In my first year of life, I fell victim to the epidemic of whooping cough that was sweeping through the infant population in England in early 1944. The availability of medicine had been curtailed by the war effort, and sophisticated drugs for prevention and treatment of civilian illnesses were not yet available. The doctor told my parents that there was only a fifty-fifty chance I would live. At that time, my mother had hired a housekeeper, Margaret Doheny, whom we called Mags for short. Mags was an Irish Catholic with a bottomless well of devotion to Our Lady of Lourdes. When the doctor's news was relayed to her, she told my sisters and brother that they were to gather each morning for nine days to say the rosary, completing a novena to Our Lady and to St. Bernadette for my recovery. On the ninth day, the final day of the novena, my symptoms cleared up and I smiled. The story of this spiritual intercession was also woven into my earliest recollections.

The deprivations of the early postwar period are also etched in my memory. I remember my mother counting out coupons from a ration book for the one bottle of precious orange juice that I was allowed. We shivered through the bitter winter of 1945–46, as Britain's capacity to produce energy was still depleted by the war effort. But I was also nurtured on scratchy recordings of Churchill's wartime speeches about what he called "the finest hour" of British history. I heard stories of Aunt Ethel's husband, Frank, who had enlisted as an RAF pilot when they returned from Singapore and had been killed in training at the beginning of the war. Ethel, left a widow with a small baby to care for, nevertheless drove an ambulance through the East End of London during the height of the blitz. These were my heroes. Their example, as well as the whole context of the British war effort, imbued me with the belief that even though an opponent might seem overwhelmingly powerful, resistance must always remain a possibility.

I grew up with an abiding hatred of tyranny and a determination to defend the rights of the downtrodden and persecuted. The national and individual stories of the Second World War also fostered in me a resolve to live by truth and integrity, and a conviction that some compromises are not worth living with. This fitted very well with my later study of medieval European history, British history in particular. I reveled in the story of the revolt by Queen Boudicca of the Iceni against the Romans, her proud defiance captured in a statue outside the Westminster House of Commons, where she rides a chariot with her great mane of hair flowing behind. Another favorite character was Wat Tyler, the Londoner who confronted King Richard II during the Peasants' Revolt at the head of the masses, chanting, "When Adam delved and Eve span, who was then the gentleman?"

These values were reinforced early on by numerous stories of Christian saints. Like many a Catholic child of my generation, I remember one of my earliest books being a colorfully illustrated *Lives of the Saints*. I spent hours entranced by the pictures and stories of the martyrs: men, women, and even children who had faced death rather than surrender to the Roman Empire. I especially loved the story of St. Lawrence the Deacon. Lawrence was the treasurer of the Church of Rome, and when he and nine other companions were brought before the Roman authorities, he alone was spared immediate execution. The Romans believed that the Church was fabulously wealthy, and they told Lawrence to go away and bring back the treasures of the Church. "Give me two or three days," he replied, "and I will bring them here for you." Sure enough, Lawrence returned. "Where is the treasure?" the authorities demanded. Lawrence led them to the entrance of the great hall and threw open the doors to the courtyard. Outside was assembled a crowd of poor, blind, and crippled humanity. "Behold the treasure of the Church," said Lawrence. He was taken away to be tortured and killed in the cruel torment of roasting on a gridiron.

In postwar England, the power to heat water was rationed and scarce, so our whole family had to take a bath in the same water. My mother would run the water very hot for the first person, usually me because I was the youngest. I would slowly squirm into the scalding water, steeling myself against the heat by imagining how I would rate if I was set alongside Lawrence on the gridiron.

When I later attended university to take a degree in history with a specialty in the medieval period, I discovered that the Church of Rome had buried Lawrence's treasury of the poor under great baubles of wealth and property. The Roman Church, from the fourth century onward, gradually absorbed the structures of the moribund Roman imperial system into its administration. A succession of popes, culminating in the thirteenth-century Innocent III, molded this secular system of imperial governance into an instrument of spiritual and political power. For me, this became and remained a source of mental and spiritual conflict, faced as I was with the disparity between ideals and reality. I was also to discover in the modern history courses that Hitler's anti-Semitic fascism—the same ideology that had taken the lives of my uncle and so many others during the Second World War—had found a welcome home in many Catholic hearts in those parts of Europe that were allied with or collaborated with Germany.

CONVENT LIFE BEFORE AND AFTER VATICAN II

I progressed from the *Lives of the Saints* to other aspects of Catholic tradition. The rigor and vitality of the best of the Catholic intellectual tradition has always attracted me. I loved the religion classes of my adolescence, which was spent in a convent boarding school in England. I was educated by the Sisters of the Holy Child at St. Leonard's–Mayfield School, which was located on two campuses, one on the cliffs above the sea at St. Leonard's, the other in a small village deep in the rolling hills of Sussex. Thanks to the stimulating company of nuns who had studied at Oxford University and who were determined to bring the girls in their care up to a level where we could aspire to do the same, our curiosity about contemporary movements both inside and outside the Catholic Church was encouraged rather than feared. Our senior religion classes left no stone unturned, and we had great class discussions about everything from sex to Socrates.

In my last year of school, I felt called to enter the Society of the Holy Child as a nun, and after a year as an au pair girl in Rome, returned to Mayfield to spend my novitiate in the same convent where I had been educated. My father was overjoyed because he had been told by the nuns at the school that I was regarded as a star candidate with a bright future ahead of me in the order. My mother was devastated because her childhood memories were colored by a convent education in a different era, an experience which had been narrow and restrictive. She wanted me to experience the world, fall in love, and start my own family.

The first year of my novitiate was spent in what was known as canonical silence. We used sign language to communicate and spoke only for forty-five minutes at the end of the day unless we were called to a conference with the mistress of novices. Our main pursuits were sewing, cleaning, and, in my case, helping in the laundry, where we washed, starched, and ironed clothes belonging to the community and the school.

This was a year that toughened me both spiritually and physically. I loathed the sewing but loved the silence, which enabled me to explore the mysticism that was beginning to draw my soul. In the second year, we embarked on a serious study of theology and Church history. This was in 1963, the momentous year that saw the opening of the Second Vatican Council in Rome. At the same time as we were reading the *Summa Theologica* of Aquinas in Latin, we were also devouring the latest books and commentaries pouring out of Rome and other theological centers. It seemed as though the Spirit had grasped the whole church and was shaking it out of the torpor of the ages.

There was one particular book, first published in 1960, that changed my whole theological orientation: *The Resurrection* by Father Francis Xavier Durwell. I still have it on my bookshelf. I found a nook on a windowsill in the novices' dormitory where I would hide myself away for hours and read and pray over it. Why was it so revolutionary? Because the Catholic spirituality and theology I had known until then focused on the passion and death of Jesus as the central events in his life, and thus the aspects to be emulated by his disciples. Obedience, discipline, endurance, humility, and suffering—these were the hallmarks of the religious life into which I had been initiated in my first year of novitiate. The resurrection was presented as an afterthought, a kind of icing on the cake which confirmed the value of Jesus' suffering but would not be enjoyed by anyone else until after death.

Durwell's book pulled the rug from underneath this spirituality. As the opening words of Chapter 1 stated:

> There is a widespread idea that the Resurrection is an epilogue; that the whole mystery took place on Calvary, and the drama was brought to its close at the ninth hour on Good Friday. Easter simply tells us of the fate of our hero after his great adventure... But Scripture sees the history of our redemption differently.[2]

Durwell was one of the first modern theologians to develop the New Testament teaching that the paschal mystery of Easter is the central fact of Christian life into which all Christians are baptized. The paschal mystery is the unbroken continuum of the life of Jesus seen as incarnation, death, resurrection, and the gift of the Spirit at Pentecost. "The paschal theme," wrote Durwell, "spreads over the whole gospel like a fine filigree." The Church would soon be described in the documents of Vatican II as the herald of the resurrection and the sign in the world of the paschal mystery. This followed the example of the earliest Christians, who celebrated the fact that Jesus is risen here and now, not in the hereafter, and lived not in anticipation of future joy, but as if God's joyful reign had already begun.

The reverberations of this controversial change toward a theology centered on Jesus' resurrection rather than a theology centered on his sacrificial death are still being felt in the Catholic Church, and will form the substance and tone of much of this book. The development of feminist theology and the movement for women's ordination to the priesthood reflect this change. If the resurrection is celebrated as *the* key event in the life of Jesus and of his followers, then the part played by women as the first heralds of the resurrection becomes central to the Church's history. If Christians are called to live as if Jesus is truly risen and as if God's reign is here and now, then all pre-resurrection constraints of gender, belonging as they do to the purely human existence of Christ, must be cast off. Joy, confidence, risk, imagination—the mighty wind of the Spirit released at Pentecost which whirled the believers away from the dark, fear-filled upper room and sent them out onto the streets of Jerusalem in a state of exaltation—become the hallmarks of the contemporary Church. Transgression of boundaries is the order of the day. Fear of the future, rigid adherence to the past, authoritarianism, and servility are not characteristics of a community for whom, as St. Paul wrote to the Galatians, "There is neither Jew nor Greek, male nor female, slave nor free: you are all one in Christ."

After my first, temporary vows as a nun, made in 1964 at the height of the ferment surrounding the Vatican Council, I was sent to take a degree in history at the University of London. Focusing on the medieval period, I discovered that the universities of Europe originated in the Church, and that theology was regarded for a long time as the queen of the humanities. I later embarked on my first degree in theology at my order's house of studies in Cavendish Square, London, and was one of the first women to take the same theological and scriptural courses as men studying for the priesthood. Week by week and day by day, the scholastics, as we were then known, eagerly awaited the latest news about the tumultuous debates and discussions that were taking place not only in St. Peter's, but in every bar and square in Rome. It is hard to convey the intensity of that new springtime in the ancient Church. As John XXIII put it, the "windows of the Vatican were being flung open" to let in the great wind of the Holy Spirit as the Church experienced again the promise of a "new Pentecost."

I remember the key debate at the very beginning of the Council, which set the tone for much of what followed. The Roman Curia, the inner circle of Church government, led by the redoubtable and conservative Cardinal Alfredo Ottaviani, had submitted their outline on the nature of the Church to the fathers of the Council for discussion. Largely a repetition of traditional theology, it described the Church as the Perfect Society, which was structured as a descending hierarchy. The Pope was the pinnacle of perfection and the laity, women in particular, were the farthest removed from godliness.

When the Council opened, the debate on the Church was the first item on the agenda. A fierce fight ensued over the order of the chapters in this first key document of the Council, *Lumen Gentium*,[3] which was to define the nature of the Church itself. The traditionalists, led by Ottaviani, insisted that the hierarchical and patriarchal nature of the Church was part of the very foundation of its essence and existence, and that the document must reflect this priority by placing the teaching on the hierarchical structure of the Church in the first chapter.

Although the odds were heavily stacked in favor of the Roman Curia at the outset of the Council, the Holy Spirit was working powerfully to shift the ground. In the end it was the progressive bishops from outside Rome who found a strong voice and directed the ordering of the chapters as follows: Chapter One, "The Church is a mystery"; Chapter Two, "The Church is the People of God"; and only in Chapter Three, "The Church is hierarchical." In other words, the mystery of the Church's existence as "People of God" takes precedence over its historical development into hierarchical and patriarchal structures.

Even those of us who welcomed this development did not realize at the time what a truly momentous change had taken place in the Catholic Church's understanding of itself and its mission. A whole new language about the Church as the "Pilgrim People of God" began to surface in the documents of the Council. This was a seismic shift, with repercussions at every level of Catholic life.

As a result of this and a whole wealth of theological and scriptural studies which were opened up to the Catholic world and beyond by other deliberations and documents of the Second Vatican Council, it became clear that wealth, princely pomp, and the stifling structures of male privilege, which had evolved within the structure of the Catholic Church, could evolve further or even be changed or set aside. The Vatican Council would describe the Church as *semper reformanda*[4]—always in need of change and internal renewal. It seemed at the time that the Holy Spirit was calling the Church to present a new face to the modern world.

The road of the future lay with the Pilgrim People of God, treading lightly upon the earth and reaching out to the contemporary world with a gesture of welcome rather than a frown of judgment. The Council challenged Catholics to return to their roots, to put aside the historical accretions of wealth and power that had obscured the gospel message over the centuries, and to return to the Church as it was in Rome at the time of my early hero, Lawrence the Martyr. I was elated.

One of the boundaries transgressed by the Council was the one that cut off the sacred from the secular and had hitherto formed an impenetrable barrier between religious and lay life. Not only was the lay state regarded as lower in the hierarchy of favor with God than the religious or priestly state, but interaction with laypeople was regarded as a danger to the vocation of nuns. Laypeople were pejoratively referred to as "seculars," and their presence regarded as a threat to the serenity and security of the cloister. Before the Council, even my own parents were restricted to visiting me only in the convent parlor, and always in the presence of a more senior nun.

I vividly remember an eight-day silent retreat I made in the summer of 1965 which blew a huge hole in these walls of restrictions. It took place at my old elementary school, high on the cliffs at St. Leonard's, and was given by a Jesuit who at the time was in charge of the Society's House of Studies in Dublin. He took us through an overview of the Spiritual Exercises of St. Ignatius, illumined by the theology of the Vatican Council and illustrated by extracts from modern writers such as James Joyce and Teilhard de Chardin, whose works had hitherto been banned from convent libraries. I read and prayed over Teilhard de Chardin's *Hymn of the Universe* in a state of exaltation:

Now Lord, through the consecration of the world, the luminosity and fragrance which suffuse the universe take on for me the lineaments of a body and a face—in you... If the fire has come down into the heart of the world it is, in the last resort, to lay hold on me and to absorb me. Henceforth I cannot be content simply to contemplate it or, by my steadfast faith, to intensify its ardency more and more in the world around me... so, my God, I prostrate myself before your presence in the universe which has now become a living flame; beneath all the lineaments of all that I shall encounter today, all that happens to me, all that I achieve it is you that I desire, you that I await... Lord Jesus, beneath those world-forces you have become truly and physically everything for me, everything about me, everything within me.[5]

What had heretofore been only an intellectual understanding of the unity of the People of God and the penetration of the whole universe by the fire of God's Spirit suddenly took passionate hold of my heart and soul.

The day the retreat ended, I joined a group of young scholastics for a walk on the cliffs. We had all been deeply moved by the retreat and were discussing our new insights. We noticed a young family walking toward us on the path. According to our training, we should have practiced what was called "custody of the eyes," which means that nuns avert their gaze from laypeople and their pursuits lest they be tempted to immodest thoughts or actions. We automatically shifted into this mode and were about to give them a wide berth. Our novitiate training had blinded us from recognizing what Teilhard called "the lineaments of the face and body of Christ" in them. I suddenly realized what was happening and said, "Stop, don't you realize that family over there is a part of the People of God! God is in them just as much as he is in us!" The unspoken thought in my mind was: "so stop thinking that they might pollute us."

The Second Vatican Council's great insight into the unity of the People of God and the equal call of all Christians, not just nuns and priests, to holiness, eventually led me out of the convent and back to the lay state in 1968. I had also fallen in love with Roger, a Jesuit scholastic whom I had met at the University of London.

My final summer in religious life plunged me into a dark night of unknowing. I remember praying before a huge crucifix on the grounds of the convent in Edgbaston, near Birmingham, where I was on an eight-day retreat. I stood there and said, "Give me a sign of some kind: should I leave or should I stay?" No word or sign was forthcoming, but all my instincts told me that I had to go. My religious superiors were heartbroken at the decision, made less than a year before I was due to take final vows. Once my dispensation came through from the Archbishop, I was told to pack my trunk in the dead of night so as not to alert the rest of the community to my defection.

The day I left the convent at Cavendish Square, I stopped to hear Mass at Westminster Cathedral. I was on my way to Victoria Station to catch a train to Eastbourne in Sussex where my parents had retired. I felt naked and raw before God—literally, because I had stepped out of my nun's habit into the era of mini-skirts and the hemline of my skirt had shot up from my ankle to above my knee, but more so spiritually, because of the enormity of the step I had just taken. The trunk that had accompanied me into the convent had been placed in the baggage compartment of the train. Left behind were the twelve pairs of black stockings, the eight pairs of bloomers and the four pairs of sturdy black shoes—all part of the "trousseau" that I had brought to my marriage with God. This time I was traveling lighter. On this journey, I was much less secure in my decision and far less certain about my future. My decision to leave deeply disappointed my father. My mother and the rest of my family received me back with open arms.

Looking now at my decision to leave the convent, I see that I was propelled back into the world by a growing but largely unarticulated conviction that holiness was not to be confined behind a carefully monitored monastic wall but lay rather in discerning the actions of the Spirit in the hurly-burly of everyday life. The theology of the Vatican Council and of writers such as Teilhard de Chardin was challenging the careful distinctions between what was religious and what was secular. The Council seemed to be saying that the future course and direction of the Pilgrim Church would be in the hands of the People of God as a whole rather than just the hierarchical elite. I can see now that my individual journey was running parallel to that of the Church in the 1960s, called out of the dogmatic certainty of the past to embark on a new path as the Pilgrim People of God.

The study of theology and history remained a lifelong passion, and my understanding of the shifts in theology over the course of time nurtured the feminist in me. In attempting to integrate the personal and the political, I have drawn on that combination of intellectual intensity, contemplative prayer, and a lived commitment to personal and global transformation forged in that unique period when my years of intense convent training coincided with the Second Vatican Council. As John XXIII lay dying in May 1963, he summed up the work of the Council in the following words:

> Today more than ever, certainly more than in previous centuries, we are called to serve humanity as such, and not merely Catholics; to defend above all and everywhere the rights of the human person, and not merely those of the Catholic Church. Today's world, the needs made plain in the last fifty years and a deeper understanding of doctrine have brought us to a new situation. It is not that the Gospel has changed: it is that we have begun to understand it better. Those who have lived as long as I have were faced with new tasks in the social order at the start of the century; those who like me, were twenty years in the East and eight in France, were enabled to

compare different cultures and traditions, and know that the moment has come to discern the signs of the times, to seize the opportunity and to look far ahead.[6]

This peaceful vision of a new springtime in the old Church barely survived the pontificate of John's successor, Paul VI. With the accession of John Paul II in 1978, John XXIII's outstretched arms of welcome would be reversed to a wagging finger of judgment, and the open smile of acceptance so characteristic of Angelo Roncalli was exchanged for Karol Woltywa's frown of severe displeasure. Like the late frost of a Canadian winter which can catch the first flowers of spring unawares, the reassertion of papal power in Rome and the clawback of hierarchical control by the Roman Curia came upon the Catholic world in the late 1980s to stunt the first shoots of the new springtime of Vatican II. But I believe that the Council's achievements live on in movements outside or on the fringes of the Church. As John XXIII foresaw, the Spirit of God released at this new Pentecost would fill the whole of creation, far beyond the boundaries of the Catholic Church.

THE SEMINARY AND MY GROWING FEMINISM

Two years after I left the convent, I married Roger, who had left the Society of Jesus. I began a career in teaching and then, following the births of our two children, Nicholas and Andrew, we immigrated to Canada in 1975. Once we had settled in Toronto, I took up the threads of my career as a history teacher with the Scarborough Board of Education and later as Head of Program at an alternative school.

One of the outcomes of Vatican II was the restoration of a permanent diaconate as an ordained ministry open to married as well as single men. Deacons, female as well as male, first appear in the Bible in the early chapters of the Acts of the Apostles and the letters of Paul. They were members of the community appointed to assist with the temporal needs of the People of God. The diaconate as a separate order in the Church later died out and became merely a temporary step on the way to ordination into the priesthood. The diaconate as a form of ordination in its own right was restored by Paul VI in the apostolic letter *Ad Pascendam* of August 15, 1972.

After a period of training and discernment (that is, seeking to know the movement of the Spirit of God in one's life), deacons are ordained to preach at Mass and assist with the conferring of other sacraments such as baptism. In Toronto, they are mandated to a ministry of the sick or the marginalized in settings such as hospitals or prisons. In 1982, Roger was accepted into the diaconate program at St. Augustine's seminary. His entry into this program was to open a new chapter in my relationship with God and with the Catholic Church. Up until then, the demands of full-time teaching and raising two small children in a new country had consumed all my energy. I had continued to pray and attended Mass regularly, but had not had the opportunity to continue my study of theology.

The wives of candidates for the diaconate were encouraged to partici-pate in all aspects of the program alongside their husbands. Couples spent one weekend every month in prayer and study at the seminary under the guidance of teachers from the Toronto School of Theology. Several of the theology professors were women, some of whom were working in the area of feminist theology and spirituality. I remember one weekend during that first year when the question of the ordination of women to the diaconate came up in one of the presentations. The possibility of being ordained as a priest had never occurred to me even in my wildest dreams, and the first time I heard it, I thought the idea was preposterous. The issue of women's ordination had not surfaced at Vatican II and, because I had been out of contact with theological circles for about ten years, I was not even aware of the fact that women had begun to write as well as to study theology.

But study, prayer, and experience were about to fuse once again to lead me to a new understanding of the mystery of God. Spiritual direction in prayer was offered as part of the training program, and I took this oppor-tunity to enter into much more intense prayer under the direction of Sister Charmaine Grilliot. Charmaine reintroduced me to the Spiritual Exercises of St. Ignatius. This form of spirituality had formed the basis of my prayer life in the convent, but there was now a renewed form, the Annotation 19, designed to foster habits of contemplation for laypeople in the midst of everyday life. Charmaine insisted that I should pay more attention to the movements of my heart and emotions in prayer. I was approaching my fortieth birthday, entering the period of upheaval and reassessment that seems to occur at that mid-stage of life.

One Sunday I sat alone in prayer in our room at the seminary. I was following the first week of the Exercises, a time when life decisions are reviewed and deep memories are stirred up by the Spirit of God, often for forgiveness and healing. Up until that time I had put off reviewing my decision to leave the religious life. With my heart and emotions finally released in prayer, I found myself turning in anger to God. "Why did you betray me? Why did you call me and then abandon me? How dare you!" I sensed myself falling into a deep, dark well. I was so terrified that I cried out. Suddenly, I was caught and held, and I felt God saying to me, "You know, there was a lot of self-seeking in your decision to enter the convent. You were secure and highly regarded and had a brilliant future ahead of you. When you left, you went not knowing whether it was the right decision, but all the time I was calling you to abandon yourself more completely to me." Far from falling out of favor, I discovered that I was held all the more closely by God.

I realized that throughout the fourteen years since I had left the religious life, I had judged my existence as a layperson to be second best. True, I had gained an intellectual understanding of what the Vatican Council meant by the Church as the Pilgrim People of God, but I had not assimilated this insight into my heart. Coming back into the seminary situation had forced me to see that my ego was still playing the old tapes of hierarchical states of perfection. Now I was beginning to understand at a soul level that nothing, not even the Church, can come between anyone and God. And God looks at us all with the eyes of love.

The Ignatian way of prayer had taught me to seek the will of God. I was discovering that complete abandonment to God means casting aside all preconceptions of who God is or what God asks. God's nature is greater than definitions and God's love exceeds all boundaries of creed or calling. God asks us only to turn and respond to love. In responding, we become aware of how we have failed to love—not by breaking rules, but by falling short of returning the unconditional love of God.

This new level of seeing was and is both a blessing and a curse. On the one hand, I loved the immersion in theology and prayer that the seminary provided, but that very immersion was leading me to question a Church whose structures reflect the message that God loves men more than women. If the Church were truly the Pilgrim People of God, why were some of the paths on this pilgrimage still fenced off from women? If women could be seminary professors, why couldn't they teach the word of God by preaching in Church? The fact that I knew more theology than any of the male candidates for the diaconate only increased my inner conflict.

There was one particular occasion when I received a rude awakening to another more subtle but more insidious source of tension. The professor of homiletics (preaching) had invited me to join the men in a dry run for a Sunday sermon. "You can show the men how to do it," he had said to me. We were divided into small groups and instructed to give feedback to each other on our performance. I prepared carefully, and when I came to deliver the sermon, I was relaxed. I moved to one side and rested one arm on the pulpit. As soon as I had finished, I could hear a buzz of reaction. I stepped down, and the men were all smiles. "Now we know why the Church won't allow women to preach," said one. "You were so sexy and inviting, we couldn't take our eyes off you." "You bet," said another, "I didn't take in a word of what you said."

I never preached again at the seminary after this incident. It was not the first or the last time in my life that I had been sized up for my sex appeal rather than for my brains, but the fact that this reaction was so universal from this particular group of men was an eye-opener. These were not men on a construction site whistling and leering or truckers driving by and shouting, "Come up here and get it, darlin'," but men I knew and respected. Their reaction made me feel as though what I had done at the pulpit was not only a sham but also shameful. It is not that they had set out to insult me, or even that they were conscious of how their words would affect me. The notion that rating a woman by her sex appeal is insulting would never have entered their heads.

This was the early eighties, when feminist analysis of the structures of sexism was just beginning to penetrate into workplaces and boardrooms, though it still remains beyond the threshold of seminaries even today. Like countless other contemporary women in all walks of life, I was getting a taste of the cost of trespassing on traditionally male turf.

I had experienced a somewhat similar situation the previous year at the Board of Education. In 1980, I had been appointed as Head of Program of a new alternative school, Alternative Scarborough Education Two. Although I was not technically a principal, I had similar status and responsibilities. There was only one other female high school principal in the Board at that time. I reported directly to the Superintendent of Program at the Board office.

As I set about the task of hiring the staff for the new school and was faced with the unfamiliar and somewhat daunting task of interviewing potential candidates, I asked the superintendent to request a more experienced colleague to assist me. He hurried out of his office right away to seek out the individual in question and came back with a smile on his face. "He's on his way," he told me, adding, "I only had to mention 'sex' and 'Joanna Manning' in the same sentence and he said he'd be right over." Suddenly a perfectly normal work situation had become supercharged with sexual innuendo. In the twinkle of an eye, with but a wink and a nod, I had changed from professional to playgirl. Since the time of that incident, structural sexism has been thoroughly exposed and challenged in the education system, and even in traditional male bastions such as the Canadian armed forces. A remark such as that made by my superintendent to me would most likely not be uttered today.

At the time, I did not have the tools of feminist analysis at hand to challenge sexist behavior or understand my own gut reactions to it. All I felt that Sunday in the seminary was that the whole exercise had been a waste of time, and that I was not prepared to subject myself to being a source of amusement. I took what appeared to be the only course available and removed myself. This event gave me an insight into the conflict that so many women experience in other contexts. Should we stay within the structure and tailor ourselves to fit the male mold in order to get to the top and then effect change from a position of power within the system, or should we withdraw in order to expose and fight the system from outside?

Shortly after these two incidents, I read a book that uses archetypes to analyze the different routes women take toward solving this dilemma. In an insightful study of Greek mythology interpreted through the lens of Jungian psychology, *Goddesses in Everywoman*, Jean Shinoda Bolen uses the profiles of the goddesses Artemis and Athena, among others, to describe different types of women. Some women are more like Artemis, who "represents qualities idealized by the women's movement—achievement and competence, independence from men and male opinions, and concern for victimized, powerless women and the young."[7] Artemis was a fearless huntress who defended the young children and animals in her care by turning the hunter Actaeon, who threatened the security of their forest sanctuary, into a stag who was then torn to pieces by his own hounds.

On the other hand, many bright and talented women succeed like Athena, the favorite daughter of Zeus, by staying within the boundaries placed on women by patriarchy and its structures. "Rather than separating," writes Bolen, "an Athena woman enjoys being in the midst of male action and power... knowing what the game is and scoring points... she naturally gravitates towards powerful men who have authority, responsibility and power." Their attitude, spoken or unspoken, is expressed in terms like "Well, look how I've succeeded, so what's wrong with you?" The Athena woman's dismissive attitude toward women who criticize the system that has conferred privileged access upon them as individuals often causes intense bitterness between Athena and Artemis types.

My prayer life, my first taste of feminist studies, and the inner conflict induced by my experiences in patriarchal settings were preparing me to take on an Artemis role. An occasion presented itself at the end of our seminary training and on the eve of Roger's ordination. The progressive positions adopted in the seminary toward allowing women full participation in the training program were beginning to be challenged by the more conservative winds blowing from Rome as John Paul's papacy got into its stride. There was a movement to return to the pre-Vatican II idea of a strict division between laity and clergy. As a cleric, a deacon is part of the hierarchy, not the general populace. Anything that compromises this distinction or blurs it must be eliminated.

The wives of deacons have two parts to play in the ceremony of ordination to the diaconate. They must signify their consent to their husbands' ordination by standing and answering yes when questioned to that effect by the bishop. It had also become a tradition in the Toronto Church for the deacon's wife to carry the stole, the symbol of her husband's diaconal office in the church, up to the altar. The wives would then assist the pastors in placing it over the deacon's right shoulder. This inclusion of the wives highlights a significant difference between a deacon and a priest. Both receive the sacrament of Holy Orders, but a deacon remains part of a couple and thus, in the eyes of the Church, the sacrament of marriage is an integral part of his ministry.

A few days before the ordination ceremony, the men went to the cathedral for a practice run. They came back with the news that they had been told by Monsignor Alan McCormack, Cardinal Carter's secretary, that one part of the ceremony was going to be changed: the stoles were now to remain on the altar and would be conferred by the priest alone. Wives were to remain in the pews. This was a small but significant step toward making it clear that the deacon was a cleric, part of the hierarchy of authority that comes down from God through the Pope, through bishop, then priest. Wives are out of this loop altogether.

"If you go along with this," I said, "then I will stand up and say no when the Cardinal asks for my consent to Roger's ordination." Hasty negotiations ensued and the proposal was withdrawn, but the authorities bided their time and introduced it without opposition the following year.

An Artemis kind of action like this creates a polarized response: people will either admire you or hate you, but it is hard for them to remain neutral. Former friends and allies may take fright and abandon you. Neither all of the men nor their wives were comfortable with my ultimatum to the Cardinal.

In following Jesus more closely in my mature prayer life, I have come to relate to the Artemis type in him. His biting exposures of the hypocrisy of the religious authorities of his day, his fierce defense of the poor and despised, his cleansing of the temple, his challenge to the disciples to leave family and familiar structures to set out on the uncharted road to the Kingdom of God all powerfully evoke the Artemis archetype within. As Jesus said, "I have come to set a fire on the earth, and how I wish it were already kindled! From now on, a family will be divided . . . fathers against sons, mothers against daughters. . ."[8]

THE ROCK OF NEWFOUNDLAND
DIVIDES THE CANADIAN CATHOLIC CHURCH

Those three years spent in the seminary diaconate training program renewed my interest in theology. In 1985, I transferred from the Scarborough Board of Education to the Toronto Catholic School Board and began to teach religion. Two years later, I enrolled in the Master of Theology program at Regis College and graduated with honors. The following year, I embarked on a doctorate in theology. The intensity of reading, writing, debating, and teaching the subject that I loved the most somehow gave me the energy to combine a new career and advanced university courses with family responsibilities. I also joined the part-time faculty at York University and began teaching summer courses in theology for teachers in the Catholic School Board. It was in this already turbulent context that the Spirit of God once more stirred the waters in my life, speaking through voices calling from the margins, far removed from any academic or political corridors of power.

In 1989, Shane Earle, a former resident of the orphanage run by the Christian Brothers at Mount Cashel just outside St. John's, Newfoundland, went public with a story of life behind the walls of that institution which would shatter the relative calm of the Catholic Church in Canada. This event had an impact on my personal journey in ways I could never have imagined. Other former residents of Mount Cashel, as well as men who had served as altar boys in several parishes in Newfoundland, came forward with similar stories, and the horrendous saga of sexual and physical abuse suffered by orphans placed in the care of the Brothers at Mount Cashel and boys serving in diocesan parishes spilled onto the front pages of Canadian newspapers.

In that fateful summer of 1989, I was teaching at York University, leading a seminar designed for teachers who were preparing to head religious education departments in Catholic high schools. I remember arriving each morning and sharing with these teaching colleagues the utter shock and dismay we all felt as each day's paper revealed not only fresh revelations of well-documented cases of abuse in Catholic parishes and institutions, but also the utter failure of those in authority in the Church to deal with the crisis. Worse still, as all of this was coming to light, no one from within the Catholic community seemed willing to voice any response other than one of denial.

As Catholic religious educators, we decided that we had a responsibility to raise our voices on behalf of the children in our community. The majority of us were parents of young children, and we could feel very keenly the vulnerability of those who had been subjected to abuse as well as imagine the horror of discovering that something similar could have happened to one of our own children. We decided to press for some measure of accountability and reform within the structures of the Catholic Church in order to ensure that nothing like this could ever happen again.

Our group of about thirty teachers proceeded to draft a letter to the Canadian bishops. We then decided to circulate it to laypeople in positions of leadership within the Toronto Church. Our plan was to present this letter as an agenda item for the Canadian Bishops' Conference, due to take place that October in Ottawa.

In August I went to Ottawa on a contract with the National Office of Religious Education to work on the high school curriculum for religious education. The seminar group encouraged me to use this opportunity to visit the National Office of Bishops, located in the same building, to request that our letter be placed on the agenda for the Bishops' Conference. I was informed in no uncertain terms by the Secretary of the Bishops' Conference that "no one ever gets to address the bishops in person." He added, "Your group should try to work through an organization that's already established. Why don't you try the Catholic Women's League?" His response struck me as yet another symptom of the inability of the Church's hierarchy to perceive the depths of this crisis, a crisis that was both a challenge and an opportunity for the Church.

After this rebuff, I called together a meeting of Catholic lay theologians, the teachers from the summer course, and other parish administrators and concerned Catholics who had heard about our initiative. As a result of the stonewalling from the National Office of Bishops, we decided to release our letter to the media immediately prior to the date of the Bishops' Conference. We hoped that at least the journalists who were allowed to attend part of the meeting would bring our concerns to the table.

One man initially sat in silence during that first meeting in Toronto. He had told us that he had come because his wife was going and he had nothing else to do. Suddenly he stood up and said, "I can't contain myself any longer. Yesterday I saw the movie *Romero*, about Archbishop Romero of El Salvador. As you're talking, I keep seeing the scene where Romero is thrown in jail and he hears the screams of his friends being tortured. He starts shouting, 'Stop the repression! Stop the repression!' Well, we're hearing the screams of the victims of sexual abuse, and we must stop this repression in the Church!" That man was John Macrae, a superintendent with the York Region Catholic Board of Education. He and I were appointed spokespersons for the newly created group that emerged from that meeting, the Coalition of Concerned Canadian Catholics (CCCC), an acronym deliberately chosen to parallel CCCB, the Canadian Conference of Catholic Bishops.

The morning after we released it to the press, our letter to the Canadian Bishops hit the front page of the *Globe and Mail*, Canada's national newspaper. At 6:30 that morning, John Macrae's phone rang. "This is CBC Radio in Halifax. Will you do a phone interview for our morning news program in fifteen minutes?" The news of our letter broke across the country in the course of that day. John and I followed its progress with a succession of radio and TV interviews which spanned the continent from Halifax, Nova Scotia, to Victoria, British Columbia.

By the end of that week, we had done interviews with everyone, from local cable TV in Toronto to CBC's "The National" with Barbara Frum. This media storm was a baptism of fire that I had neither anticipated nor imagined. With camera or microphone thrust in my face and fear of the wrath of Church authorities gnawing at my stomach, I felt petrified most of the time, but somehow managed to speak. I felt like the prophet Ezekiel, as though I had been yanked up by the hair and carried by the Spirit of God right into the eye of a raging storm.

My telephone started ringing off the hook. Catholics were calling, from St. John's to Vancouver. A deluge of rage, grief, and hope poured into my ears. I heard from hitherto silent victims of sexual abuse by Catholic clergy with accounts that made my hair stand on end and often caused me to weep. Their stories ranged from sexual fondling in sacristies to priests practicing sadomasochism on altar boys in parish basements. Nothing in my long and intimate personal experience of the Catholic Church had ever prepared me for anything as horrific as this. The volume of mail grew so great that the CCCC had to rent a mailbox. The media exposure, like a nine-day wonder, eventually died down, but in its wake a Canadian movement for reform within the Catholic Church was born.

In late 1989, stung into action by the public revulsion at the continuing revelations of sexual abuse, the Archdiocese of St. John's, Newfoundland, commissioned a public inquiry to be headed by the former lieutenant governor of Newfoundland, Gordon Winter. The Winter Commission report was published in St. John's in June 1990.[9] Catholics who had expected at least a denial of responsibility or even worse, a whitewash from the Catholic Church, were pleasantly surprised by the commission's report. Based on raw data from interviews and submissions from victims, their families, parishioners, religious congregations, and also analysis from experts in the field of child abuse, the two-volume report pulled no punches. It declared that the root cause of child abuse within the Church lay not only with the individual perpetrators, but was endemic within the structure of the Church itself.

According to the Winter Commission report, there are five ways in which patriarchy has corrupted the Catholic Church: first, by legitimizing the abuse of power by those in authority; second, through an authoritarian denominational education system which inculcates blind obedience and fear of the Church; third, through instilling a fear of sexuality in the young, which inhibits the development of healthy sexuality in the clergy and leads to an exaggerated fear of the feminine; fourth, through a diocesan structure which has no mechanisms for accountability and shuts out the majority of Catholics from decision making; and finally, through an internal corporate culture in the Catholic Church which focuses on self-preservation and the avoidance of public scandal at any cost, including the sacrifice of truth. In this way, the opportunity for far-reaching reform, which the Catholic Church had failed to implement after Vatican II, was once again placed before the Church in the voices of children and their families. Would the Canadian Catholic Church be open to recognizing this persistent call?

One immediate result of the publication of the Winter Commission's findings was the resignation of Archbishop Penney of St. John's. Some lawsuits and efforts at compensation by the victims followed. Since 1990, however, the Winter report has been quietly laid to rest by the hierarchy of the Canadian Church. Although it sold out within weeks of the first printing, it was never reprinted. Bishops have dealt piecemeal with the claims and lawsuits arising out of sexual abuse in local churches without taking a serious look at any of the five underlying factors identified in the Winter report. Issues of the abuse of power, celibacy, and the exclusion of women and laypeople from decision making have been swept under the carpet once again.

In the summer of 1990, I visited the provinces of Newfoundland and neighboring Nova Scotia. Earlier that same year, Roger and I had decided to separate. The breakdown in our marriage had begun several years earlier and my increasing public involvement exacerbated the division between us. There were times during the year that followed when I seemed to be swimming in an ocean of grief, the tears of my personal loss joining with the outpourings of the victims of sexual abuse and their families.

I had been invited to Newfoundland by a group of local Catholics who had joined the Coalition of Concerned Canadian Catholics. During the trip to Newfoundland and Nova Scotia, I found common ground with many lay Catholics. This trip also marked a step forward in my own thinking and commitment to the issue of women in the Catholic Church. That journey to Atlantic Canada exposed me directly to the devastation that the secrecy and denial around child sexual abuse was causing in the Church at large. Faithful Catholic laypeople, some of whom had served the Church for the best years of their lives, were sickened, angry, and desperate for some plain-speaking and truthful answers from their pastors.

I remember one particular morning when I sat on Signal Hill, which overlooks the harbor of St. John's. I watched the whales frolic in the bay below and felt the pulse of the Atlantic Ocean as the waves broke over the rocks beneath me. It came to me clearly, in the ebb and flow of history that I was caught up in, that there was another issue threatening to cause a similar crisis in the Church, and that was the denial to women of equality within the Church. The low status of women within the Catholic Church was continuing to fester beneath the surface of a paternalistic concern for women's well-being.

I realized that any work I did to raise public awareness about this issue would lead to my being labeled an enemy of the Church, with repercussions for my job and reputation. I thought of the thousands of women in other parts of the world who face torture, rape, death even, for speaking out, and decided that no matter what the consequences, I had to begin to speak the truth about women and the Catholic Church as I saw and experienced it.

LEAVING MY FATHER'S HOUSE

At the time of my visit to the Atlantic coast, I was serving as the Metro Separate School Board (MSSB) delegate on the Archdiocese of Toronto's High School Curriculum Committee for religious education. This committee had been formed as a result of pressure from the heads of religious education departments in the MSSB schools who had refused to accept a new, conservative set of curriculum guidelines.

The story of these curriculum guidelines had unfolded over the previous school year in a manner that had revealed another abusive aspect of Church governance, this time right in my own backyard. With a startling disregard for the professional process, Archbishop (now Cardinal) Aloysius Ambrozic of Toronto had simply set aside curriculum guidelines drawn up by a committee of department heads, and ordered a much more conservative set of guidelines, which had been written by a group of his cronies, to be secretly substituted for the original by administrators of the School Board.

When this sleight of hand was discovered and brought to the attention of the religion heads, I was one among several teachers who spearheaded resistance by forcing the issue into open discussion. Despite intimidation in the form of a visit from the Archbishop and threats from the Board to remove us from our jobs, we stood firm, relying on the due process of the School Board, which in 1989 had become a publicly funded and accountable institution in Ontario. The Archbishop's substitute guidelines were withdrawn and a new curriculum committee was formed with representation from both sides of this dispute. The following year my colleagues elected me chair of the MSSB's Religion Heads Subject Council. In this capacity I began to serve as one of two Board representatives on the Curriculum Committee. Archbishop Ambrozic was also a member. I was eventually selected by this Curriculum Committee to be the general editor of the new religious education guidelines.

In the spring of 1990, Archbishop Ambrozic was elevated by Pope John Paul II to the rank of Coadjutor Archbishop with right of succession to

Cardinal Carter of Toronto when the latter retired. In this capacity, Ambrozic gave several interviews to the Toronto media, which outlined the direction he would follow for Canada's largest metropolitan diocese. He made it very clear that he would make a point of cracking down on any elements of feminism in the Toronto Church. Girls must not be permitted to serve at the altar, he stated, because this might give them ideas of wanting to be a priest (a position since reversed by Rome: girls are now allowed to serve at the altar); the question of women's ordination was not even to be discussed; and inclusive language about God could never be permitted. God must be referred to only in male terms, because "otherwise," said Ambrozic, "we're going to end up with a hermaphrodite God."[10]

All these memories flashed through my mind that day on Signal Hill in St. John's, as I sat and reflected on the impact of my visit to Newfoundland. I decided that as a religious educator in a position of some prominence in the Toronto archdiocese, I had to voice my opposition to the Archbishop's position on the place of women in the Church and their relationship to God. Silence on my part would indicate acquiescence, especially since I was working directly with the Archbishop on the Curriculum Committee.

In the course of my brief visit to Newfoundland I had heard and felt first hand the devastating effects of the silence of Church authorities on the young victims of clerical sexual abuse. I knew that my position of leadership within the school system carried with it a responsibility to the female students in the Catholic classrooms of Ontario to take issue with the Archbishop about the effects his statements would have on young Catholic women. I decided that I must resign from the Curriculum Committee and make public my reasons for doing so.

On my return to school in the fall, several of my teaching colleagues tried to talk me out of resigning. They argued that if I took this step, a strong, progressive voice would be removed from the Curriculum Committee. Was I called to be an Athena and continue to work from within, or must I take the Artemis role in this issue to be effective? This dilemma plunged me into turmoil. My younger son, Andrew, was attending

St. Michael's Cathedral Choir School at the time, and I was the head reader at the same cathedral. As I attended the solemn High Mass celebrated by the Archbishop one September Sunday in the cathedral and listened to the choir sing Mozart's *Ave Verum*, tears poured down my face as I wrestled with the prospect of taking a step that could be seen as disloyal to a tradition I loved so dearly.

I realized that if I was to speak out for women within the Church, this would necessarily make adversaries of "the fathers." I would lose the approval of the Church's hierarchy and years of loyalty as a favored daughter of the Church would be called into question. Perhaps I could continue to work within the limits of my role in the Church and stop questioning or criticizing the structures. When I finally made the decision to resign, I felt that I at least owed "the fathers" the benefit of a personal explanation before it came out in public. I made arrangements to speak to the Archbishop, but he canceled our original interview and refused to reschedule.

When the news of my resignation and the letter I had written to the Archbishop reached the media, letters and phone calls of support poured in. One of the most moving was a card signed by the first-year education class at York University, saying, "You are an inspiration to young people. We need more teachers like you." I knew, however, that this step would mark the beginning of the end of my career in Catholic education. Shortly after my resignation from the Toronto Curriculum Committee, I applied for a one-semester leave of absence from teaching. As a co-founder of the CCCC, I had been invited to travel across western Canada to speak to various groups of progressive Catholics. These groups had sprung up around the desire for reform, particularly in reaction to reports of sexual abuse by clergy. Shortly before my departure, I happened to meet the Director of Education in the front hall of my school. "Would you like me to buy you a one-way ticket to Vancouver?" he asked, only half in jest.

Just as I was beginning to get more publicly involved in a struggle with the Church over women's issues, an incident occurred right in my own classroom that showed that the Vatican's teaching on the ordination of women has a direct impact on the lives of Catholic girls here in Toronto.

In 1990, I was teaching a course on World Religions to a class of grade 11 students. There were twenty-two boys and seven girls in the class. I had begun to notice considerable sexual innuendo from the four rows of boys who were seated behind Maria, a very attractive girl who sat in the front row of the class. As she came into class each day and took her seat, the boys would comment on the length of her skirt, or make remarks on what her parents had been doing together in bed the night before. They would suggest that "maybe she'd like to get a piece of the action." All of this was accompanied by leering and chortling by other boys. I could see that Maria was very uncomfortable, but she would simply smile and pretend that it didn't bother her.

I spoke to the individual perpetrators, but the harassment only increased and became more overt. One day, I heard one of the boys say, "Hey Maria, wouldn't you like to come over here and suck my cock!" At that point I announced to the whole class that we were going to drop the assigned topic for the day and deal with what was going on in our classroom. Although the school at that time had no policy on sexual harassment, I told them that from now on it would be subject to disciplinary action. This suggestion was greeted with incredulity and derision. "Come on, Miss," one of the boys said, "you know that the girls love it." The rest of the boys grinned and nodded in agreement. Another said, "I wish some of them would do it to me!" "Oh yeah!" yelled the male chorus. The girls were silent.

We then went on to discuss the topic of dating: who decides what, and how a couple negotiates their relationship. The majority of boys were convinced that they had the right to tell their date what to wear, whom to talk to, and that if she was not ready to have sex after he had taken her out and paid (which they assumed he would do), she was just a tease. I explained that judging girls based on their potential for sexual activity interferes with their right to study and concentrate in the classroom. I also told them that even if they disagreed with this, when they left school they would be in workplaces where any kind of sexual harassment was now against the law.

"But, Miss," said one of the boys, "you can't change thousands of years of attitudes by passing laws. And anyway, you know that God is a man, and Jesus was a man, and the Church will never ordain women, so you will *never* be equal." The boy who said this evidently thought he had played a trump card. Against all that society might do to advance the equality of women, the authority of the Catholic Church would always succeed in reinforcing male dominance. In the mind of this adolescent boy, the ordination issue clearly legitimized male dominance on a daily basis, even harassment within the classroom.

In a flash, I saw women in all the Catholic cultures of the world, from Canada to Chile, from Portugal to the Philippines, imprisoned by the Church's patriarchal principles and practices and often condemned to a life of subjection, including abuse and violence. I remembered reading about the callous attitude of Catholic priests in Croatia to the suffering of women who had been subjected to repeated rape during the civil war in Bosnia. In no way would the local clergy condone making contraception or abortion available to rape victims in the refugee camps under Catholic-dominated Croatian control. But neither were there any reports that they had offered to adopt the children or support the women, who were twice victimized, first by the war and then by Catholic policies.

The issues surrounding the nature of God and the ability of women to represent God are not abstract or academic for a vast number of Catholic women in the world today. These are not merely obscure theological debates for scholars to pronounce on in the calm of libraries and lecture halls. They are life-and-death issues for thousands of women. The final struggle for women's equality will only be won when the world's religions, through the transforming movement of the Spirit of God, recognize the equality of women.

In February 1992 I set out for western Canada full of hopes, dreams, and not a little dread of what or whom I might meet on the road from Winnipeg to Victoria. I spent three months on the road, traveling across the continent by Greyhound bus, a portable typewriter clutched in one hand and a suitcase in the other. All that I would experience within my soul and among the people I encountered served to confirm that I had put my hand to the plough and could not turn back.

I spent my first weekend at a women's retreat at St. Benedict's monastery just outside Winnipeg. Until 1990, St. Benedict's had been given the customary designation of a priory, lower in status than a full-fledged monastery. The Benedictine women decided that there was no reason why women's monastic communities should continue to accept a second-class station, so they raised it to the status of a monastery. This was an encouraging start for me, as was the theme of the weekend, which was that of "journey." We watched a video on Nelle Morton, a Presbyterian feminist theologian. "There is no road ahead," said Morton. "We make the road as we go."

All along "the road I was making," as word of my arrival spread to towns or cities ahead, the organizers of my trip encountered opposition from the local clergy. I was banned from Catholic Church premises in Winnipeg, Calgary, and Vancouver, and so we met in public libraries or in churches and halls belonging to other Christian denominations.

As I trundled across the Canadian Prairies on the Greyhound early morning milk run, I was engrossed in reading *Hope Within History*, a book written by the Scripture scholar Walter Brueggemann. This book fueled my prayers and gave me the energy for an often grueling schedule of public appearances and media interviews at each stop.

Brueggemann outlines three stages in the faith development of the people of Israel at the time of the Exodus,[11] the event that symbolized the basic experience of faith and deliverance for the People of God and also served as the paradigm for the ministry of Jesus. The first step toward faith and the liberation from slavery was their awakening to the destructive power of the rule of Egypt. They sensed a need to find the freedom to act apart from and against this power.

The second stage of Israelite faith development was the crossover from private complaints about individual problems to public speech. It is only through a public process that a common critique of the dominant and oppressive ideology can emerge. This involves individuals and groups breaking through relationships that have created a dependency and passivity, carefully cultivated by the dominant system. "As long as the people experienced the pain of slavery in their individual private isolation," writes Brueggemann, "no social power is generated, but where there is public meeting a risky, passionate power is generated ... this going public is an irreversible act of disobedience." It has the effect of breaking through the domestication of the people's anger, caused by their own inner assent to the imperial mythology. What a powerful model this offered for the initial steps of the women's movement and also for the revelations from victims of sexual abuse by clergy.

This dangerous second step is a necessary prelude to the third, which is the formation of a new community. "Juices are set free," writes Brueggemann,

> which enable those who have not hoped for a long time to hope, those who have not imagined for a long time to imagine ... The kind of mature faith that is generated through this process is never neutral: it is always passionately partisan ... God's transformation of the people is disjunctive, painful, hidden at first. Biblical literature focuses on the wrenching transitions and new disclosures of the power of the Spirit happen at these points of disjunction, not in situations of equilibrium.[12]

My own journey of faith up to that point had been a living example of the pattern described by Brueggemann, and this was replicated in my experience in the West. The dominance of the patriarchal power of the Catholic Church, mythologized and enforced through authoritarian structures, was being challenged by the cries from the victims of sexual abuse, and from women, excluded for too long from full participation at the table.

Shortly after I finished reading Brueggemann's book, my western pilgrimage took me to the farming community of Busby, north of Edmonton. My host had arranged for me to meet with a group of women who had been instrumental in bringing to light a whole cycle of sexual abuse of young boys perpetrated by the local priest. We sat around a large wooden table in the kitchen. One of the local farm owners started to describe what had happened to her son. "The priest was an alcoholic and used to get so pissed whenever he came to visit that someone always had to drive him home," she said. "One night about ten years ago, my teenage son took him back to the rectory. When he came home, he told me that while they were in the car, Father had tried to put his hand down my son's pants. This made me wonder what else might be going on there."

"We asked around, and gradually the truth came out," said one of the other women. "There were at least fifteen victims of sexual assault. One of the boys has now become an abuser himself, one is mentally ill, and one has died of a mysterious, unnamed disease." When the abuse came to light, the priest in question was taken to court, convicted, and fined. "When it all came out," she went on, "I stopped my son from going to camp with the priest. This priest used to give the boys cigarettes and make them drunk. The night before they were due to leave for camp, the priest came round and took my son out to the truck to talk to him. I went to get Rory and saw that Father had his arm around him and they were smoking. I nearly vomited. I made up an excuse to get him out of that truck. I told him he couldn't go with Father the next day. Later on when the priest phoned to talk to Rory, he told Rory he should come anyway and not take any notice of me." Rory's mother went to the police, and the priest was charged.

These women were horrified to hear that shortly after this, Emmett Carter, Cardinal of Toronto, had the same priest placed in a parish in Toronto without his history as an abuser being made known to the parishioners. They decided to go public with their story. "We took the decision to go to the *Edmonton Journal,*" said another woman, "because we were thinking of the children in Ontario and the danger they were in. The neighbors were furious about all the publicity because they believed that it showed the community in a bad light. The men didn't want to talk about it at all. We all had real problems at home with our husbands. They have no idea of the depth of feeling we have for our kids."

We broke and shared freshly baked bread, and we cried together. Brueggemann's description of Moses rising up, killing an Egyptian overseer, and exposing the slavery of the people of Israel in Egypt came into my mind. The courageous choice made by these women had led them into similar acts of disobedience against their Church and husbands, acts which had freed the children of Busby and saved other potential victims in Ontario. As a result of their action, the story had come to light in the Toronto media and the fury of the parishioners forced the Cardinal to move the offending cleric out of parish work, though not out of the priesthood.

These women paid a price in breaking out of their dependence on the dominant system within their community and in their homes. Their actions on behalf of their children brought about recriminations from perplexed husbands and neighbors. The struggle against patriarchy in the Church was advanced by their public and political action, but poignantly painful on a personal level. I was soon to discover parallels to this halfway across the world.

I returned to Toronto from western Canada in April. In July 1992, I went to Africa. I had been invited there by an African friend whom I had met at the Ontario Institute for Education, where he had studied for a doctorate in education. He had returned to Africa to take up a position as regional Director of Education in the northwest province of Cameroon. I spent two months in the village of Nkor, located in the remote and rugged mountains bordering on Nigeria.

Most of the time I just sat and talked with people or helped out in the health clinic. Every week I walked the eight kilometers to and from the nearest market, listening to conversations along the way. One of the first things I noticed in the health clinic in Nkor was a government poster about the risk of HIV and the need for safe sexual practices. But the illustration of how to put on a condom had been covered up with masking tape. When I remarked on this to the pharmacist, who was paid and trained by the government, she replied: "Yes, it's crazy, but this is a very Catholic village, and the government has to be careful not to offend the Catholic Church."

Soon after this incident, I was walking to market with a mixed group of men and women. One of the men started talking about the problems of finding clothes for his family of five. Another woman said that she did not know if any of her children would be able to finish school, because they had no money to pay for education beyond sixth grade. Margaret, who happened to be the president of the local Catholic Women's League, added, "You know how Africans love children, and we would never reject any of them. But we don't want to have so many. We want a better life for our children, but we can't even clothe and educate them. Yet we are desperate, because the Church tells us that we can only use the rhythm method. It doesn't work, but we don't know how to argue with the priests."

It struck me that so many women in Africa, like their sisters in the West, remain loyal to the ideal of the Church but reject Catholic Church teachings on women's lives. These African women knew that the fathers who make the laws of the Church were in grave error. Another woman joined in: "And do you know that now I'm afraid of losing my husband? I tell him we can't have sex on certain days, and now he is threatening to look for another woman. What can I do?"

These two conversations have haunted me ever since. I had spoken and written about the injustice, the lack of credibility, and the health risks which are the result of the Vatican's intransigent opposition to contraception. Never before had I heard such a direct statement of the pain of poor families, especially women, when faced with the autocracy of the Church. I knew then that my decision to defend women's rights within the Church, whatever the cost, had been the right one.

So now, when people ask me why I still bother about the Vatican, I tell them some of these stories. Though most Catholics in Europe and North America have long since ceased to pay attention to papal teachings on sex, the long finger of the Vatican reaches directly into the lives of the poor, especially poor women, in the most remote corners of the earth, limiting their access to better health, education, and mutual relationships. As a white Canadian woman, I do not have to face the struggle for survival, which is a daily reality for most women in two-thirds of the world. I have also enjoyed unique opportunities in my life to become theologically educated and literate in the language of the Church. I can read Latin, and I am in a position to "argue with the priests." But with this privilege comes the responsibility to struggle against injustice.

My African experience also opened me to a whole new way of looking at life and living as a human community. In Africa, the individual is never an island unto herself. What touches one person is a matter of concern to all. I was to see these values in action when I heard about Anthony. The women came one day and told me that they had found a sick man staying in the hut of a leper who lived outside the village. The man was very ill, but because it was the rainy season, no doctor or nurse could make the hazardous trip through the mountains for at least two months. They wondered if I had brought any medications with me from Canada. I picked up my small first-aid kit and a bottle of Aspirin and set off with them.

When we entered the hut, the first thing that hit me was the stench of rotting flesh. The injured man lay on the leper's pallet. His right foot had been severed almost in half. The bone was sticking through the flesh and pus had collected in a pool in the middle of his foot. I realized that because I was providing the only source of relief, I was expected to be both doctor and nurse. We gathered some large leaves to place under the man's foot. The sight and smell were overwhelming, but I prayed for the strength to be able to treat Anthony as if my hands were tending the wounded Jesus. While the rest of the women started to say the rosary, I poured the pus onto the leaves and began to try to bind the two halves of his foot together with my small bandage. "Oh, thank you, thank you," murmured Anthony.

He was not from the village, but had apparently been herding cattle in the nearby mountains when a cow had stepped on his foot and severed it. He had managed to drag himself down into the village, where the first person he encountered was Pa Dzinum, the leper. Pa, whose leg had been removed and whose fingers were eaten away with the disease, had taken this man in, given up his own bed, and fed and tended him as best he could. I marveled at the fact that here, the poorest of the poor can still find room to share the little they have with a fellow human being in need. Anthony spoke pidgin English, so he could understand what I said, but I found it hard to make out his responses.

Every day for the next two weeks, I would walk with a group of women to the hut to tend him. I managed to get some more bandages at the clinic so I could clean out the wound and change the dressing each day. Along the way to and from the hut, the women would often ask me about life in Canada. "Canada must be a wonderful and rich place," they said. I told them that life is good for most people, but the poor really suffer, and that last winter, poor people had frozen to death in bus shelters and on the street. This shocked them. "It would be a disgrace to our whole community," they said, "for someone to be left outside with nowhere to live. That would never happen here."

This response became like a mantra for me. "It would be a disgrace to the community... disgrace to the community." What if I could convince people in Toronto to adopt that way of thinking, to bring home the African vision of human solidarity, working through the Catholic school system to reach the streets of the city? With the resources and people available in our schools, we could change the face of our city! Ideas began to take shape in my head.

I had been invited to spend a few days in a neighboring village, so the day of my departure, I bade farewell to Anthony, who seemed in good spirits and less feverish. He said he would wait to see me when I returned. I said to him, "You know, Anthony, when you die you'll go straight to heaven even if you aren't baptized. When you're sitting up there at God's right hand and you see me coming before the throne of God carrying all my sins on my back, I want you to put in a word for me and tell God that this white woman wasn't all bad." He laughed and nodded. A week later I returned to find that Anthony had died that same morning. I was heartbroken. "We must bury him right away, before the rains come," the women said.

I offered to provide the coffin, so I ran over to the carpenter's hut and he set about making one. I also purchased a large vat of palm wine. Everyone in the village found something to bring, and a great procession made its way to the hut. The women picked flowers from the fields as we walked and wove them into garlands. When we arrived, we found that the men had dug a grave behind the hut and were rhythmically stomping the earth and singing a song. "Where is Anthony, where is our brother? He has gone to the father, he has gone to the mother." We said the rosary and other prayers and threw the garlands onto the grave. After praying at the grave, we gathered in a large hut where a group of women had materialized out of nowhere with musical instruments and everyone ate, drank, danced, and sang.

At one stage, some people stood up to make speeches. One was the unofficial leader of the women. I was so moved by what she said that I wrote it down as soon as I got back from the funeral. "The women of this area have learned a big lesson from you," she began. "You have shown us that women in Canada have concern and sympathy for people. We thought this was only true of African women. We have been observing you since you came here and seeing all you have done. Whatever we eat, you eat; whatever we drink, you drink; and you have participated indiscriminately. Most especially we want to thank you for the love you have shown our brother Anthony. Now we understand through your actions that no matter the color or religious group, we are all one."

THE COST OF COMMITMENT TO WOMEN'S EQUALITY

My experiences in western Canada and in Africa in the spring and summer of 1992 left me feeling a sense of deepening commitment to the global struggle of women and a conviction that I was being called to be a voice for the voiceless, especially for poor women. The reality of this commitment was soon to be put to the test. A week after I returned from Africa, I was summoned to the Metropolitan Toronto Separate School Board office and told that I was as of that day forbidden to teach religion or be involved in chaplaincy work in any Catholic school. I was henceforth restricted to teaching social science. The reason cited for this move was an article I had written which had been published in the *Toronto Star* in May 1992, "Vatican Plays Roulette with the Fate of the Earth." In this article, I had criticized the Vatican obstruction of the agenda at the United Nations Summit on the Environment in Rio de Janeiro, and in particular

Vatican attempts to remove any reference to contraception as a solution to overpopulation.

This was not the first article I had published. Ever since 1989, when the silence surrounding the scandals of sexual abuse by clergy in Newfoundland was broken by the Canadian media, I had begun to speak out on radio and TV, and to publish critical commentaries on the Church's reaction to sexual abuse by clergy. The widespread publicity which this attracted nationally in Canada served to highlight the need for reform in the Church, but also trained a spotlight of negative as well as positive attention onto me personally.

By 1992, I had been demonized by some members of conservative Catholic groups. These groups were enjoying a revival as a result of encouragement from John Paul II and his episcopal appointees. I had become a regular target of tirades in reactionary Canadian Catholic journals such as *Challenge* and *Catholic Insight*.[13] I had been denounced from the pulpit in several churches, including the parish beside the school where I was teaching. Deputations went to the Metro Separate School Board to demand that I be fired. The controversy was becoming too much for senior Board officials, and their ban on my teaching religion was regarded as a measure of appeasement which would cool the heat they were getting from right-wing spokespeople and from the Toronto Chancery Office.

It had the opposite effect. My union, the Ontario English Catholic Teachers' Association (OECTA), immediately launched a grievance under the recently won "Just Cause" clause in the Toronto Secondary Teachers collective agreement, which states that a teacher may not be fired or disciplined without a just cause having been established.[14] This began a long and bitterly contested suit against the Board. Students at my school were shocked at the Board's action, and they and their parents wrote letters in my defense. The chair of the parents' association went to bat for me in the media. Not a single complaint had ever been made about any of my classes, and I was one of the Board's most popular and well-respected religion teachers.

The grievance ended in a labor relations court hearing in 1993. In his opening statement to the court, OECTA's lawyer, Paul Cavalluzzo, stated that the reason I was there was that I had challenged the patriarchal power of the Catholic Church. In a precedent-setting action, which served to demonstrate the importance the Board attached to winning this case, the Director of Education himself took the stand to testify against me. When the judgment eventually came down in the summer of 1994, it was a complete vindication of my position. Chief Arbitrator Gerald Charney castigated the Board's surrender to what he called "political pressure" and ordered not only that I be restored to the religion classroom, but that I also be given the next religion headship for which I applied. In September 1994, I was back teaching religion for the Metropolitan Separate School Board.

Raising issues of justice in the Church and in society had led me to a deep soul-searching. I began to see that by speaking out as an advocate of women and victims of clerical sexual abuse, I was calling for the Catholic Church to adopt what the contemporary theology of liberation describes as "the preferential option for the poor." This was in turn calling me to conversion in my own life. Africa had intensified this call. I had better start looking at what was going on under my own roof if I was not to become, as St. Paul put it, "a clashing cymbal or a tinkling brass."[15]

I considered what I had learned from people in Africa and decided that the time had come to try to put their values of community living into practice. So in March 1993 I entered into an arrangement with a teaching colleague, Domenic Raco, to purchase a property in Kensington Market and open it for refugees and people on welfare in downtown Toronto. I and my two sons would also live in the house.

The previous summer, I had been invited to Germany to give a presentation at an international progressive Catholic meeting in Munich. I took the opportunity to make the short train trip to Amsterdam, to visit the Anne Frank House. I had brought back a poster of Anne Frank with one of her sayings on it in Dutch and English: "We must always hold on to our ideals because who knows when the time will come for us to put them into practice." We hung this up in the hallway of the Kensington Market house. "We have to have a name for this house," said my son Nick, the night we finished moving in. I looked up at the picture and said, "Well, I think we should call it Anne Frank House."

The figure of Anne Frank fused my earliest memories from wartime into the reason for my present direction in life. Anne Frank died in 1944, only a year after I was born. As an adolescent girl I had read her story. Anne's hiding place had been betrayed, but the Anne Frank House would offer a secure place of refuge for people in flight from civil war, violence, poverty, or any other type of persecution. Since the house opened, some forty-five people have lived here at different times. Nine people live under the same roof at any one time, from the displaced refugees of civil wars in Africa and Latin America to Canadian "refugees" seeking relief from abusive relationships, homophobia, homelessness, or poverty.

Many of the issues explored in this book have been aired around the kitchen table at Anne Frank House. Day-to-day living in a community that includes people of different race, gender, age, and sexual orientation has been profoundly challenging. Structures of gender and power have unraveled when men arriving from patriarchal societies are faced with a female head of household. Some men from more traditional societies have felt threatened by the change that takes place in their wives when the latter realize that Canadian law does not permit a husband to use force with his wife. One African man told me that when he had first married, his father had berated him for not beating his wife to keep her under control.

It is the African women who have continued to teach me about the meaning of community. Grace (not her real name) was a refugee who lived at Anne Frank House for two years. She had fled to Canada from the civil war in northern Uganda. Her family belonged to the minority tribal group which was being persecuted by the government. One day, soldiers came to her house in search of her husband. He was out. They caught Grace and raped her in front of her three small children, then took her away with them, leaving her children behind. She was taken to an army barracks where she was kept against her will with other women who had been captured. There, she was forced to act as servant for the wives of the officers. Because of the trauma she had suffered, she became ill and was moved to the hospital.

At the hospital, she met a nurse from her village who offered to help her escape. The nurse managed to send word to Grace's father. Then she acquired an extra nurse's uniform for Grace, and the two women walked out of the barracks undetected when the evening shift changed. Grace's father had concealed his car in the bush, and as soon as the coast was clear, he drove her to Kampala and from there she found her way to Canada.

A woman of extraordinary inner strength and resilience, Grace was also skilled in mediating conflicts in Anne Frank House. Once, when a serious conflict over a couple's relationship had erupted and was affecting everyone else in the house, Grace suggested that we follow the customary way of settling disputes that she had learned in Uganda. Each of the parties chooses an advocate to help them present their position. One person from outside their immediate circle is chosen to preside. The whole community listens to both parties and their advocates and then discusses the issue until they have reached a resolution which is fair and satisfactory to both parties. The same community gathers one month later to see if the solution is working. Some of the Canadians in the house felt uncomfortable at the prospect of working out personal matters in this way, but by the time we had gone through the process together, they came to see the advantages of communal input and discernment as opposed to the rugged Western individualism which often leaves a couple bereft of support in their relationship.

The wisdom and resilience of another African woman, Assumpta, also left a deep impression on the house community. Assumpta was a Tutsi who had fled from Rwanda when the civil war broke out. She had been forced to leave her four children and her cousin behind. Day and night after she arrived here, Assumpta petitioned Canadian Immigration to grant emergency visas for her children. Andre, a young gay Jewish man, was living in the house at the time and working as an interpreter with the refugee court system. The civil war in Rwanda was closing in around the area where the children were staying, and day and night Andre and Assumpta called,

faxed, and agitated. They engaged Catherine Kerr, one of the best immigration lawyers in town, to work out the legal issues. Finally the word
came through. The children could come, but we had to find ten thousand
dollars immediately for their airfare. I was attending a Catholic teachers'
conference at the time, and I stood up that day to ask for help. Within half
an hour, I had seven thousand dollars pledged.

The story of Assumpta's escape and the children's imminent arrival
attracted the attention of the Toronto media, and the press and TV carried
several reports of their arrival. The next day I began to receive hate mail
and calls from white supremacists. One letter addressed to me arrived with
the words "VD Test Results" scrawled on the envelope in large red letters.
Inside was a newspaper photo of Assumpta and her youngest child which
had been ripped apart, together with some white supremacist literature and
a scrawled note to me: "Hey, Joanna, you asshole! Next time you want to
invite an uneducated skill-less piece of shit like this to our country, why
don't you pay for it all! Because we real Canadians are sick of being the
welfare office for the whole world! And just the fact that you name your
house after some silly Jewish fart who produced phony diaries shows
where your empty head is! Just go away, mad Manning, just go away!"

I didn't tell anyone else in the house about this at the time because I
was ashamed that my fellow Canadians could be so racist and hateful, but
I eventually took the letters to the police because I was concerned about
security as the address of the house was known to these extremists. This
was not the first time I had received threatening mail or calls. Whenever
I speak or write publicly about issues in the Church, there are angry
letters and phone calls telling me that I am doing the "work of the devil."
These threatening voices can sometimes catch me off guard and make me
fearful. But I keep coming back to the question: how can we begin to live
now as though God reigned? I think again of Nelle Morton, who said we
must "make the road as we go," often in the darkness of faith but always
fired by the light of love.

As a result of community living and communal discernment at Anne
Frank House, in 1996 I decided to take a leave of absence from teaching in

order to found the Centre for Justice, Peace, and Creation with a board drawn partly from the Anne Frank House community. This was a small step toward realizing the dream that had come to me in Africa of belonging to a Catholic school system that practiced as well as preached the preferential option for the poor.

The goal of the Centre is to give students and teachers within the Catholic educational community an opportunity to respond more directly to the needs of the poor and the call for justice. Through retreats conducted by means of walks on the streets of Toronto, visits to women's shelters or to drop-ins for homeless people, and through outreach projects such as a breakfast every Saturday for about 150 street people, we are attempting to "let the poor be our teachers." The response to this venture has been overwhelmingly positive and is one of my sources of hope for the future of the Church.

Despite my present orientation toward a Church of the poor on the streets of the city, away from direct involvement with the institutional Catholic Church, I could no longer postpone the writing of this book, which is deep and necessary "soul work" for me. Even though raising the issues of women and the Catholic Church carries the risk of further censure, there is a fire within me that no fear can quench. This is the Church that I love, and I will not let it go.

Some conservative Catholics have hailed Pope John Paul II as the saviour of the Church from the evils of change inflicted by the Second Vatican Council in the 1960s. I hazard a prediction that instead, future historians will view the pontificate of John Paul II as marking the beginning of the collapse of institutional Catholicism in its present form. Paradoxically, the dismantling of the Church of power may well proceed more quickly in reaction to the policies and practices John Paul II has put in place in his attempt to reverse the changes introduced by the Vatican Council.

This reassertion of papal power and the centralizing control of the Roman Curia have been challenged by three movements which grew directly out of the spirit of renewal unleashed by the Second Vatican Council: liberation, feminist, and creation-centered theology. The Pope and the Roman Curia have fought against these movements on the political as well as religious levels, as this book will demonstrate.

John Paul II's views on women have been a key factor in the general reversal of Vatican II within the Church. The Pope has defined the role of women in the world and in the Church through the restricted lens of his very personal view of God's "eternal destiny" for her. This perspective is at the root of John Paul II's opposition to women's ordination and is the key to understanding the Vatican's position on a multitude of contemporary women's issues.

The following two chapters of this book will present a critical analysis of John Paul II's views in the light of feminist understanding and historical experience. The fourth chapter will outline the effects of this Vatican teaching in Catholic schools. Chapter 5 takes a global perspective on the Vatican's attempt to place obstacles in the way of the realization of women's equality. In the final chapter, I will suggest ways of sustaining and carrying forward the struggle for women's equality in the Catholic Church.

Chapter Two

What Is a Woman's Worth?

W omen and women's issues have taken center stage in the second half of John Paul II's papacy. Indeed, feminism seems to have replaced communism as the archenemy of the Church. In 1988, ten years into his papacy, the Vatican published a document written by Pope John Paul II titled *Mulieris Dignitatem: The Dignity and Vocation of Women*.[1] Unlike John Paul II's later teaching denying the priesthood to women, this "meditation" on the place of women in society was not released to the world under the guise of an infallible document, which would have meant that it contained teaching that was to be held as an article of faith. It is, however, directly linked to the Pope's subsequent teaching on women and the priesthood. According to John Paul II, God designed a totally separate human nature for women, which renders them unfit for ordination. Priesthood is not part of the Creator's eternal and unchanging destiny for women, a destiny writ deep within their feminine nature. What, then, is the role and destiny of women in the eyes of the Catholic Church hierarchy?

A salient point which must be made about papal statements on women such as the 1988 teaching is a self-evident one, but one which bears repeating in this context. All of the Catholic Church teachings on women have been formed and delivered from the particularity of a male perspective. Because of the universality of clerical celibacy, this perspective is not even mitigated by the influence of life experience with a female partner.

In the Vatican scheme of creation, women are always treated as objects of commentary and concern, but never as subjects who can define their own destiny. That their destiny has even been defined at all is only by virtue of men's commentaries on their nature and role. Women's own experience and definition of themselves do not count. It is ironic that John Paul II, who has insisted in all his writings that women's nature is so different from men's (and that this is one of the reasons they cannot be priests), nevertheless finds the capacity within his male self to be an expert on women's lives and experience and the arbiter of their destiny.

There is no evidence that popes have ever consulted with women before writing voluminously about them. In recent years, the Vatican has wised up to the public relations problem of having men in priestly soutanes delivering its messages on women. At the Beijing Conference on Women in 1995, it was Harvard law professor Mary Ann Glendon who presented the Vatican's views. But in two thousand years of history, up to and including the last decade of the twentieth century, the Catholic Church has not consulted women in the preparation of its teaching. If women protest that the reality of their lives does not match the clerical pronouncements on their nature and destiny, then they, the women, must be at fault. It is thought that women who question the wisdom of the fathers do so only because they have been infected by the dangerous "secular" influence of feminism. John Paul II in particular has worked vigilantly to prevent any male authority figures in the Church from consulting women about any matter, even those which deal intimately with women's lives.

THE U.S. CATHOLIC CHURCH AND WOMEN

The checkered history of the U.S. bishops' aborted *Pastoral Letter on Women*[2] illustrates the depth of determination in the Vatican to keep the definition of the role of women in male hands, and also to negate the effects of what it has come to regard as the pernicious influence of the feminist movement in North America. In 1983, the U.S. bishops, in preparation to write their *Pastoral Letter on Women*, conferred widely with women's groups. As a result, the emphasis in the first draft, which appeared in 1988, reflected a shift from the Church's usual "women as they are seen by men" approach to an emphasis on women's concerns, such as sexism and patriarchy.

More than 75,000 women were consulted, and many of their opinions were quoted in the first draft. Sexism was named as "a pervasive sin that depersonalizes women." The bishops called for a speedy review of the prohibition on the admission of women to the diaconate, and for further discussion on the issue of women priests. They pledged to work to combat sexism in the Church, society, and family life. "All members of the Church," the bishops state, "are called to a profound interior renewal to reverse sexist and discriminatory attitudes," which have denied women opportunities, ignored or trivialized their contributions, and placed unequal burdens on them.

That same year, John Paul II produced his own treatise on women, *Mulieris Dignitatem: Dignity and Vocation of Women*. The U.S. bishops were instructed by the Vatican to write another draft and to bring the *Pastoral Letter* more in line with the Pope's thinking. By the time the second draft appeared in 1990, the voices of women had been expunged in favor of a heavy injection of the Pope's ideas. Then the Pope summoned the bishops to Rome for an "international consultation" on the *Pastoral Letter*. Bishops from around the world were invited to give their fraternal advice on this fractious problem of women. Needless to say, no women were invited.

In his opening remarks, Cardinal Sodano, the Vatican Secretary of State, told the bishops that "the Vatican can offer you important elements of judgment, so you can present the Catholic doctrine on the mission of women in a way that is understandable to modern society without, however, betraying the integrity and originality of the Christian message."3 One observer to this secret consultation stated that the meeting had been called because there was "general concern" at the Vatican that the U.S. bishops had been overly influenced by "radical feminism." The role of the bishops, Sodano told them, is to teach, not consult. They must form Catholic consciences that conform unquestioningly to Church teaching, most notably to the Pope's latest treatise on the role of women.

As a result of this Vatican "correction," sexism was accepted as the natural pattern of relations between men and women, sanctioned by the Church. This shift is reflected in the American bishops' third draft of the *Pastoral Letter*, which states: "To identify sexism as the principal evil at work in the distortion of relations between men and women would be to analyze the underlying problem too superficially." In a massive shift from naming sexism as a sin, the draft goes on to condemn the successful efforts of the women's movement to combat sexism in society by bringing in legislation on equal rights, equal pay, and equal access to jobs and benefits, not to mention reproductive choice, because these "owe more to the tradition of the Enlightenment than to Catholic tradition," especially as advanced by "radical feminism, which has brought in its wake a new ambivalence toward motherhood."

In a shocking blanket condemnation of equal rights for women, the third draft concludes that "the development of social legislation which offers the same benefits to women and to men actually deprives women of the special kind of provisions they need for maternity and family support. It is inadequate." This shallow judgment on decades of struggle waged by the women's movement would provide Catholic support for the backlash against feminism emerging from Christian fundamentalist movements such as the all-male Promise Keepers.

In December 1992, the Church of England voted in favor of the ordination of women. By the time a fourth draft of the U.S. *Pastoral Letter* was produced for approval at the American bishops' meeting in 1992, it contained an extensive restatement of Catholic arguments *against* the ordination of women. But by this time, the Vatican's fierce opposition to issues raised in the *Pastoral Letter* had so alienated Catholic women and so deeply divided the U.S. bishops and the international Church, which was keenly watching the outcome of this debate, that the American bishops voted the *Pastoral Letter* into oblivion.

As a high school teacher of some thirty years' experience, I find it bizarre that anyone could purport to teach in total ignorance of the receiving audience. Jesus' statement about the Pharisees, "the blind leading the blind," seems to fit the Vatican's pronouncements on women. The bishops at least had the sense to realize this when they chose not to publish the *Pastoral Letter*. When Jesus taught, he sat with and walked among women, men, children, and animals. He listened. He based his teaching on stories from people's lives. But in the vast silence of the chaste halls of the Vatican, amid the rustle of silk robes, nary a woman's voice or child's cry is heard.

It seems that very early in life, Karol Wojtyla, later Pope John Paul II, formed views on the nature and role of women which grew out of the context of his all-male family (his mother died when he was eight years old) and the seminary environment in 1940s Poland.[4] These views have remained uncritically accepted and intellectually unchallenged ever since. Yet John Paul II never acknowledged that his views on women might have been limited by the context of his personal history and ethnicity. The Vatican is wont to portray feminism as a cultural development that has arisen out of the narrow context of white, liberal, materialistic culture, yet Rome is unable to accept that any of its teachings on women have arisen out of the narrow confines of a white, conservative, seminary-bred male culture.

John Paul's narrow experience of women has been elevated to the level of a universal doctrine. The Vatican now proposes to teach not only women in the Catholic Church, but women in the world at large, concerning the nature and purpose of their station and role in life. A close scrutiny of these views on women reveals that they are based on discredited anthropological theories and distortions of traditional Church theology. It is these views, used in the 1980s to force the U.S. bishops into submission over their *Pastoral Letter on Women*, which have informed the Vatican's increasingly strident and public stand in the 1990s against the progress of women toward equality in the Church and in the world.

MALE AND FEMALE HUMAN NATURE

In his writings, especially in *Mulieris Dignitatem*, John Paul II proposes an anthropology of total difference in nature between men and women. "Equal but different" has been the rallying cry of the conservative backlash in the Catholic Church which has gathered momentum under the sponsorship of John Paul II. This has served as justification for denying women ordination within the Church, and furthermore, jeopardizes the safety and equality of women in the world at large.

This view of gender—of masculine and feminine identities being mutually exclusive and unchanging biological endowments which fundamentally and immutably set the role of men and women within the world and the Church for all time—does not stand up to the scrutiny of modern scientific research. In a study released in the July 1998 issue of the U.S. medical journal *Pediatrics*, a group of Canadian researchers found evidence, based on studies of male babies who had suffered trauma to the genitals, that a person's sexual identity is mutable and does not develop in some cases until after birth. "The outcome of our case," stated Dr. Kenneth Zucker, head of the child and adolescent gender identity clinic at the Clarke Institute of Psychiatry in Toronto, one of the four authors of the study, "at least with regards to gender identity, suggests that it is pliable after all."[5]

This study is only one recent example of a number of findings on gender that have resulted from studies in the fields of anthropology, psychology, biology, history, and sociology. Far from being fixed and immutable from conception onward, gender identity is in fact variable and diverse and arises over a long period of time as a result of the interplay of complex cultural and other forces which go to make up the environment of human development.

But in the view of John Paul II, men and women are polar opposites. Each gender possesses unique attributes to which the other half of the human species has only secondary or indirect access. So men can learn to nurture and be compassionate only by being raised by good women: men do not have this capacity within their human nature. Another fundamental difference is that women's attributes are always conditioned by biology, whereas men's are not. Men's attributes, such as the right to priesthood, power, and authority, are derived from their resemblance to God. Women cannot learn these particular attributes from men, because in God's eternal design, only men are formed in His image, and thus the exchange of human qualities is not a reciprocal one.

According to John Paul's *Mulieris Dignitatem*, women's destiny lies within the natural law of their biological construction, imprinted on every woman since the time of creation. These patterns have always existed as the natural law of God and remain untouched and unchanged by culture or other influences. This is the religious equivalent of Sigmund Freud's "Biology is destiny." It is in the fulfillment of this unique destiny that women are to "find their true equality with men." "The personal resources of femininity," writes the Pope, "are certainly no less than the resources of masculinity: they are merely different."[6] One cannot help gasping at the sheer intellectual duplicity of a man who tells women that they are equal to men, but in the same breath subverts this so-called equality by stating that women are still fundamentally different from men.

"Hence a woman as well as a man," he continues, "must understand her fulfillment as a person, her dignity and vocation, according to the richness of femininity which she receives on the day of creation and which she inherits as an expression of the 'image and likeness of God' which is specifically hers."[7] There is, however, very little detail in any of John Paul's teachings that defines how women are made in the image of God.

The Vatican has long preferred to think of women as having been made either in the image of Eve, the rebellious temptress, or in the image of Mary, the obedient daughter and perfect mother. In John Paul II's writings, the Virgin Mary rather than Jesus is constantly upheld as the true model and path of salvation for Christian women. In his view, virginity is the superior choice for women over marriage, and dedication to Christ as a nun is still considered to be the best choice for a woman.

The mythology centered on Eve and Mary in the Catholic tradition has resulted in a complex legacy of internalized misogyny and self-denigration for Catholic women. No woman can simultaneously live up to Mary's role of being a mother and remain sexually a virgin, so most women feel that by default they must fit the role of Eve the temptress. As an eleven-year-old girl preparing for confirmation, I listened to the priest caution us against "tempting" the boys into sin. This was not my experience of myself, but all through my adolescent years it shaped my perception of who I must be.

GOD CANNOT BE CALLED MOTHER

Despite a wealth of nurturing images from Scripture, images that figure increasingly in the lives of believers, the Catholic Church hierarchy is unable to accept the possibility that any maternal aspect, even that of Mary, Mother of God, could reflect the inner life of God. If motherhood is woman's supreme fulfillment and destiny, and women are made in the image of God, doesn't it also follow that motherhood has its source in God?

In Genesis it is clearly stated that both women and men are made in the image of God. This truth cannot be overtly denied, as it is writ large on the first page of the Bible. John Paul II, however, has gone to extraordinary lengths to reconcile Genesis with his teaching on the separate nature of women and men. In a section in *Mulieris Dignitatem* entitled "The Anthropomorphism of Biblical Language,"[9] John Paul II admits that "in the Bible we find comparisons that attribute to God 'masculine' and 'feminine' qualities... If," he continues, "there is a likeness between the Creator and creatures, it is understandable that the Bible would refer to God using expressions that attribute to *him* [emphasis mine] both 'masculine' and 'feminine' qualities." I draw attention to the use of the male pronoun in this passage because if there was ever a need for the use of nongendered language for God, it surely must be in this sentence.

These significant details from *Mulieris Dignitatem* reflect the determination to prove at all costs that God must be male, even at the risk of intellectual dishonesty. "The biblical language about 'generating,'" continues John Paul II, tying himself into more mental knots, "points directly to the mystery of the eternal 'generating' which belongs to the inner life of God." In fact, human reproduction involves the joining of a male sperm and a female egg. Does this mean that the inner life of God contains a feminine as well as a masculine principle? Apparently not. "This generating has neither feminine nor masculine qualities," writes John Paul. "It is by nature totally divine. It is spiritual in the most perfect way, since 'God is spirit' and possesses no property typical of the body, neither feminine nor masculine."[10]

So far, so good. It would seem that he had the same insight as the liberation theologian Gustavo Guttierez, who described God as "the synthesis of a sexed humanity."[11] In other words, God is beyond male or female but contains the fullness of both. But no, for John Paul II, "generation" is all about fatherhood. "Although it is possible to attribute human qualities to the eternal generation of the Word of God, and although the *divine fatherhood* [emphasis mine] does not possess 'masculine' characteristics in the physical sense," he writes in the next paragraph of *Mulieris Dignitatem*, "we must nevertheless seek in God the absolute model for all generation amongst human beings." What is this divine mode of generation, the one which is the absolute, unchanging, and supreme model for all human beings?

John Paul's train of thought continues with a quote from the Letter to the Ephesians: "I bow my knees before the Father, from whom every family in heaven and earth is named."[12] He concludes from this that "all generating in the created world is to be likened to this absolute and uncreated model. Thus every element of human generation which is proper to man and every element proper to woman, namely human 'fatherhood' and 'motherhood,' bears within it a likeness to or analogy with that *fatherhood* [emphasis mine] which in God is totally different, that is, spiritual and divine in essence: whereas in the human order, generation is proper to the 'unity of the two': both are 'parents,' the man and woman alike."[13] Thus, according to this logic, even motherhood in women is derivative of fatherhood, which contradicts John Paul's earlier assertion that motherhood is woman's unique and supreme attribute.

This description of parenting reflects little knowledge of the present state of academic discourse in biology, psychology, or theology. John Paul II's views might have been acceptable in the days when Aquinas, following Aristotle, taught that, as the Monty Python song puts it, "every sperm is sacred," and men were thought to generate human life by depositing miniature human beings in empty female wombs. For John Paul, as for Aquinas, generating still means ejaculation, and motherhood takes over from there. What this actually signifies is that women will always be one step removed from "the eternal and uncreated" method of generation, or fatherhood, which is the inner life of God. However exalted the Pope's language on motherhood may be, it is still secondary to the male role even in that aspect of the human project, parenting, for which women are, according to John Paul II, so uniquely endowed by God with natural abilities.

MARY AS THE MODEL FOR WOMEN

According to John Paul II, women's way of birthing new life into the world is purely human, whereas men's way of "generating" is divine. Even though the prophet Isaiah speaks of God "crying and panting in labor,"[14] the Vatican still views the actions of labor and giving birth as purely human, having no direct connection with any divine activity. Motherhood is modeled on the image of the human Mary, not derived from the divine nature of God. The model for mothering lies along an axis connecting Eve to Mary and missing God altogether. Men's power to "generate," on the other hand, runs along a God-Adam-Christ axis, one that follows a direct line from God to the human Adam and directly on to the Second Person of the Blessed Trinity.

John Paul II's exclusive use in *Mulieris Dignitatem* and throughout his later writings on women of the Eve-Mary model of womanhood effectively cuts women off from any direct line to God. One consuming fear about the influence of feminist theology which has gripped the Vatican in recent years is that it will succeed in establishing a direct line between feminine human nature and the divine nature of God. This preoccupation emerges even more clearly in John Paul II's teaching on women and the priesthood, which is examined in some detail in the next chapter.

In the person of Mary, God the Father found a perfectly passive and pure womb for "generating" Jesus. After the birth of Jesus, Mary is metaphorically relegated to hearth and home. In the teaching on the priesthood, as we shall see, there is not even speculation that Mary was present at the Last Supper. Her role on Calvary, at the resurrection, and at Pentecost is a private one, always secondary to the public role of the male apostles.

The exaltation of this domesticated Mary as a model for women devalues actual women in practice. To use Mary as a model of womanhood serves to emphasize the superiority of virginity. It also aligns the ideal of "true womanhood" with motherhood, but a motherhood derived, like Mary's, from an immaculate or at least asexual conception. This kind of symbolism also promotes obedience, passivity, and subordination as key religious values for good women, the very values that were thrown out of the window by the women who announced the resurrection of Jesus to the apostles.

In psychological analysis, the beautiful virgin and asexual, compassionate mother are often seen as projections of the masculine desire for the "eternal feminine," one which seems to hold a special fascination for the celibate mentality. It is not surprising that the papacy of John Paul II has fostered the cult of Mary. At the same time, John Paul II's conservative allies have encouraged a broad movement to restore traditional family structures, with men assuming headship following the model of Christ.

In this conservative framework, the masculine role in parenting is confined to a short moment of ejaculation. From then on, the mission of nurturing life is reserved for women. In order to fulfill this role, women must have a nest of protective custody in the home. In the privacy of this protective custody, women teach men how to be fathers. This sublime domestic vocation discourages women, except in cases of dire necessity, from any fruitful work in the public realm.

Within this framework of parenting, a domestic role for men barely exists. Men's public work, which carries along with it the right to authority and power in Church and society, is their way of showing the human face of the divine image. Men are free-ranging human beings. It is simply assumed that they are the norm for everything human outside the boundaries of hearth and home. Once they cross the threshold into the home, their competitive tendencies must be reined in by the calming touch of a woman.

This ideal of womanhood also portrays all women as alike, because all women participate, actively or passively, in the common maternal nature which collectively forms the universal definition of woman. As a result of this role, women's life choices are strictly limited. All women are destined to be mothers in one way or another, either spiritually or biologically. Men's roles and destinies are variable, taking on different patterns as men move freely to shape the external world. Men's lives are a matter of choice, whereas women's lives follow a biological design.

DIVISION OF ROLE, DIVISION OF WORK

The fact remains, though, that in this century women have crossed the threshold into public life and work and have entered the work force in unprecedented numbers. The Vatican ideal of the traditional family with its strict division of gender roles is an increasingly rare experience for the majority of women. But since the papal definition of women's destiny and vocation depends so directly on a home-based maternal role, the entry of women into the work force has presented John Paul II with a major challenge. The twentieth century has seen a flowering of social teaching in the Catholic Church, teaching which has provided support for workers' rights and compassionate social policies. The "worker" and the "union," though, have been viewed solely in male terms.

John Paul II wrote that women should work outside the home as the exception rather than the rule. When they enter the public domain, they must never forget that this is a deviation from their true role of motherhood. One of the first issues addressed in John Paul's pontificate was the rights of workers, in the encyclical *Laborem Exercens: Human Work*, in which women in the world of work are mentioned only in passing. Work outside the home and motherhood, the Pope states, are basically incompatible.[15] To quote from the fourth draft of the Vatican-amended and later aborted *Pastoral Letter on Women* (1992): "... having to abandon the tasks of motherhood in order to take up paid work outside the home is wrong from the point of view of the good of society and of the family when it contradicts or hinders the primary goals of the mission of the mother."[16] The two-thirds of North American women who work outside the home would have been amused by this pronouncement had it seen the light of day.

Men's work is their free choice; whether or not they are parents is irrelevant. Women, though, should work outside the home only as a last resort. It is a small step from this way of thinking to the assertion that a whole number of contingencies should be placed on women in the workplace, namely: women are only in the workplace on sufferance; the conditions of work should continue to reflect male ideals and norms; women should take what they are given and be content; because they are not the primary breadwinners, women should be the last hired and the first to be laid off; a woman boss is an aberration; and, if women experience sexual harassment at work, they are asking for it by trespassing onto male turf. As a person who has worked on issues of employment equity, I have been on the receiving end of every one of these arguments, thrown up as excuses for the barriers that still exist to women's advancement. The Catholic hierarchy's views on the nature and role of women serve to legitimize these excuses.

INTERNALIZED MISOGYNY AND EXTERNAL VIOLENCE

These Catholic teachings, perpetuated by John Paul II in what may appear to some as quaint and innocuous teachings on women, still have the power to create a negative environment for women within families and in society at large.

In the course of my 1992 journey across western Canada, I spent an evening with the women's studies class at Newman Theological College in Edmonton, Alberta. At the end of an evening of discussion and prayer, one woman who had remained silent throughout the proceedings suddenly spoke up. "When I was younger," she said, and her eyes filled with tears, "I always prayed to be old and ugly. My brother went into the seminary, and whenever my parents took me to visit him, he and his friends treated me as though I was the devil. They would keep telling me not to come near them, and they looked on me with angry faces as though I shouldn't be there at all."

This caricature of women as instruments of the devil, somehow responsible for the sins of men, as well as the exaltation of virginity as the path to holiness, reflect the celibate male's fear of women's sexual power and their attempts to keep it in check. This was recognized by the Second Vatican Council as a distortion of the teaching of Jesus. The Council reached back to the shared patterns of discipleship and ministry in the early Church and called for a renewal of the universal and equal call to holiness of all the People of God, whether married, single, ordained, or in a religious community.

I often hear or read the opinion of educated Catholic women, many of whom have left the Church, that writings such as *Mulieris Dignitatem* are merely the quaint ramblings of an old man and modern women do not need to take his writings seriously. This is the Pope they have seen on TV as he smiles and waves, bending over to embrace children or bless the sick and handicapped. I believe that this is a naive view of what is in fact a dangerous situation.

In the latter years of this papacy, a different image of the Pope has emerged. It is of a warrior Pope, determined to lead his troops into the third millennium on a crusade to subdue what he sees as a feminist revolt against women's divinely appointed destiny. John Paul II's views, outlined some ten years ago in *Mulieris Dignitatem*, have informed and directed a prodigious international effort by the Vatican in the 1990s to subvert the progress of women to full equality. These views have helped to fuel the backlash against feminism which has been experienced in North America as government cutbacks and the cancellation of legislation on employment equity have been approved at the whim of conservative politicians, often under the banner of "family values."

It is true that in *Mulieris Dignitatem*, John Paul II goes to great lengths to show that violence and discrimination against women are not rooted in Scripture, nor is it part of the Creator's eternal plan. The Pope exhorts men to avoid violence, and this is considered sufficient to prevent abuse. But no amount of sweet papal words can shield women from the consequences of the suppression of equal rights for women within the household of the Church.

A report published by UNICEF in July 1997 states that violence against women is actually on the increase in the contemporary world: "In today's world, to be born female is to be born high-risk." Somewhere in North America a woman is abused by her partner every nine seconds. "For tens of millions of women today, home is a locus of terror."[17] The director of UNICEF's programs commented that "this has to do with the social construct of power. Over the centuries, men have assumed certain things as their birthright, and women are less valued."[18]

One of the greatest achievements of the women's movement in this century has been to discredit the old idea that violence against women is the problem of a few sick individuals. Courageous women activists have persisted in exposing the roots of violence in the structures of discrimination against women which prevail in the family and in the workplace. This systemic discrimination arises out of the traditional division of roles between men and women, the kind of rigid division of masculine and feminine roles advocated by John Paul II. The imbalance of power between men and women at every level derives from a paradigm of male domination and female subordination in relationships, and male activity and female passivity in its definition of separate natures and roles. While it may be laudable for a pope to denounce male violence, it is disturbing that he cannot acknowledge that it is precisely within his kind of thinking on the nature of women that the roots of violence against women are found.

Indeed, it is in the belief in two separate human natures for men and women that the division of male and female roles in society has its origin. The "woman as nurturer, man as breadwinner" polarity has resulted in a strict definition of roles in society and a corresponding ranking of unequal worth attached to the two genders. The relegation of women to the domestic sphere and their consequent lack of power and influence in the public domain has led to multilayered structures of dominance by men over women.

The gender hierarchy which has been the rule in the West until very recently and still holds fast in many parts of the world has its roots in male images of God. Where God is male, the male is god. "Equal but different" is all very well, but one must look to who is defining the differences and who is benefiting from the very unequal division of power within the Church which these differences are said to legitimize. Just as the "separate but equal" argument which sanctioned racial segregation has now been completely discredited, the same argument used by male religious leaders to ban women from direct participation in any active role at the altar is seen as equally dangerous and discriminatory. Apartheid in the sanctuary justifies abuse and violence in the streets.

This is both the scandal and tragedy of John Paul II's writings on the separate natures of men and women: that the roots of societal violence against women can be traced along the line of his argument. If God did not invent violence against women as a result of His plan for hierarchical gender relations, then how did gender violence arise? Precisely as a result of men like John Paul II who, down through the ages, have said that the male God has given them the right to define the role of women for them and to set the boundaries of that role along the lines of their biological function as mother.

"Women's attempt to gain a share of power," states the 1997 UNICEF report cited above, "has destabilized relationships between the sexes. Change will not occur unless women demand it and men find a new role for themselves which does not involve exercising power over women."[19] According to Pope John Paul II, God's will as interpreted by men has consistently shown that women's destiny is laid down for all time within the biological imperative of motherhood. It is hard not to conclude that the tragic result this has had—the domination and abuse of women by men—is connected to the fact that men have arrogated the right to interpret the mind of God for women. Their male God has told them that men are superior by nature, and so their rightful place is to be in control.

The religiously based nature of systemic violence against women is well analyzed in another, very different pastoral letter which appeared in 1989, on the heels of *Mulieris Dignitatem*. This is the letter from the Assembly of Quebec Bishops entitled *A Heritage of Violence: A Pastoral Reflection on Conjugal Violence*. Perhaps because the Vatican was engrossed in the struggle over the U.S. bishops' *Pastoral Letter on Women* at the time, this Canadian bishops' pastoral letter got by the scrutiny of the Holy Office without intervention. This letter is unique in that all four members of the working team and fifteen of the sixteen resource persons consulted by the Quebec bishops were women.

In their analysis of the causes of violence, the Quebec bishops outline the problem of violence against women as "supported by a whole hierarchical system of social, political, economic, and religious structures" from Old Testament times to the present day. The cultural roots of violence clearly lie within an environment "where woman acquired social status solely through her sexual functions as wife and mother and not through her personal worth or basic dignity as a human being."[20]

Violence as a social problem, the Quebec bishops continue, is generated by patriarchy, which they define as "a social system which supports and authenticates the predominance of men, brings about a concentration of power and privilege in the hands of men and consequently leads to the control and subordination of women, generating social inequality between the sexes."[21] The sexual stereotypes, the inequitable distribution of roles and tasks, and the unworkable model of family which this system generates are reinforced by the economic system and by the Church. This section is worth quoting in its entirety, because it provides a diametrically opposing analysis to the one offered by John Paul II.

> In the ecclesial institution itself, is there not still a patriarchal mentality:
> • when the Church continues to specify the function of women by insisting almost exclusively on their role as mothers and on their own distinct psychology;
> • when it uses exclusive language;
> • when Canon Law excludes women from certain functions and positions of responsibility, for example lectors, from sacred ordination, from giving homilies; from positions such as judicial vicar or diocesan judge.[22]

In their final list of recommendations, the Quebec bishops include the following:

> Recognize women, not only in their role as wives and mothers, but as human persons with vast potential as well as limitations, who are entitled to their autonomy . . . Before being a mother, a woman is a person with her own identity. Motherhood, however noble, is not what defines womanhood. While many women find fulfillment in physical or spiritual motherhood, others also find it elsewhere.[23]

WOMEN'S RIGHTS: SECULAR OR SACRED IN ORIGIN?

In asserting categorically that women are full and autonomous human beings in their own right with a human identity not intrinsically linked with their reproductive capacities, the Quebec bishops place the Catholic Church within a framework that can support the decades of struggle to define the personhood of women in law and social policy as equal in all respects to men. The goal of full recognition for women's rights as universal human rights, not subject to diminishment by social custom, has not yet been fully achieved. While religion did and still does play a role in sanctioning discrimination against women, it also has the potential, as in the case of the Quebec bishops' teaching, to play a major role in encouraging both Church and society to undergo conversion.

For the majority of male Catholic leaders, however, the topic of women's rights appears to be one on which society, not the Church, needs to undergo conversion. They choose to assert that society has been led astray from the path assigned by God for humanity because it has fallen under the demonic influence of "radical feminism." It is up to the male Church to provide all the answers this deluded society needs on the rights and place of women.

The strict dichotomy of male and female human nature promoted by John Paul II has also produced a strange paradox in the Catholic Church's understanding of human rights. "The Church must in her own life promote as far as possible the equal rights and dignity of women," he states in *Mulieris Dignitatem*, "but clearly all of this does not mean for women a renunciation of their femininity or an imitation of the male role, but the fullness of feminine humanity which should be expressed in all their activity, whether in the family or outside of it."[24] The only thing that is clear from this tortuous statement is that John Paul is laying the groundwork for the Church to justify its own internal practice of granting superior rights to men.

According to John Paul II, universal human rights do exist, but they apply only to men. Women's rights are not universal human rights; rather, women's rights fall into a separate category which is strictly limited according to women's biological constraints. "In our time," he states in *Mulieris Dignitatem*, "the question of 'women's rights' has taken on new significance in the broad context of the rights of the human person. The biblical and evangelical message sheds light on this cause by safeguarding the truth about the 'unity' of the two, that is to say, the truth about the dignity and vocation that result from the specific diversity and personal originality of man and woman."[25]

The concrete outcome that emerges from statements such as these is that John Paul II's anthropology supports the position that women are not full human beings in the way that men are. Women should under no circumstances try to be "like" (read equal to) men, even when their personal safety is at stake. "Even the rightful opposition of women to what is expressed in the biblical words, 'He shall rule over you,' must not under any condition lead to the 'masculinization' of women... There is a real fear," insists the Pope, "that if they take this path [to equal rights] women will not reach fulfillment but will deform and lose their essential richness."[26] In this context, women's "essential richness" can only mean their submissiveness, sweetness, and passivity, even while suffering in silence the imbalance of power in and outside the home, which can lead to sexual assault and physical battering.

This kind of thinking is not only illogical, it is also downright harmful and threatening to women. It has led to the emergence of some questionable people as defenders of the Catholic Church, as will be seen in Chapter 5. A special kind of virulent hatred toward anyone who promotes any kind of rethinking of the position of women has spread like a cancer in the heart of the Church, a cancer that has fed off the direct encouragement of these papal teachings.

The Vatican's contemporary determination to crush the movement toward women's equality marks a sharp change of course from the path set for the Catholic Church by Pope John XXIII. In his 1962 encyclical *Pacem in Terris*, John XXIII lauded the women's movement as one of the signs of the activity of the Spirit of God in the world and stated clearly that "Human beings have the right... to set up a family with equal rights and duties for man and woman."[27] He continued, "It is obvious to everyone that women are now taking part in public life... Since women are becoming ever more conscious of their human dignity, they will not be tolerated as mere material instruments, but demand rights befitting a human person both in domestic and public life."[28]

But under John Paul II, the notion that universal human rights apply to women as well as men became suspect in the eyes of the Vatican because this notion rests on the assumption that there is one universal human nature, not two distinct ones. A recognition that the role of women and their status in society has varied within different cultures and over time is absent from the Pope's extensive discourse on the dignity of women. In fact, John Paul II has refused to acknowledge the validity of any kind of analysis of discrimination based on gender. For the Pope, such analysis is too "secular," even "feminist."

History shows that up to the present time women have had limited social and economic rights under the law, but not full political or civil rights. Abuses of women, such as battering, rape, and genital mutilation, have been considered private and therefore not subject to universal jurisprudence. The women's movement has fought long and hard during this century to achieve full and equal recognition of women as citizens, beginning with the granting of suffrage and personhood, to bring these abuses to public attention.

THE WORK OF THE DEVIL

John Paul II and his conservative allies in the Catholic Church have also attempted to force Catholics back into pre–Vatican II confines of thought, where there was a sharp division between the secular and the sacred. This dualistic thinking parallels his dualistic anthropology of male and female, and is part of the backlash against feminism into which John Paul II has directed so much of the energy of the latter half of his papacy.

This world view relies on a central tenet that there are two mutually antagonistic forces at play in the unfolding of the history of the universe: one directed by God, the other directed by the devil. The idea owes much to one of the most celebrated works of St. Augustine, *The City of God*. Written in 415 C.E. as the Roman Empire was collapsing from within and without, *The City of God* proposes a view of history that has had enormous influence over the Catholic Church ever since. All human history,

Augustine held, is a struggle between the Kingdom of God and the King-dom of the World. According to Augustine, the Kingdom of God, to be realized fully in heaven, is present in earthly form in the Church, which offers a perfect model of the structure of relationships in the kingdom willed by God. The Kingdom of the World is present in the State, that is, the Roman Empire, which was in chronic decline at the time. The struggle between good and evil is played out in history. The State is in decline and thus under the dominion of evil. To find salvation, all must take refuge in the Church, which is a foretaste on earth of the eternal Kingdom of God. The State must be subject to the rule of the Church if it is to be redeemed.

For many centuries after the collapse of the Roman Empire, the Church did in fact wield control over the secular as well as the spiritual world. As the nation-states of Europe began to fight for independence from papal control, the Church fought back and in so doing proved itself to be inimi-cal to the rights of kings. The Church also fiercely opposed the series of revolutions that ushered in democracy in Europe and North America.

The ideological foundations of papal monarchy and with that, papal control of territories and the taxes thereof, were threatened by the over-throw of the divine right of kings, which gave the monarch rather than the Church the license to tax and control the life of the peasant. Later, to the founders of democracy in Europe, the Church was as oppressive as the State, and along with the abolition of the rights of kings came the abolition of the rights of clergy. In 1791, Pope Pius VI condemned the Civil Consti-tution of the Clergy in France, and declared the consecration of bishops elected under new rules of the National Assembly "sacrilegious."

Papal opposition to the French Revolution came fast on the heels of the great rift between religion and science, which dated from the censure of Galileo in 1616 and grew more pronounced as the Enlightenment pro-gressed. Once the Church lost power over the State, popes started to describe the State as sinful and became determined to keep the Church pure, unsullied by secular ideas—Augustine's politics with a modern twist.

In 1864, Pope Pius IX issued a *Syllabus of Errors* in which he attempted to lay down rules to stop Catholics from falling into what he perceived to be the traps set for them by the modern world. The Pope lists the "principal errors of our time." Among these errors are freedom of conscience, the denial of the temporal power of the papacy and its right to use force to impose the Churches rulings, the attempt to undermine the immunity of the clergy from civil laws, the challenge to the exclusive rights of Catholicism as a state religion to the exclusion of all other religious worship anywhere, and the assertion that "the Roman Pontiff can and should reconcile himself and come to terms with progress, liberalism and modern civilization."[29]

This *Syllabus of Errors* is enjoying something of a revival in right-wing Catholic circles today. In 1990, at one of the early gatherings of the Coalition of Concerned Canadian Catholics, I was leading the meeting when a member of a right-wing Catholic group thrust a copy of the *Syllabus of Errors* into my face and started shouting about the errors of liberalism and false secular progress. Like Pius IX, this group evidently believed they had the right to use force and intimidation in the name of the Church. Some of them stood in the aisles and screamed out passages from papal writings while the business of the meeting was in progress; other members of the same group started to shout out the rosary. Some of them stood right over the speakers, another woman and me, and thrust other papers into our faces. We regained control of the meeting by singing the old hymn "Holy God, We Praise Thy Name," which eventually calmed them down.

The attitude that intimidation is an appropriate tool to be used in defense of their version of Catholicism is also witnessed in the more extreme views of right-wing anti-abortionists who have killed or maimed doctors and staff and bombed clinics in recent years. These same groups will often dismiss the Winter Commission report on child sexual abuse by clergy as a "secular" document because the head of the archdiocesan commission of inquiry was a layperson.

It is paradoxical that here in Canada, reactionary Catholic groups find justification in the Pope's writings to argue that concepts drawn from the Canadian Charter of Rights and Freedoms, including equality provisions for women, have no relevance within the Church because they derive from a "secular" mentality. When it comes to the rights of denominational Catholic schools in Canada, though, they will accord complete validity to the secular Canadian Constitution and insist on the inviolability of the rights of Catholic schools because these rights were granted under the British North America Act of 1867, never mind that the BNA is a secular accord.

The struggle for women's rights is the latest in a long line of movements for liberation which the Catholic Church has attempted to label as the work of the devil.[30] The condemnation of modernity at the First Vatican Council (in the 1870 decree *Pastor Aeternus*) was followed by the anti-modernist inquisition under Pius X. In the twentieth century, the Church has buttressed its own reactionary structure by making common cause with like-minded political movements. From Franco in Spain and Le Pen in France to Reagan in the United States, popes have raised their standard in defense of reactionary governments.

Now that communism has fallen, due in no small part to the efforts of John Paul II, the new "evil empire" is mistakenly perceived to be feminism and the struggle for universal and equal human rights for women. The many-headed monster of women's equality is seen as a threat to God's rightful order, which according to the Vatican is inherently patriarchal. It is feared that the wave of successful arguments for women's full equality in the secular realm will flood through the Church. Viewed from a historical perspective, this struggle can be compared with the Church's reluctance to accept "secular" arguments against slavery and in favor of freedom of conscience.

The Roman Empire, according to St. Augustine's *City of God*, fell into decay owing to slavery, luxury, and debauchery. Christians had to flee to the safety of the Church, the new City of God, to escape destruction. In modern times, so Pope John Paul II and his supporters have argued, society is facing decay because the struggle for women's equality has resulted in the evils of contraception, promiscuity, abortion, and equal rights not just for heterosexual women but also for lesbians. In order for women to protect themselves against feminism, they must find refuge in the Church.

From this it follows that the Church is perfectly justified in upholding practices within and without its structures that are more exclusionary than those operating in secular society. Women must not fight for ordination because this is not a right but a calling from God. And since the Vatican holds that God has called only men to represent *him* as priests, it follows that this is God's eternal will, a position which will be more fully analyzed in Chapter 3.

LIBERATION AS A SPIRITUAL JOURNEY

This unrelenting war against the feminist movement, in particular against the articulation in feminist theology of the call of women to priestly ordination, has resulted in anger, grief, despair, denial, or even exile for many individual Catholic women. Patriarchal structures and the use of language that evokes images of Satanic possession also reinforces internalized misogyny and self-doubt in many women. I am aware that it has taken me more than twenty years of experience and continual prayer and study after the end of the Second Vatican Council in 1965 to come to terms with my own internalized misogyny, and it still often catches me unawares. I sometimes share this long journey toward liberation with other women who are struggling with the contradictions of Catholic faith and feminism. It is the support of faithful friends, the refreshment of reading Christian feminist writing, and fidelity to prayer which have sustained me.

During the course of the prayer cycle of the Spiritual Exercises, which I have already alluded to as one of the formative influences on my own life, the individual following the Exercises enters into a deep contemplation of the life of Jesus. This involves actually entering into and participating in the gospel story at the levels of imagination, heart, mind, and soul. In common with most people who embark on this journey of prayer, I found myself initially comfortable only to participate in the prayer experience as an imaginary and passive observer, content to stay on the fringes of the crowds of people who surrounded Jesus.

In the course of the first week of following the Exercises, the retreatant, under the guidance of the spiritual director, is called to a gradual and often painful stripping-away of the barriers that prevent us from coming close to God. The retreatant discovers that it is not God who keeps us at arm's length because we are bad, but we ourselves who hold back from falling into the arms of the all-merciful God. As my experience of divine love grew deeper in this contemplation, and with the encouragement of Sister Charmaine, I was able to enter into the gospel scene as a more active participant.

At the beginning of my experience of doing the Spiritual Exercises, I started off the gospel journey following Jesus in prayer with an assumed personality of a male child scampering along at his side. As this child, I experienced a contemplation in which I was carried on Jesus' shoulders in the gospel scene where he walks through the field of corn on the Sabbath and, to the anger of the religious authorities, allows the people to eat the ears of corn in contravention of the law. Later, I would find myself assuming the role of an adolescent, one of the boys helping Peter and Andrew with the boats on Lake Galilee. It was in this assumed persona of a young man that I followed Jesus as the scenes of the gospel moved through the villages and towns of Galilee.

More than halfway through the pattern of prayer laid down in the Spiritual Exercises, the retreatant is invited to accompany Jesus on the final road to Jerusalem. One day, meditating on the scene at the house of Mary and Martha at Bethany, I found myself alone with Jesus, sitting outside under a large tree. I was feeling extremely agitated. The reason was that I had suddenly changed into my real self, and I was there seated beside him as a mature, sexually active married woman. Jesus turned toward me and asked me what was wrong. I tried to conceal the truth of what I was feeling, but in the end I couldn't help blurting out: "I shouldn't be here! I'm a woman, I'm 'doing it' and I like it, and I'm afraid I'll turn you on!"

To my astonishment, the Jesus I was accompanying in prayer threw his head back and roared with laughter. "Don't you realize," he said to me, "that everything in your feminine nature and sexuality is a gift from God? God made you who you are, and that's how you're called to serve

87

God." From that moment on, I followed Jesus into the passion and resurrection narratives in all my glory as a fully flowering woman, "doing it" and all. What also began to happen is that after this breakthrough to my true self, I began to notice all the other women around Jesus, and to form in prayer a deep attachment to and identification with these other women in his life. For the first time, I paid attention to my namesake, Joanna, the wife of Chusa, King Herod's steward, who had left her husband to join Jesus' ministry.

As I wrote in my journal about this experience and talked with Charmaine, I realized that a great weight had been lifted from my relationship with God. The stages of my personal encounter with Jesus were steps toward mature adult faith and an empowerment of myself as a woman. Taught for so long by the Catholic Church to cultivate a childlike relationship with God, to remain subservient to men, and to fear my own sexuality, I found that Jesus' words to me in prayer came as a total affirmation of myself as an adult woman and as a sexual human being. When my personal experience of liberation coincided a few years later with studies in feminist theology, the result was a deep conviction that in trying to turn women back into obedient plaster madonnas, this Catholic Church is placing obstacles in the way of the liberating work of God in the world. Pope John Paul II in particular has attempted to close the ears of the institutional Church to the call of the Spirit speaking in and through women.

Digging deep into my own internalized misogyny, I also realized that in early childhood I had absorbed some negative messages from my family's expectations about who and what I would be. One of my earliest memories is a casual remark my mother made to me when I was about five years old. "When you came along," she said, "we had wanted a boy, a brother for Tony [my nearest sibling]. We had already settled on the name John. We called you Joanna because it is the feminine version of John."

The impact of my parents' disappointment at producing a third girl rather than a boy remained with me and only increased over the years. I became determined to prove that I was not second best, and that I could be the equal of any boy or man in any sphere of life. No doubt many will nod their heads and say that this proves that feminists like me are just motivated by penis envy, but there is more than mere envy in the wound left by ambivalent love or rejection experienced in childhood. It was only as a result of the deep experience of God's love bestowed through the gift of prayer that I came to understand that every one of God's children, women and men, are loved simply for being who we are. "Each of us is God's work of art," as the author of the Letter to the Ephesians expresses it, loved for ourselves and not for who we can be or what we can do.

In the course of a day-long retreat that I made shortly after completing the Spiritual Exercises, I was led into a healing of these memories. The gospel reading assigned for that day was Jesus' saying "Consider the lilies of the field: they neither spin nor sow, and yet your heavenly Father loves them all."[31] I found myself in prayer that day identifying with the flowers of the field, growing from a seed in the rich, moist earth. All of a sudden I was back in my mother's womb. I knew my parents wanted me to come out as a boy, but within the womb, I felt the loving presence of God bringing me into being. "I want you to be a girl," said God, "gifted in many ways."

In my prayer experience that Sunday, I relived my birth. I heard the voices of the nurses who had gathered to help bring me into the world, and felt the love and care which surrounded my birth. "Thank God, she is safe," I heard one say. I sensed my mother's enormous relief. I was washed by the nurses and cuddled in a warm blanket. My mother had been saying the rosary, and I realized that the housekeeper had also gathered my sisters and brother at home to pray for my safe delivery.

In the presence of God in prayer, I was able to engage my mother in conversation. So certain was my conviction of God's love for me that I was able to forgive my mother for the disappointment she had conveyed to me and heal those aspects of my childhood memories. In conversations with many women, I have heard similar stories of childhood hurts sustained through being unfavorably compared with male siblings, or simply being the wrong answer to a parent's prayer for a boy child.

The Catholic Church teachings on women perpetuate this internalized misogyny. Many families instill an understanding in their female offspring that they are second rate compared with their more desirable male siblings. The Church sustains this on a spiritual level by giving women the message that they are second-rate Christians, fit to follow Mary but not fit to exercise the fullness of Christian discipleship reserved for those made in the image of God.

In the course of my seven years as a nun, I spent the final two years at London University. I lived in the Holy Child convent in Cavendish Square in the heart of London. The Superior at the time, Mother Mary Paul, had participated in the suffragette movement in England. Mother Paul was about five feet tall, with a genial face and a deep, hearty laugh. She had known Emily and Christabel Pankhurst, and she was one of a group of suffragettes who had chained themselves to the railings outside the House of Commons in London in 1918. Mother Paul kept that suffragette spirit alive. She encouraged the young nuns to excel in all areas of studies, and she kept the whole convent up to date with the latest communications flowing from Rome as a result of the Vatican Council. We experimented freely with new designs for habits with shortened skirts and smaller veils. We were encouraged to invite university friends in for discussion, and to take part in peace movement rallies in Trafalgar Square.

I satisfied my youthful intellectual and spiritual thirst in an atmosphere which was like wine for the soul. Whenever Mother Paul passed me in the hallway, there would be a wink and a smile. As a result of this, I began to see that as the Vatican Council was telling the Church, the Spirit of God was at work in the modern world, giving sight to those blinded by prejudice, causing those crippled by social and religious bondage to hope, and freeing those imprisoned by poverty and discrimination. The secular struggle for civil rights for blacks and later for women became one with the liberating movement of the new Pentecost unleashed in the Catholic Church.

Later, my experience of the Spiritual Exercises brought me into contact with a God who does not use fear to draw us into union, but instead surrounds us with love—all kinds of love: sisterly and brotherly love, parental love, the love of friends, even erotic love. We taste God's ecstasy and completeness in mutually self-giving sexual love. Held in our mother's arms, we are wrapped in God's tender care. We are challenged by a sister or brother and consoled by a friend. All human love is a reflection of the power of God's love, the passion which fires the universe and sustains all life within it.

This does not mean that I do not struggle with the Christian notion of a male saviour, and do not always succeed in reconciling the dissonance this produces in a feminist context. But this and other experiences of Jesus as a liberator flourish deep within my being, and I remain immersed within the Christian story.

Chapter Three

God Is Male:
The Church's Position

ontroversy over the ordination of women to the priesthood has
by no means been confined to the Catholic Church. One has only
to recall the number of departures from the Church of England
when that Church decided to ordain women in 1992 to appreciate that this
movement of the Spirit in modern Christianity has resulted in intensive
soul-searching and shattering upheavals. I am convinced that the movement for the ordination of women to the priesthood in the Catholic
Church is part of this same unfolding of God's plan under the direction of
the Holy Spirit, and that it is a development of doctrine fully consonant
with the course charted by the Second Vatican Council. This is why I dare
to state that Pope John Paul II's fierce opposition to any discussion on the
issue of women's ordination constitutes an impediment to the working of
the Holy Spirit both within the Catholic Church and in the world at large.

In his opening speech to the Second Vatican Council in 1962, Pope
John XXIII outlined the overarching vision which should guide the Council in its deliberations. God, he stated, was "leading us into a new order of
human relations which, by humanity's own efforts and even beyond its

very expectations, are directed toward the fulfillment of God's superior and inscrutable designs ... New conditions and new forms of life introduced into the modern world," he continued, "have opened new avenues to the Catholic apostolate... The substance of the ancient doctrine of the deposit of faith [the substance of faith handed down since the time of the apostles] is one thing," he concluded, "and the way in which it is presented is another. And it is the latter that must be taken into great consideration with patience if necessary, everything being measured in the forms and proportion of a *magisterium* [the teaching authority of the Church] which is profoundly pastoral in character."[1]

Until the pontificate of John Paul II, the question of women's ordination had never been treated in the Catholic Church within the category described by John XXIII as "the substance of the deposit of faith." Although the Second Vatican Council did not debate the issue, it placed the modern Catholic Church on a theological and cultural trajectory toward a much more open, inclusive, and pastoral relationship with the contemporary world, with all its deep spiritual yearnings and ambiguities.

Very soon after Vatican II ended, the Canadian bishops were the first episcopal group in the Catholic Church to open the debate on women's ordination right in the heart of Rome. In 1970, the Canadian Conference of Catholic Bishops invited seventy women from across Canada to meet with them immediately before their annual general assembly. The bishops were preparing for a synod of bishops scheduled to take place in Rome in 1971. In a speech made to the 1971 synod, Cardinal Flahiff of Winnipeg stated that in the context of the need for "diversification of the priesthood," and as a result of "informal consultations with highly qualified representatives of Canadian Catholic women... our Episcopal Conference almost unanimously adopted the recommendation... to establish a mixed commission of bishops, priests, laymen and laywomen, religious men and religious women to study in depth the question of the ministries of women in the Church."[2]

This mixed commission was never formed, but the Canadian bishops continued to press the issue. In 1975 they requested that nonordained ministries in the Church be extended to women, and in 1976 they requested a theological examination of the issue of women's ordination. During the early 1980s, the Canadian bishops continued to speak loud and clear in Rome with a voice informed by the insights of the growing feminist movement in Canada, especially in the province of Quebec. At the 1980 general synod of bishops devoted to the topic of the family, Bishop Robert Lebel spoke of the secular feminist movement as "a positive reality" and "a step forward in the establishment of the Kingdom." The role of women, he pointed out, extends beyond the family, and he suggested that women should be made "co-responsible" for the Church as a whole.[3]

Another remarkable intervention took place at the 1983 general synod of bishops devoted to the topic of reconciliation. Archbishop (later Cardinal) Vachon of Quebec, then Primate, or most senior bishop, of Canada, defined relationships between men and women not only in terms of "equality of origin and destiny" but also of "equality in mission and involvement." This, it is important to note, was but a few years before John Paul II corrected such "misguided" ideas with his excursion into anthropology in *Mulieris Dignitatem*. Vachon continued with a quite extraordinary appeal for repentance and reconciliation on the part of his fellow bishops. "As for us," said Vachon, "let us recognize the ravages of sexism, and our own male appropriation of Church institutions and the numerous aspects of the Christian life." He further called on the bishops to recognize "the archaic concepts of womanhood which have been inculcated in us for centuries."[4]

Before Pope John Paul II breathed new life into these archaic concepts of womanhood and made them the foundation of his teaching on women, Pope Paul VI had decided to excavate the biblical foundations on the issue of women priests, and he gave a mandate to the Pontifical Biblical Commission to study and report back on the biblical arguments for and against women's ordination. This Vatican commission reached the conclusion, in its 1976 report, that "the New Testament by itself alone does not conclusively permit us to settle in a clear way and once for all the problem of the accession of women to the priesthood."[5] In other words, it is impossible to use the gospel accounts of the Last Supper to prove that Jesus intended only men to be priests. This was a key finding, because it overturned what had hitherto been considered as the main scriptural argument against the priestly ordination of women: namely, that when Jesus celebrated the first Eucharist, there were no women present, and therefore women should never be present in a priestly role presiding at the Eucharist.

It is therefore shocking but not surprising that this report, which came from the Vatican's own commission, was quickly suppressed, but not before the results of a vote taken by the members of the Pontifical Biblical Commission were leaked to the press: a majority of twelve to five of its members had voted in favor of women's ordination, with one abstention.

In 1976, Paul VI issued an apostolic letter titled *Inter Insigniores*: *Declaration on the Question of the Admission of Women to the Ministerial Priesthood* in which he ruled out the ordination of women. The main argument advanced by Paul VI was that there is an unbroken tradition in the Church of restricting the priesthood to men, and that furthermore, women are incapable of acting *in persona Christi*, or as a personal representative of Christ. The Canadian biblical scholar Father David Stanley immediately tendered his resignation from the Commission, stating that "it has become patently obvious that the laborious, patient, scholarly, and honest efforts of last April's commission meeting have been deliberately consigned to oblivion."[6]

Debate on women priests continued in the Catholic Church after 1976, with bishops, priests, and laypeople calling for a reversal of Paul VI's teaching. Like the teaching on clerical celibacy, the teaching on an exclusively male priesthood has ranked on a much lower level of importance than, for example, the divinity of Christ. Prior to John Paul's 1994 teaching on the ordination of women, few theologians would have placed the ban on women priests at the heart of Catholic belief. The male priesthood was a practice traditionally followed in the Church but was not accorded the truth of revelation.

By emphasizing a link between the nature of God and the ban on women priests, and by using this argument to elevate the teaching to a central doctrine, John Paul II has, I believe, forced the Catholic Church into a heretical position. His teaching on the maleness of God, which will be explored in this chapter, has dramatic repercussions on other central Catholic beliefs as well, such as the resurrection of Christ and the effects of the sacrament of baptism.

In the Catholic Church there is what is called a "hierarchy of truth" among its teachings. This does not mean that some teachings are more true than others, but that some are more important and must be given a deeper assent of faith. The farther down the hierarchy a teaching is, the easier it is for the Church to change it. The 1994 declaration moved the prohibition of the ordination of women to a higher level in the hierarchy of truth. John Paul II has not only elevated it to a place at the center of the Church's teaching, but in the process he has entrenched the idea of God as male in a way which distorts history and flies in the face of contemporary experience.

In January 1997 the Vatican issued a book titled *From Inter Insigniores to Sacerdotalis Ordinatio*, which presented a comprehensive overview of its position against the ordination of women. Bishop Angelo Scola told reporters that "the Church does not have the power to modify the practice, uninterrupted for two thousand years, of calling only men to the priesthood. This was willed directly by Jesus." "Rejection of the ban on women is not heresy," added Cardinal Joseph Ratzinger in a later interview, "but it is clearly erroneous and incompatible with the faith."[7] Two months later, the Vatican issued an edict barring women from the diaconate. At a later news conference, several reporters questioned the legitimacy of the ban, given the practice of the early Church as recorded in the New Testament, where women served as deacons. Cardinal Pio Laghi, head of the Vatican Congregation on Education, replied that "the women referred to in the Bible were blessed by church leaders, but not sacramentally ordained."[8]

In 1998 the teaching that bars women from the priesthood was elevated in importance yet again; denial of it is now subject to canonical penalties. "Pope Changes Canon Law in Defence of Faith" ran the front-page headline in the Toronto *Catholic Register*.[9] This document, an apostolic letter titled *Ad Tuendam Fidem* (To Defend the Faith) inserts three new paragraphs into the Code of Canon Law. Canon law is a summary of the rules and regulations which govern the lives of Catholics. This apostolic letter raised certain "definitively held" teachings to the level of infallibility and attached a sliding scale of penalties for denial of these teachings, ranging from admonition to excommunication.

The Congregation for the Doctrine of the Faith at the Vatican issued a simultaneous commentary on *Ad Tuendam Fidem*, written by the Prefect of the Congregation, Cardinal Ratzinger. After explaining that truths on the second level of the hierarchy of truth are those which are connected logically to the faith even though they are not expressly revealed in Scripture, he places the truth that "priestly ordination is reserved only to men" within this category. In a sweeping statement that bears little resemblance to historical accuracy, he claims that "this doctrine is to be held definitively since, founded on the written Word of God, constantly preserved and applied in the Tradition of the Church, it has been set forth infallibly by the ordinary and universal *magisterium*." He then adds that there is a "possibility in the future that the consciousness of the Church might progress to the point where this teaching could be defined as a doctrine to be believed as divinely revealed."[10]

In Canada, the 1990 Newfoundland Winter Commission on the sexual abuse of children by members of the clergy, as well as countless other contemporary studies of violence against women and children, have concluded that patriarchal structures, whether these be within the Catholic Church or in other institutions such as the military, have provided fertile ground for the abuse of power. John Paul II's insistence that patriarchy, as exemplified in the male-only priesthood, is sanctioned by God as the sole means of sacramental grace and thus of salvation, has coincided with a period in history when the scandal of child sexual abuse by male Catholic clergy has erupted in many parts of the world.

Yet the Vatican continues to turn a blind eye to this mounting evidence that the priesthood is in deep trouble. The arrogant response of so many in positions of authority in the Catholic Church to the sexual and physical abuse of children by its clergy has caused many people to turn away from the Catholic Church in disgust. Does the Vatican's male God also turn a blind eye to the cries of patriarchy's victims just as his representatives on earth have done in so many cases?

A NATURAL RESEMBLANCE TO CHRIST

At the heart of the Vatican's teaching on women's ordination lies a notion based on an outdated biological fundamentalism which does not stand up to the light of serious theological scrutiny. The teaching on ordination gives a theological twist to John Paul II's anthropology of the intrinsic differences between men and women, which was examined in the previous chapter. According to his analysis, men and women are two completely separate and different manifestations of human nature. In John Paul II's view, the different manifestations of these two separate male and female forms of humanity are the result of biology, and cannot be altered as a result of historical or cultural influence.

Jesus Christ, God in human flesh, came to earth as a male human being. According to John Paul II's anthropology, Jesus' human nature must therefore have been completely different from any woman's human nature, even that of his mother, Mary. So, this argument continues, the priest at the altar must be male because only a man bears a "natural resemblance" to the human Jesus. The priest, stated John Paul II, becomes a kind of icon or image of God for the people. And only a male human being can truly portray the humanity of Jesus to the people.

But how can this "natural resemblance" of the priest to Jesus be physically measured? What precise physical features would qualify to make a human being into a living icon of the human Jesus? It is evident that there are women who look like men, and men who look like women, especially when they are dressed in priestly vestments. Some men develop breasts; some women are flat chested. Some women have hairy bodies; some men are smooth. Some women are stronger than most men; some men are physically weaker than many women.

Where do we draw the line on the details of the "natural resemblance" to this person of Christ, the human Jesus of Nazareth? Jesus was ethnically and religiously Jewish. We are not sure how tall he was. He probably wore a beard. Does a "natural resemblance" to the human Jesus, then, not call for all priests to be circumcised, Semitic, and bearded? But there are short priests, tall priests, fat priests, thin priests, black priests, bald priests—does anyone ever imagine Jesus as bald? Does an Oriental priest, for example, have a "natural resemblance" to Jesus? Where exactly does this "natural resemblance" lie?

If we eliminate variables like the above, which are too fluid to constitute a decisive standard of measurement of any "natural resemblance" to Jesus, we are left with the one and only constant feature about all men that differentiates them from women: the shape and construction of male genitals. Just as the Vatican teaches that the womb makes the woman, is it the penis that makes the priest?

It is on this basis, a sheer accident of physiology over which women have no choice or control, that the Vatican insists all women are to be barred forever from full participation in Jesus' redemptive work. It is on this basis that the Vatican teaches by inference that women, once described by the philosopher Aristotle as "deformed" males, are now to be viewed as "deformed" Christians. There is something always incomplete and beyond reach in the way that women disciples can imitate Christ. This is what the Vatican teaching on the vocation of the priesthood, which is at the heart of Christ's work on earth, actually signifies: it is contingent upon the possession of male genitals.

To accommodate a theological position based on genitalia rather than one based on the Genesis account of male and female both made in the image of God, Pope John Paul II and those who agree with him have been forced to distort other doctrines of the Catholic Church. These include what theologians call christology, or teachings on the nature of Jesus; soteriology, which describes the work and redemptive mission of Jesus; the resurrection of Jesus; and ecclesiology, or the nature of the Church and in particular, the sacrament of baptism.

99

As the Church has taught from the beginning, a "natural resemblance" to Christ is enjoyed by all human beings who are transformed through the sacrament of baptism into a new creation. Human beings grow into the likeness of Christ by what they do, not by the way they look. Within a very short period in recent Catholic Church history, the frantic attempts of the opponents of women's ordination to stifle any discussion on the issue has led them into an extraordinary number of distortions of the Church's two-thousand-year-old teachings. Even more frightening is the fact that no one in high places in the Church is saying anything about this. Sometime in the future, the Catholic Church is going to be mightily embarrassed by these errors. Some future pope or Council will explain away this teaching with phrases like "what John Paul II really meant was..." or "as it has been the constant teaching of the Church, men and women are equal..."

Many priests and bishops remain unconvinced of the validity of this teaching on women's ordination and yet they do nothing to challenge it. Individual priests have confided to me that they are totally against the Pope's teaching on women, but they are too afraid of reprisals should they speak out. The fear of what Walter Brueggemann refers to as the prophetic call to "speak the truth to power" permits this erroneous and dangerous teaching to hold many in the Catholic Church captive.

THE NATURE OF JESUS

One of the foundational beliefs of the Christian faith is that God is revealed by Jesus Christ as a Trinity: Creator, or Father; Word, or Son, and Holy Spirit. "The Word became flesh," as the first chapter of the gospel of John puts it. God became human. "Et homo factus est" says the Latin version of the Nicene Creed, which is still sung in many Catholic churches.

This "taking flesh" by the second person of the Trinity is also referred to in theology as the incarnation. Over the centuries, the Church has continued to meditate on the meaning of these great mysteries, seeking always to make them accessible in terms within the grasp of contemporary thought. The traditional doctrine of the incarnation is that at a certain moment in time, God entered human history in order to save the human race from sin. God, in the person of Jesus Christ, had two mysteriously linked natures: human and divine. Both were equally real, both equally active in the makeup of Jesus' nature. Just exactly how this union of divine and human is worked out has been a matter of interpretation in the Church over the centuries. At one time in history it has been the divinity of Christ that has been emphasized, at another, his humanity.

The teaching on women priests which has issued from the Vatican in the past ten years represents a new and, in my view, erroneous interpretation of the doctrine of the incarnation—one which has seen the light of day only in the latter part of the twentieth century. This teaching accords new and overly significant weight to the gender of Jesus Christ. According to this interpretation of the nature of Jesus Christ, the male gender of Jesus is now to be regarded as a constitutive element of Jesus' divinity as well as of his humanity. This has never been taught before within the tradition of the Catholic Church.

As was outlined in the previous chapter, Pope John Paul II taught that there can be no such thing as a common human nature shared equally by both men and women, but that there are in fact two distinct types of human being: male and female. Let us apply this anthropology to the humanity of Jesus. The second person of the Trinity became incarnate as a male human being. According to John Paul II's anthropology, as a male human being, Jesus' human nature must have been completely different from that of any female human being. It follows, then, that Jesus' male humanity must exclude women. When he became human, Jesus could only represent the male half of humanity. Jesus' humanity does not, as the Church has always taught, encompass or recapitulate the whole human race, women as well as men. Thus it would follow that the defining feature of the incarnation reveals not the humanity of the second person of the Trinity, but rather his maleness.

Never before in the history of the Catholic Church has Jesus' maleness ranked as more important than his humanity. If the recent Vatican teaching on women's ordination is correct, then the Latin translation of the Nicene

Creed should be changed from the generic "Et homo factus est" (and he became man) to "Et vir factus est" (and he became a male). The Vatican's latest teaching on women's ordination means that Catholics must believe and confess that only a specifically male God in human flesh is to be worshiped as God's revelation of Himself. This in turn means that male gender is an essential characteristic of the inner nature of the divine essence of God. Is this not a travesty of two thousand years of Catholic tradition?

REDEMPTION IS UNIVERSAL

Jesus became human to carry out a mission from God. According to Catholic tradition, the Word was made flesh for a purpose: God sent Jesus to save humanity from its sins and to bring us to a new creation as children of God, far beyond the limitations of the first creation of Adam and Eve. But according to the latest teaching on women's ordination, it is through God made male that we are saved. If it is only male human beings who can bear a "natural resemblance" to Jesus, and if it is only in their flesh that the nature of God is inscribed, then how does this male saviour, Jesus, represent and save women? Was Jesus a saviour only of men, or was Jesus a saviour of the whole human race? Exactly how can women be redeemed by a saviour whose male nature, according to John Paul II, is so intrinsically different from their own?

A similar question was debated much earlier in the Church. This one concerned the sexuality of Jesus. Catholic tradition has held that Jesus was celibate and remained a virgin to the end of his life. Does the perpetual celibacy of Jesus deny that he was a fully sexual being with fully operative sexual organs? Was he just a spirit clothed in the mere outward appearance of a body?

A group called the Docetists (from the Greek *dokesis*, or ghost), one of a number of sects that arose during the second century when the nature of Jesus was a hotly debated topic, denied that Jesus was a sexual being. He had only the appearance of being human, so his body did not perform the "lower" bodily functions associated with sex and excretion. If sex was not included within the human nature of Jesus, sex was not part of the new creation redeemed by God and was still a cause of sin.

Given the negative associations with sex that began to permeate the Church as it came under the influence of a Greek philosophy heavily indebted to the anti-materialist philosophy of Plato, the Docetists found a ready following. But their ideas were countered by the official Church. One of the early Christian writers, Irenaeus, Bishop of Lyons, wrote what was to become a crucial statement about Jesus' humanity. Irenaeus taught that Jesus was fully human, in every detail, and that "Quod non assumpsit, non redemit." That is, what was not assumed or included within the human nature of Jesus could not have been redeemed. In the year 451, the Council of Chalcedon set the final seal on this debate by stating that Jesus was a full human being with all his bodily parts intact and functioning. This means that sexuality is indeed a part of the new creation brought about by the redemptive work of Christ.

We now have a contemporary parallel to this debate. If the Vatican denies that women can represent the human Jesus, then how does Jesus represent women? If John Paul II's position that male and female natures are ontologically different is correct, then women's human nature could not be "assumed" by Jesus. Place the Pope's teaching alongside the "Quod non assumpsit" criterion of Irenaeus about Jesus' humanity, and the staggering but logical theological conclusion follows that women cannot be redeemed by a saviour who could not assume a female human nature.

But if the more traditional teaching that Jesus' humanity included women as well as men is true, as it must be according to the doctrine of the redemption, then the Vatican's insistence that all priests must bear a "natural resemblance" to Jesus as male makes no sense theologically. According to the traditional doctrine of redemption, Jesus became incarnate as a universal human being beyond the confines of gender, and his humanity includes all humanity: black, white, female, male—in fact, all human beings, past, present, and to come.

The "natural resemblance" argument used by the Vatican to keep women out of the priesthood also breaks down if, as a criterion of priesthood, it is applied to sexual orientation. The Catholic Church forbids homosexual sex, but it does acknowledge that there is a separate gay or lesbian sexual orientation which is not sinful in and of itself. Was Jesus gay or straight? If Jesus was straight, can a straight male saviour redeem gay men? Could a homosexual Jesus have redeemed heterosexuals?

There has been much shifting of ground on sexual orientation within the contemporary Catholic Church. The situation at present is that providing a gay man agrees to abide by the rule of celibacy still enjoined on all Catholic priests, he can be readily admitted to the Catholic priesthood. Recent statistics even indicate an increase in the number of gay men joining the priesthood and that at least a third of men now applying to Catholic seminaries have a homosexual orientation. The Catholic Church places no barriers in the way of their ordination.

But who bears a "natural resemblance" to Jesus? The gay priest or the straight priest? Which one is the "icon" of God? If both gay and straight males can bear a "natural resemblance" to Jesus, and males of either sexual orientation can be accepted for priesthood, why should gender continue to present an impenetrable barrier to priesthood? Jesus, the Word incarnate, could not have been both gay and straight at the same time, just as he could not have been both male and female at once. In a mysterious way, his human nature includes all possible variations.

It is impossible not to conclude that only a deep-rooted fear of feminism could have led the Vatican to take such desperate steps to prevent women from establishing a direct connection between themselves and Emmanuel, "God with us." In so doing, they seem to be excluding women from the path to salvation.

WOMEN AND BAPTISM

St. Thomas Aquinas, the theologian behind so much of traditional Catholic thinking, wrote eight centuries ago that the reason women could not be priests derived from the natural order of human affairs. Political and social life in the world have developed within a patriarchal structure, and accordingly, only men could hold authority within human institutions. Aquinas accepted without question the hierarchical and patriarchal rankings of medieval Europe and in so doing effectively elevated them to God's blueprint for the world. It was part of this natural order that men should rule and women should obey.[11]

Aquinas also accepted the philosopher Aristotle's dictum that women are "misbegotten" or "deformed" men. According to this notion, women derive their humanity only through men. So, Aquinas wrote, it was only fitting that the second person of the Trinity should be a man rather than a woman, because only men possess the fullness of humanity. But Jesus' humanity included women. This was because women's humanity in the natural order is subsumed under men's, so in the supernatural order of redemption, women were also subsumed under the male humanity of Christ, and were therefore included in all his work.

Aquinas taught that Christ's work of redemption overthrows the natural order. The redemption of the whole human race by Christ places women on a new and equal level with men. The "temporal" or "natural" order of the first creation of female subordination gives way to the new creation wrought by Christ. Through the sacrament of baptism, women as well as men enter into a new order of salvation, and women become equal to men in the sacred order of salvation established by Christ. Although unequal to men in secular society, women are full members of the Church and fully redeemed. Patriarchal structures, in other words, cannot be projected into heaven.

The reason that despite all of this work of redemption which makes them equal in the spiritual sphere, women still cannot become priests, Aquinas taught, was that the Church still exists as part of the temporal order here on earth and so its structure must be patterned after that order. This is the only way the Church can function in society without becoming a source of scandal. It would cause grave consternation for women to be placed in positions of authority over men as priests in the Church; therefore, they should not be ordained as priests. The female members of the

Church, Aquinas stated, will have to wait for heaven to realize the fullness of the new creation established by Christ.

Notice that the line of Aquinas' argument banning women from the priesthood is purely pragmatic. It has nothing to do with the theological nature of priesthood or the incarnation and redemption wrought by Jesus. Despite Aquinas' views of women as inferior human beings, he never for a moment denies that they are as fully represented and redeemed by Christ as men. In order to keep women out of exercising any authority in the Church, the Vatican has now reversed Aquinas' line of argument. The twentieth-century teaching elevates the inequality of women into the sacred rather than the secular sphere. It is not women's equality here on earth that is in question; it is their spiritual status that John Paul II's theology places in jeopardy.

In the light of the developments in society over the centuries since Aquinas, and the achievement of a measure of equality for women in public life since the 1950s, the Vatican realizes that it can no longer put forward a teaching which is based on the natural inferiority of women to men, although John Paul II's anthropology, as we have seen, actually depends on this concept. So how can the Vatican continue to hold the line against women priests? By shifting the ban on the ordination of women to the spiritual realm.

Women are now barred from ordination because their inferiority to men resides not in the temporal order of this earth, but in the spiritual order sanctioned in heaven. While obstacles to the realization of women's equality are slowly being removed here on earth, in the eternal, sacred realm, women will remain as a kind of permanent spiritual underclass because Jesus' maleness bars women forever from equality at the level of the sacred. The Vatican now teaches that patriarchy is in fact projected into heaven.

The sacrament of baptism is the foundational sacrament not just in the Catholic Church, but in every Christian denomination. "All who are baptized into Christ," writes St. Paul, "become a new creation."[12] But the Vatican's teaching on ordination calls into question the universality of the sacrament of baptism. The full effects of baptism, described in the words of St. Paul as "putting on the person of Christ," are actually limited only to men. According to the latest teaching on ordination, it is impossible for women to "put on the person of Christ" because they don't possess a "natural resemblance" to him.

IS CHRIST TRULY RISEN FROM THE DEAD?

According to Christian belief in the resurrection, Christ has "entered into glory." He is now in a completely different state of "being with God." Although he has entered into glory as a human as well as a divine person, all the limitations of his human nature have been overcome. Jesus is beyond time, place, suffering, and death. But according to the Vatican's teaching on women's ordination, this cosmic Christ is still limited by the boundaries of the male gender.

The Church has always taught that all of the seven sacraments, through which Catholics believe that human beings participate ever more deeply in the life of God, are part of the "new creation" brought about by the death and resurrection of Jesus. The Vatican's most recent teaching on women's ordination effectively removes the sacrament of the Eucharist from this post-resurrection sacramental order, because it makes the life and gifts of Jesus which flow through the sacrament subject to a contingency which places a limitation on Jesus' action. The hierarchy of the Church now states that only those human beings who bear in their genitals a pre-resurrection resemblance to Jesus may stand at the altar and take his place. This teaching means that the conduit for the sacramental graces of Eucharist must be limited to the confines of a male body.

John Paul II has proclaimed as an infallible doctrine that a baptized woman may not stand *in persona Christi* and cannot represent the risen Jesus because she lacks a "natural resemblance" to his earthly image. This contradicts a fundamental teaching on Eucharist which the Catholic Church has always held from the beginning: namely, that although the Eucharist commemorates the death of Jesus, the bread and wine used in the Mass are not transformed into the dead male human body of Jesus of Nazareth, but into the living, risen Jesus. It is the Risen Lord who is made present by the actions of the priest and the community celebrating Eucharist.

The Catholic Church has always taught that through the resurrection, Jesus burst the bonds of all human constraints, even death. But the current teaching on women's ordination states that Jesus' risen nature is still incomplete. Christ, having broken through the bondage of death to sit at the right hand of God, will be held captive for all eternity within the limitations of his gender. The Vatican is now teaching that earthly realities transcend those of heaven: that who Jesus was before the resurrection is an eternal aspect of the meaning of his life.

When I read John Paul II's 1994 statement on women's ordination, it truly made me wonder whether he believed in the resurrection, or whether he would not have preferred to have the Church left beside the cross on Calvary. "If Christ be not risen," says St. Paul, "our faith is in vain, and we are still in our sins." Mary Magdalene, Joanna, and the other women present at the empty tomb on the first Easter Sunday were mocked by the original male apostles to whom they announced the good news of the resurrection. It seems that women are still trying to get through to the men in the Vatican, who are sheltering in fear in their upper rooms, but the Catholic hierarchy shutters the windows to keep from being rattled by the breath of the Spirit.

THE TWELVE APOSTLES

Another line of argument employed by the Vatican to deny priestly ordination to women is based on their interpretation of how Jesus designated official leadership within the Christian community. Jesus ordained only twelve men to the priesthood. These men are specifically identified as the apostles. It is from these twelve that the Christian priesthood originated, and hierarchical authority in the Catholic Church is ordered in direct succession to the twelve apostles.

This literalist interpretation of the New Testament has come under considerable challenge in recent years. First of all, the concept of "apostle" is much more fluid in New Testament writings than the papal argument against women's ordination would have us believe. The word "apostle" in Greek signifies a "commissioned messenger." It is used in the letters of Paul, which we now know predate the writing of the four gospels, to refer to a variety of people, including women. Paul himself was not one of the twelve, but is most certainly counted as an apostle and celebrated Eucharist.

The twelve apostles do not feature at all in the gospel of John, neither does John highlight the breaking of bread at the Last Supper, choosing instead the washing of the disciples' feet by Jesus as the ultimate symbol of Christ's ministry. The only gospel accounts that do name the twelve (Mark 3:16–19, Matthew 10:2–4, Luke 6:12–16, and Acts 1:13) list only men. Does the sum total of this evidence for the naming of twelve male apostles mean that Jesus regarded maleness as an essential component of their mission?

In response to this, it might well be pointed out that with the exception of John, all the men named in these lists were married. Yet the overwhelming number of married men in the list of the twelve apostles has not been taken as an indicator of Jesus' preference for married leaders for the Church. In fact, quite the opposite view has prevailed in the Catholic Church, and since the twelfth century, married men have been barred from the Catholic priesthood. It does seem illogical to isolate only biological maleness as the characteristic for ordination of the twelve apostles while ignoring all their other human characteristics.

There is one passage in the New Testament which lays down much more specific criteria for a priesthood based on the example of Jesus. This occurs in the Letter to the Hebrews. Hebrews, long attributed to St. Paul but now known to have been written after his death, offers a long meditation on the priesthood of Jesus spread over several chapters. Hebrews is one of very few books in the New Testament in which Jesus is named as a priest and in which the characteristics of Jesus' priestly office are laid out in detail. Not a single one of these has anything to do with the gender of Jesus.

Jesus, says the author of Hebrews, is "the great High Priest who has gone into the presence of God." What are the characteristics of Jesus the High Priest? Jesus "was tempted in every way as we are." He "feels sympathy for our weaknesses" and so will help us to approach the throne of God, "where we will find mercy and grace to help us when we need it... In his life on earth, Jesus offered up his prayers and requests with loud cries and tears to God." God made Jesus a priest "because he was humble and devoted... he learned through suffering to be obedient."[13] Many would see the characteristics of Jesus as priest that are identified by this author as the very same qualities of nurturing and tenderness that are constantly extolled by the Vatican as more characteristic of women rather than men.

A priest, according to the author of the Hebrews, "is called and chosen by God... is weak in many ways, so must be gentle with others... and because he himself is weak, he must offer sacrifices not just for his own sins, but for those of the people." And, the author adds, "no one chooses for himself the honor of becoming a priest... it is only by God's call"—a call that the Vatican now declares is beyond the possibility of God to make to any woman, thus arrogating to themselves the power to curtail the actions of God in the world.

But to return to the twelve apostles. The number twelve is a literary device which is used to associate Jesus' followers with ancient Israel, which consisted of twelve tribes. This link is also made in the Book of Revelation to show that the creation of a New Jerusalem will be in continuity with this ancient pattern.[14]

In the gospel of Matthew, the power granted to the twelve is that of healing and exorcism, powers which are also granted in the other gospels to all disciples.[15] Mark's gospel, which was the earliest to be written down, conflates the twelve into the disciples in general and shows that in the crucial events of Jesus' passion and resurrection, it is actually the women disciples who show true fidelity and leadership. It is ironic that the Church has chosen to bar women from leading the sacramental reenactment at Mass of the very events of Calvary and Easter to which they were witnesses. In the gospel of Luke, it is seventy-two disciples who are called and sent out.[16] Given the motley crew of people of both genders who followed

Jesus, and his propensity to break down the barriers of propriety, it is highly likely that these seventy-two included women disciples.

After the ascension of Jesus, references to the twelve apostles disappear from the records of the early Church. At Pentecost, an event often taken to mark the birth of the Church, the Spirit was poured out equally on the whole community of men and women disciples gathered in the upper room. The leadership of the Church in Jerusalem passed to James, the brother of Jesus, who was not one of the twelve apostles. Leadership in the early Church as it is described in the Acts of the Apostles and in the letters of Paul was varied and variable, according to the gifts of the Spirit. The twelve were not specifically replaced as they died out. In the later writings of the New Testament, it does not appear that even the twelve apostles regarded their leadership as exclusive in the early Church community. The argument for a male-only priesthood based on the image of the twelve apostles is therefore a tenuous interpretation that stretches the texts beyond the intention of their New Testament authors.

BRIDES AND BRIDEGROOMS

Another argument often used by the Vatican to bar women from the priesthood is based on an interpretation of the text of the fifth chapter of the Letter to the Ephesians. Pope John Paul II, as well as other contemporary supporters of an exclusively male priesthood in the Catholic Church, often make use of the metaphor of marriage used by the author of the Letter to the Ephesians to describe the relationship between Christ and the Church. Like the Letter to the Hebrews, the Letter to the Ephesians was formerly ascribed to the apostle Paul, but modern scholarship attributes the authorship to a follower of Paul, probably writing around the year 90 C.E.

The Letter to the Ephesians reflects a toning-down of the radical equality of discipleship practiced in the early Christian community. As a result of the effects of the journeys of Paul, small communities of Christians had grown up in cities and towns, such as Ephesus, which were more open to influences from Rome and other parts of the empire. The Letter to the

Ephesians is thought to incorporate material from household codes which were in circulation within Roman society at the time. These codes were a sort of Roman family etiquette, and gave instructions on how various ranks within the household—women, children, slaves—should show respect for the authority of those above them in the household hierarchy. It was not long before these hierarchical rankings began to infiltrate the structure of the household of God, as is evident from this letter.

In the Letter to the Ephesians, the author admonishes wives to be subject to their husbands, and husbands to love their wives, "just as Christ loved the Church and gave up his life for her." He continues, "He did this to dedicate the Church to God by his word, after making it clean and washing it in water in order to present the Church to himself in all its beauty—spotless and without blemish or any other imperfection."[17] The author of Ephesians used nuptial imagery for Christ and the Church to emphasize that human marriage is based on mutual respect and self-giving. John Paul II comments on this passage in *Mulieris Dignitatem* as revealing "the spousal love of God."[18]

The nuptial language used in this passage, beautiful though it may appear on the surface, is always posited on an imbalance in the relationship between an all-powerful God, who is masculine, and an inferior and often wayward human spouse, who is always feminine. In biblical terms, this feminine human race is often in need of correction by God, just as in the letter to the Ephesians, the sinful female bride/Church has to be washed clean by the male bridegroom/Christ. The bride's love will always remain inferior to that of the bridegroom. As God, he is always the initiator, she the receiver. The repeated use of this imagery as a symbol of male dominance in the Church often serves to legitimize the behavior of some men to extend this sanction for male dominance into actual marriages.

Male commentators such as John Paul II who favor this interpretation have a view of the bridegroom not so much as the lover of the bride, but rather as the dominant head of the household. Their agenda in making use of this passage seems to be to show that there is a natural, God-given structure in marriage which is defined along traditional gender roles, and that this paradigm of human marriage must model the passive and subordinate position accorded to women in the Church. The whole orientation of this argument is toward marriage as a carefully controlled and structured power relationship rather than spontaneous reciprocal love and empathy. Even on its own terms, then, the symbol as used by the original author is effectively falsified.

In this way, the poetic metaphor of marriage, used to describe the relationship between Christ and the Church, is distorted into a justification for barring women from the priesthood. This metaphor, according to John Paul II, is a good way to describe what happened at the Last Supper when Jesus "gave the sacramental charge" to the twelve apostles. Leaving aside for now the controversies around the question of who exactly was at the Last Supper and what actually took place, let us look at how the Pope makes a connection between the Last Supper and the nuptial imagery of the Letter to the Ephesians.

In instituting the Eucharist at the Last Supper, writes John Paul in *Mulieris Dignitatem*, "Christ wished to express the relationship between man and woman, between what is 'feminine' and what is 'masculine.'"[19] This seems like a far-fetched interpretation of what was in the mind of Christ as he broke bread with his friends in the upper room the night before he died. I have enormous difficulty imagining Jesus, his mind full of the events of his last days in Jerusalem, sitting down at the Last Supper table and then doing all the mental conjuring necessary to make sure that not a whiff of anything that could smack of "the feminine" should be present.

But John Paul II tries to prove that the image of the bride and bridegroom means that the Church must be essentially feminine. In spite of this, though, men can still be full and equal members of the Church. Men can belong to the Church, because the "bride," or Church, is a "collective subject." This is because, writes John Paul II, "in the human sphere, masculinity and femininity are distinct, yet at the same time they complete and explain each other." Men can be brides and so belong to the Church. But women can't be bridegrooms. This is because, he continues, "bridegroom" is a singular noun, and thus the bridegroom can only be an individual male.

There is something desperately wrong in the logic here. A symbol is a symbol is a symbol. It cannot be distorted in such a reductionist fashion. Women feel all the more degraded because such weak arguments are used to serve an agenda that is blatantly biased against them. Whenever the argument is about giving women power, as in this case, John Paul II twists the Scripture to suit his rationale. One could argue with the same logic that if "bride," which is a singular noun, is a "collective subject," why cannot "bridegroom" also be? If the gifts of femininity and masculinity can complement each other in the Church, then why should they not complement each other in the priesthood? If we are to accept a literalist position that only a male human being can be a bridegroom, then let's pose another literalist question: at what stage of growth does that male human being who has been a "bride," washed clean in the waters of baptism, suddenly become eligible to become a bridegroom? And if the Church is intrinsically feminine, then wouldn't it also make sense for her priests to be only female?

Cardinal Ambrozic of Toronto was quoted in Chapter 1 as stating that we must not call God by feminine terms because that would make God into a hermaphrodite. By the same kind of reasoning, then, if we have men in the female Church, does that not also make the Church into a hermaphrodite? If "bride" is a collective subject, then why is the noun "God" not also a collective subject, especially given the Christian belief in the collective mystery of the Trinity. In order to avoid calling God "Mother," John Paul II falls back onto the argument that God is pure spirit. And yet when the tables are reversed, and men's access to the sacred is at stake, men can be called by the female term "bride." Women may never usurp male language, especially when it comes to God, but men can usurp female language at will.

These specious arguments developed from nuptial imagery to "prove" the case for a male-only priesthood have appeared only in recent years in the Church. The traditional arguments have always relied on the now

discredited theory of women's "misbegotten" human nature as a derivative of the fully human male. The nuptial bed analogy first occurred in
Pope Paul VI's apostolic letter *Inter Insigniores* in 1976. It is another twist
in the new teaching which the Vatican has invented to justify male dominance in the Church.

THE CHURCH AND CHANGE

The Vatican has not only invented new Catholic traditions to ban contemporary Catholic women from the priesthood. In his 1996 instruction on
women priests, Pope John Paul II solemnly stated that the Catholic
Church simply does not have the power to change the male-only priesthood, which he claims was part of Christ's eternal and immutable will for
the structure of the Church. This is a most outrageous assertion for a
Catholic to make. It relies on a view of tradition, and of the Church's place
in forming that tradition, based on the *sola scriptura*, or fundamentalist,
approach to revelation contained in the Bible.

To accept that God had an "eternal will" for the structure of the
Church is to assume that Jesus left detailed instructions with the apostles,
which they simply followed without debate of any kind. Taken to its logical conclusion, this approach would mean that when Jesus ascended into
heaven, the whole Roman structure of the Church was already present on
earth, complete with bishops' miters and scarlet socks for cardinals. The
power of the Holy Spirit, released upon the Church at Pentecost, would
be reduced to an imprimatur on an already existing, detailed structure for
the community.

This view is disproved almost from the first moments of the Church's
existence. Shortly after the resurrection of Jesus, the Church was seriously
divided over the admission of the gentiles to baptism. The Acts of the
Apostles and the Letters of Paul contain resonances of this, the first
of many great theological debates in the Church. Should non-Jews be
admitted to the Church? If they are admitted to baptism, should they be
circumcised first?

The Pope's predecessor, the first Peter, did an about-face on this issue. God enlightened Peter very directly through a vision Peter received on the occasion of his visit to the house of the Roman captain Cornelius. Peter realized that, in his own words: "God has shown me that I must not consider any person ritually unclean or defiled."[20] In one fell swoop, the whole structure underpinning Jewish purity laws and ritual exclusiveness was put aside. Cornelius and his family were baptized by Peter without being subjected to circumcision or any other ritual purification.

Peter subsequently came under great pressure from a conservative faction of the Church, then centered in Jerusalem, who believed that this action was a threat to their community. In response, Peter reneged on God's inclusive vision and abruptly ceased to eat with gentiles or admit them to baptism. "When Peter went to Antioch, he and the other Jewish brothers who had started acting like cowards along with Peter" were rebuked in public by the apostle Paul for going back on God's word to the gentiles.[21]

A Council of the Church was summoned in Jerusalem to settle the issue. The whole company of believers—women and men—debated, prayed, and eventually reached a consensus. This was a community decision, not one made by Peter alone. Peter was brought to task by the community. The decision was reached after differing viewpoints had been thoroughly aired. Factions had formed around these differing viewpoints, each one no doubt convinced that they represented the "mind of Jesus" on this issue. Jesus himself had never baptized anyone, let alone a gentile. How was the Church to deal with this new circumstance and proceed on its path through history?

The request for baptism had come from gentiles themselves, as many felt called to join the Christian community. The apostle Philip had already baptized an Ethiopian official.[22] The gentiles were already receiving the power of the Spirit without any intervention from the Church.[23] After the discussion at the Council of Jerusalem, "the apostles and elders" wrote a magnificent statement to be delivered to the gentile converts of the churches of Antioch, Syria, and Cilicia, who had asked for guidance. "It has seemed good to the Holy Spirit and to us not to lay any burdens on you beside these necessary rules. Eat no food that has been offered to idols..."[24]

Notice how this process unfolded. The Spirit of God started to work in unexpected ways, outside the boundaries of the early Christian community. As Walter Brueggemann has expressed it, God's work is "disjunctive." From the very beginning, God's Spirit is shown to be active outside the boundaries of Church tradition and apostolic control. The Spirit descended on people who were not officially included in the inner circles of Jesus' ministry. Jesus left no specific instructions on the admission of gentiles to baptism. But Jesus' example and teachings were always in the direction of more rather than less inclusiveness. Jesus, they remembered, often broke down religious traditions and rules when these became barriers to the free exercise of God's love.

If we make a parallel with the issue of women's ordination in the present day, it becomes evident that according to the pattern laid down through the action of the Spirit in the early Church, the matter of women's ordination should now be very much open to debate. God is empowering women all over the contemporary world in a multitude of ways to take their full place in all spheres of society. God is calling women to the priesthood within all the Christian Churches, including the Catholic Church. New life is springing up in churches where women have been ordained.

The Second Vatican Council called the Catholic Church both to return to its roots and to "discern the signs of the times" in order to find the direction for witnessing to the gospel in the contemporary world. That "the Church is always in need of reform"[25] was another theme of the Council. To acknowledge that, historically, there has been a long tradition of not ordaining women does not necessarily lead to the conclusion that therefore Catholic tradition must forbid the ordination of women for all time.

But contemporary successors of Peter, just like the first Peter, have resisted the liberating message of Pope John XXIII and the Second Vatican Council. Reactionary factions such as Opus Dei have seized power and control in the Church. Now the modern successor of Peter, a figure whom both the New Testament and the history of the Church have shown to be often fallible and inconsistent, claims to have unilateral access to the mind of Jesus. The mind of Jesus, in his interpretation, is closed on the issue of women, and he is desperately trying to extinguish the work of God's Spirit, which is now speaking through women inside and outside the Catholic Church.

In so doing, he and others who bow before the idol of male supremacy in the Catholic Church have jeopardized much of the traditional theology of the Church. Their theology of male-only ordination has put the theologies of baptism, incarnation, redemption, resurrection, and the Eucharist in question and in contradiction among themselves. It is not only what sexism says about women that is dangerous; it is what sexism says about God that is basically heretical.

This God, who is pure spirit and dwells in unapproachable light, who can raise the dead, draw water from a rock, and lead a whole people out of slavery is, so the Vatican says, unable to work as fully through a woman as through a man. Is the grace of God, then, gender specific? Of course not. Could God have sent Jesus in the form of a woman? Of course. God, in the words of the theologian Carter Heyward, is "the power of the all-possible."[26] This God is at work today inspiring women, who are made in God's image, to call the Catholic Church and the world to conversion from the discredited and increasingly dangerous doctrine of patriarchy.

Does God, who created women as precious images of Her inner being and as beautiful in His eyes, really want women to receive a message from the Catholic Church that they are not worthy to serve at the altar? Does this God, who opens His hands to feed the hungry and who wipes away every tear from the face of Her beloved people, turn women away with all the hardness of stone rather than offering the bread of life?

Would the machismo of this Catholic culture flourish if God was addressed as Madre as well as Padre? Would a Catholic man be so ready to raise a hand to slap his wife if he had seen the hands of women lift up the body and blood of Christ at the altar? Would Catholic soldiers in places like Bosnia or Rwanda consider the rape of women just another act of war if they knelt in confession before the female face of God as presented by a woman priest? This is not simply a theological debate within the Catholic Church, but one with wide repercussions in the contemporary world.

Chapter Four

Girls in the
Catholic School System

I n the years since the publication of *Mulieris Dignitatem* in 1988, many Catholic women have fled the Church, alienated by the virulence of John Paul II's personal crusade against feminism and his intransigence on the issue of women's ordination. But what of the new generation of Catholics now in their teens and twenties? Do the anthropological and theological arguments over the issue of women's ordination examined in the last two chapters have any direct impact on their lives? Based on my experience of more than thirty years teaching high school, I believe that indeed they do.

I remember the young women in the classrooms of Catholic high schools in Toronto, many of whom come from traditional Catholic cultures—Portuguese, Polish, or Italian, for example—where religion is deeply woven into the fabric of daily life. I remember Silvana, who told me that she was expected to make her brothers' beds every morning before she left for school. I thought of Anna, who had been informed by her parents that even though she was a year older than her brother, she must wait until he had made his choice of a university before she could apply.

She would have to attend the same university as her brother so that she would be available to keep house for him.

Now some people would argue that these are cultural norms for women which have nothing to do with the influence of the Church. But these norms emanate from the very roots of Catholic cultures, where the rule of the "Fathers" and the second-class position of women in the Church have legitimized and enhanced the dominance of Catholic men in general, whether they be fathers, brothers, husbands, or boyfriends, over "their" women. If the girls are among that minority of young Catholics who still go to Mass, they are certainly not getting the message from Catholic priests that women are made in the image of God and created equal to men.

The 1980s and '90s have seen major United Nations world conferences on global issues such as social development and the environment. Most significant in the last twenty years have been the number of UN gatherings devoted specifically to the topic of women and girls. The first world conference of International Women's Year (1975) was hosted by the UN in Mexico City, followed by conferences on women in Nairobi in 1985 and in Beijing in 1995, not to mention the International Conference on Population and Development held in Cairo in 1994. These conferences have focused attention on the plight of the world's children, and in particular on that half of the world's children born female. Examining the fate of "the girl child" has exposed the fact that these children face problems of poverty, abuse, and violence which are linked specifically to their gender.

In 1991, the United Nations published a report titled *Women: Challenges to the Year 2000*. The legacy of religious traditions, the report states, still presents numerous obstacles to the achievement of equality for women throughout the world. "Monotheistic religions were often interpreted in ways that devalued and subjected women," the report states. This analysis is supported by a quote from Thomas Aquinas: "A necessary object, woman, who is needed to preserve the species and to provide food and drink... man is above woman as Christ is above man. It is unchangeable that woman is destined to live under man's influence, and has no authority from her lord."[1]

Catholic girls, even in a relatively prosperous society such as Canada, are still destined to "live under man's influence" because of the influence of the Church on Catholic families and Catholic schools. When the highest authorities in the Church teach in the name of God that women cannot define their own destiny, that women are not subjects of their own actions but the objects of reflection and action by men, and that only men can stand in the place of God as a priest, then the authority over women's lives that this God is said to place in the hands of pope, bishop, or parish priest is logically extended to that of husband over wife and brother over sister in the Catholic home.

Even though most high school students who come from Catholic homes no longer attend church, the message and role models that they see at home are deeply influenced by the opinions and teachings of the Pope, as examined in the last two chapters. The role models for men and women as these are lived out in the values and customs of the Catholic family have been deeply influenced by the patriarchal patterns of Catholic theology and Church structure. These patterns now form a serious impediment to teachers in Catholic schools who wish to promote healthy relationships between women and men.

In its analysis of the causes of child sexual abuse by clergy, the Winter Commission of Newfoundland (1990) pointed out that the denominational Catholic school can actually be an accomplice to all kinds of abuse because it reproduces and reinforces the patriarchal patterns of the Catholic Church. "The acceptance of patriarchy," the report states in Chapter 5, "begins early in the life of Church community members. The denominational educational experience, while providing in many cases an important experience of community, may also have tended to compound paternalistic and patriarchal attitudes." The report cites "the fear of the Church's administrative role in education" and the "lack of curricula and teaching strategies to address the problems of violence and male domination . . . which are so deeply ingrained in our culture and in the Church community"[2] as factors that have allowed abusive attitudes to become entrenched in Catholic schools. It goes without saying that these factors are by no means confined to classrooms in Newfoundland.

The Catholic Church continues to legitimize male dominance through sexist attitudes and practices in Church structure, which in turn have an impact on the school and the family. The Church's teaching that women cannot represent God is often used as a justification for a subservient role for women in the home and in society at large. Pope John Paul II has gone out of his way to insist that female inferiority is a matter of divine revelation, and that "secular" norms and practices of equal rights and status for women do not apply to matters which concern the Church. If good Catholic homes and denominational Catholic schools are supposed to be patterned after the example and inspiration of this same Church, then structures of male dominance are part of the orthodoxy that will be inculcated there as well.

I know from long experience dealing with issues in adolescent relationships in the co-ed classroom that many a Catholic male thinks that this "orthodox tradition" gives him the right to dictate to his girlfriend what she wears, whom she talks to, and what she does, even when they are apart. If she does not comply, he has every right to "teach her a lesson" about who is in control. Take this attitude into a marriage, and you have a situation ripe for abuse and violence.

The effects of an anthropology and theology that support male dominance are profound in the Catholic school, even in a country such as Canada which has been a leader in the advancement of women to full equality in society. Under the Canadian Constitution, specifically the British North America Act of 1867, denominational schools are exempted from anything within the Constitution that would impinge on matters classified as denominational or religious in nature. The Act states that:

In and for each Province the Legislature may exclusively make laws in relation to education, subject and according to the following Provisions: (1) Nothing in any such Law shall prejudicially affect any right or Privilege with respect to denominational schools which any class of persons have by law in the Province at the Union (2) All the powers, privileges and Duties at the Union by Law conferred and imposed in Upper Canada on the Separate Schools and School Trustees of the Queen's Roman Catholic Subjects shall be the same as are hereby extended to the dissentient Schools of the Queen's Protestant and Roman Catholic subjects in Quebec.[3]

This provision of the Canadian Constitution has had the effect of protecting sexism in denominational schools. The Pope insists that discrimination against women within the structure of the Catholic Church is now a part of divine revelation. When I moved from the Scarborough Board of Education and started to teach religion for the Toronto Catholic School Board in 1985, one of the real differences in the two systems that I came up against almost immediately was that according to members of the Canadian Church hierarchy such as Archbishop Ambrozic of Toronto, papal teaching on the role of women is part of the "Catholicity" or denominational status of Catholic schools in Canada. That is, Canadian Catholic schools must teach young women what their true destiny in life is.

In 1986, Archbishop Ambrozic published a report on a pastoral visitation to Catholic schools in the Archdiocese of Toronto which he undertook from 1985. His report found fault with several aspects of the schools. The Archbishop's severest criticism was reserved for teachers of religion, whom he accuses of being "infected with the disease of liberal orthodoxy." According to the Archbishop, these teachers have led students to believe that "Jesus was a nice guy who would not let them go to hell"; and furthermore, they were "averse to teaching the traditional doctrine on mortal sin." He complains that "priesthood and religious life are not given sufficient prominence. And," he adds, "I suspect there is some agitation for female ordination."[4]

In his list of recommendations to remedy this situation, the Archbishop states that the central issue is that schools should "strive for Catholicity and the acceptance of integral revelation." The details of what the "Catholicity" of a school actually means are further spelled out in recommendation number 9, which is specifically about curriculum. The curriculum, the Archbishop states, must include "the divinity of Jesus, Sunday Mass, daily prayers . . . and girls are to be impressed with the importance of motherhood."[5]

This directive on teaching women their role is stated by the supreme authority on religion in the Catholic school. By virtue of his ranking in the Church, the Archbishop is the *ex officio* Chair of the School Board for all the separate school boards in the archdiocese. Even though the trustees who run the separate school boards are elected by Catholic ratepayers, their decisions can be overruled at any time by the authority granted in canon law to the "local ordinary," or bishop. School trustees are accountable in most matters to Catholic ratepayers; the local archbishop is accountable to no one. If the right of the bishop to run the Catholic school board were ever challenged in a Canadian court, the canon law of the Church, which accords him his religious authority, would probably take precedence over Canadian civil law because of the denominational privileges granted to Catholic schools under the British North America Act. Ironically, the bishop's power to tell Catholic school boards what they must teach young girls about the role of women is protected by the Canadian Constitution, even if it is contrary to the equality provisions of the 1982 Charter of Rights and Freedoms.

In recent times, the secular curriculum for schools in the Province of Ontario has reflected the improvements in the status of women that have been taking place in Canadian society. New teachers in Ontario are trained in awareness and sensitivity to issues such as sexism and racism, which can be systemic within the curriculum, school texts, classroom management, and school life in general. In contrast, Catholic school boards received a clear message from the Archbishop's 1986 report: to impress girls with the importance of motherhood is tantamount to a test of the Catholicity of the Catholic school. This is but one example of the painful dissonance inherent in the life of the Catholic school, dissonance which hampers the best efforts of Catholic teachers to inculcate and model equality and mutual respect between men and women.

THE HIDDEN CURRICULUM IN CATHOLIC SCHOOLS

On Mass days, a special timetable comes into effect in the Catholic school. School Mass is one of the central and compulsory components of contemporary Catholic education and one of the most intractable components of Catholic sexism. School Mass is supported by taxes in the Province of Ontario, where Catholic schools are publicly funded and constitutionally protected.

Does a school Mass celebrate the reenactment of the life and death of that radical rabbi, Jesus of Nazareth, who brought women into the inner temple in defiance of religious laws and often transgressed the boundaries men had placed around the sacred? Quite the contrary. As was shown in Chapter 3, the Catholic Church inculcates specific exclusionary and discriminatory behavior toward women through its religious rituals. It legislates that the Mass and all other sacraments are reserved for priests to administer. By virtue of priestly ordination, men control all decision making in the Church. It is through this modeling of male dominance that the Church implicitly teaches young girls that they are of less value in God's eyes, they are not equal to men, and their place within religious structures is subordinate. The Catholic school legitimizes and reinforces this every time students participate in school Mass.

Blatant sexism is not spelled out in the religion curriculum in Catholic schools, but what educators call the "hidden curriculum" is often a more powerful influence on student attitudes than what is contained between the covers of textbooks. This hidden curriculum encompasses issues such as whether male and female sports rank equally and obtain equal funding, the relative power of male and female teachers, the subjects and departments that have status in the school, the management of the classroom, and the kind of images displayed in the classrooms and hallways.

In Spike Lee's movie *Malcolm X*, there is a scene that depicts the conversion of Malcolm to Islam while he was in jail. A black Muslim guard takes him to the prison chapel and shows him the images of God and goodness that are on display. "Look, Malcolm," he says, "don't you see that this is the white man's religion, and it's just being used to keep you and me in slavery?" I was often reminded of this scene as I accompanied students from my classroom to the local church for school Mass. Sexist conditioning is part of the ethos of every Catholic church building. The images and rituals teach students that God is male. Whatever they may have heard in the classroom about equality, and however hard teachers have tried to challenge misogynist attitudes and behavior, sexism kicks right back in again as soon as Catholic students step into the church for Mass.

What is the gender of the God addressed in the prayers? Male. Who is God's minister at the altar? A man. Who preaches the sermon to the school community? A man. Whose experiences does he draw on for his preaching? Men's. What language is used to describe human beings in the readings and the hymns? Almost exclusively male. How are women portrayed in the statues and paintings inside the church? Like the Virgin Mary, beautiful, passive, and obedient.

Catholic students study the same curriculum as public high school students in all subjects except religion. They learn about democracy, about the Canadian Charter of Rights, and about laws that have been fought for and enacted to prevent discrimination and abuse. The mission statements of most Catholic schools contain clauses about equality, a safe school environment, and mutual respect, all of which are underlined by "gospel values" and "following the example of Jesus." And yet there is a malignancy in the Catholic school environment which eats away at these values: the patriarchal structures in the Catholic Church and the portrayal of God as a man.

Imagine the impact on young women of years of this religious conditioning, inculcated at an unconscious as well as a conscious level in the Catholic home, school, and parish. Every domain over which the Catholic Church has control speaks volumes to the Catholic girl that whatever society may be doing to rectify the inequality of women and men, in God's domain she can never be fully accepted as an equal.

It is the more intelligent young Catholic women who are now particularly aware of these contradictory signals, and who are most likely to give up on the Church in disgust for its contempt for them. In 1996, the

Toronto Secondary Unit of OECTA published an *Equity Report* based on input from 70 percent of the teachers in Catholic high schools in Toronto. This is what one chaplaincy team leader had to say about working with young Catholic women:

> I have been a chaplaincy team leader for a number of years and have experienced great difficulty in dealing with the clergy in the course of my job. The overlay of the Church's teaching on women and the way the Church discriminates against women is a constant source of difficulty for a female chaplaincy team leader. On many occasions I have been overruled by a priest—sometimes in liturgies which I have taken a long time to prepare—simply by virtue of the fact that he has a collar and is therefore the supreme decision maker in any matter which touches the Church. I have an extensive theological background, but have been contradicted by clergy who have not opened a book of theology since they left the seminary. I have tried to encourage young women to take a leadership role in prayer groups and retreats, but the brightest and best are hostile to anything to do with the Church because they know it does not take their gifts and talents seriously.[6]

The first draft of the U.S. bishops' *Pastoral*, before the Vatican censors got their hands on it, noted that "clearly women feel alienated when clergy patronize them and treat their concerns as trivial." The same document also pointed to a sense of alienation among women in general, noting that this was particularly apparent among "college-age and single women who have leadership abilities but feel excluded from decision-making roles."[7] This alienation starts in high school and sometimes earlier. Girls who develop a sense of social responsibility and assume leadership roles in student councils, in anti-racist or in social justice activities in school find no outlet for their skills within the Church. Gone are the days when young women would consider it a privilege to wash the altar linens.

Even though Pope John Paul II's 1988 apostolic letter on women, *Mulieris Dignitatem*, condemns discrimination and violence against women in society, the Catholic Church's internal hierarchy of entrenched male privilege undermines this message. The Pope's teaching that it is God's will for discrimination against women to continue in the Church speaks louder to the world than his views on God's "preferential option" for the poor. In fact, his teaching on the separate and biologically determined role of women is a direct contradiction to the preferential option for the poor, the majority of whom are women. This fact is not lost on today's generation of young Catholics.

SEEN AND NOT HEARD

Cristina was a grade 12 student at the school where I was teaching. She was enrolled in a religion class taught by one of my colleagues. We had worked hard to ensure that the grade 12 religion program, which is the last religion course that students take before leaving high school, would be exciting and intellectually challenging. We were determined that students would receive the best theology the contemporary Church could offer in the hope that they would be encouraged to move into an adult relationship with God.

Cristina was a lively and articulate young woman, a leading participant in school life, especially in plays and musical productions—an ideal student and a parent's pride and joy. She was also among a very small minority of students who not only attended Mass every Sunday, but also took an active part in the parish liturgy as a lay reader. Her religious beliefs had been formed in a devout Italian family, and during her adolescence, the religion programs at the high school had stimulated her mind and nourished her spirituality.

Much of the grade 12 religion course in Catholic high schools deals with the relevance of Church teachings to the social and economic issues of today. The students in Cristina's class had studied the 1987 encyclical letter of John Paul II, *Sollicitudo Rei Socialis: Concern for the Social Order*. In this letter, the Pope urges Catholics to take a leadership role in making what he calls a preferential choice for the poor of this world. "This," he writes, "is an option or a special form of primacy in the exercise of Christian charity to which the whole tradition of the Church bears witness. It affects the life of each Christian inasmuch as he or she seeks to imitate the life of Christ, but it applies equally to our social responsibilities and hence to our manner of living, and to the logical decisions to be made concerning the ownership and use of goods... Our daily life as well as our decisions in the political and economic fields must be marked by these realities."[8]

Cristina became inspired by the Pope's words. It happened that just at this time, the parish church which she attended received a bequest of several thousand dollars. The priests decided to use this money to cover the church steps with marble, refurbish the Marian altar inside the church, and erect a large statue of the Virgin Mary in the courtyard outside.

After Mass one Sunday, Cristina spoke to one of the assistant priests. She told him she did not agree with the way the parish was disposing of the bequest by using it to decorate the church building. Could it not be used to make a downpayment on a house which the parish could support to shelter the homeless? The priest was noncommittal but said he would convey her opinions to the pastor, who was absent at that time.

Cristina heard nothing further until a few weeks later, when the entire school went to the same church for the last Mass of the school year. As she was leaving the church with her friends, she was stopped by the pastor. He had just stepped down from the altar, and was arrayed in all his priestly vestments, the regalia of his divine office.

"Cristina!" he called. "I want to have a word with you. What's this I hear—that you have been criticizing the Church? Just who do you think you are!" His tone of voice and demeanor oozing scorn, he continued, "Little Cristina, you think you have the right to take on the Church? How dare you! You come from a good Italian family. Your parents must be ashamed of you! You must be possessed by the devil!" Those who witnessed this scene said that the priest was screaming by the time he finished this diatribe.

Cristina, stunned and shocked by this sudden public attack in front of her friends and other students and teachers, fled to the school religion office and tearfully choked out to several teachers what the priest had just said to her. She was frightened as well as angry. "What if he tells my parents I am possessed?" she cried. "They will go crazy, because they're going to believe the priest." Over the next few days her initial shock grew into anger and a deep feeling of betrayal that her first steps into adult faith and responsibility in a church she had loved since childhood should be so brutally rebuffed.

Within a couple of days Cristina received a phone call from the assistant priest. He apologized for the way the pastor had spoken to her. "We don't agree with what he said to you," he told her. "But," he added, "we've decided to remove you from the readers' list because you don't agree with the way the church is run. We know it's not your fault, though. It's the ideas those feminist teachers at your school are putting into your head."

Cristina related this conversation to several teachers. It struck us that the reactions of the parish clergy were a throwback to the days of witch hunts and the Inquisition. An "uppity" young woman raises questions. She must be possessed by the devil, like her ancestors who had dared to practice the healing arts or had shown signs of independence from their husbands and were burned by the Church as witches. Would the priest, we wondered, have attributed her "feminist" ideas to her teachers if they had been male? We also speculated that a priest might not have used language of demonic possession if he had been dressing down a male rather than a female student.

It is ironic that the priest labelled these ideas "feminist" in that it was Pope John Paul II's encyclical that had inspired Cristina's action. But Cristina was most angered at not being taken seriously. "That remark about my teachers putting ideas in my head really got to me," she said. "It's as though he doesn't accept that I can think for myself." Cristina stopped going to church. "It makes me too angry," she told me. "I can't help remembering what happened." I told her that if she stayed in the Church, her experience would help her to work for change. "Why should I bother?" she responded. "The Church doesn't care about young people or take us seriously."

Cristina's story sums up the pain and paradox of Catholic youth, especially women, who are trying to remain faithful to the Catholic Church within contemporary society. Educated at school to believe in values of democracy and civic responsibility, and encouraged in all their studies to question and articulate their concerns about society, they run smack up against the hard face of an autocratic and paternalistic Church if and when they ever decide to actually attend Mass and participate in parish life. This situation has worsened under Pope John Paul II, who has made issues such as contraception, homosexuality, and the place of women—all of which are normal issues for adolescents to discuss as they wrestle with present and future life choices—into matters of faith which must be followed with blind obedience to the authority of the Church rather than by an inner conviction of the inherent moral worth of the Church's teaching.

INCLUSIVE LANGUAGE

Another issue which has profound implications for education, and one on which the Vatican has sought to enforce religious obedience to its man-made rules, is that of inclusive, or gender-neutral, language. This is another area where the denominational character of Catholic schools in Ontario leads to a direct conflict with attempts in Canadian society to combat sexism.

In the academic world, as well as in government and in business, it has come to be recognized that language is not neutral. Words both shape and reflect our perception of reality. Language has power. With the exception of religion courses and school worship, Catholic school boards have in other respects followed the lead of Canadian society in introducing the use of gender-neutral language within the norms laid down for general language usage in official documents, textbooks, and student assignments.

Language evolves to reflect social and political shifts in human society. As democracy has progressed in the West, titles have all but disappeared. When I was a child, I was taught to add the word "Esquire," or "Esq." for short, when addressing correspondence to a man. To do that now would be considered anachronistic. In response to the changing status of women, the word "man" as a collective noun to describe male and female humanity has become less and less acceptable. Whatever may have been the meaning of "man" in the past, to use it now as a collective noun conveys the impression that the writer believes that the male gender is the norm and that women have a subordinate place subsumed within the humanity of men. However "correct" the use of this noun may have been in the past, it now bears the burden of sexist language.

An African friend of mine who was doing a doctorate at the Ontario Institute for Studies in Education told me about an incident in one of his classes which illustrates how our sensitivity to systemic racism has affected the use of language. A woman was giving a presentation on some aspect of educational history and used the word "Negro" to describe blacks. "Please don't use that word," said my friend. "But it's the correct term and it's in all the books which deal with the topic," she responded. "If you use that word again," he answered, "I will get up and walk out of this class." She changed the word. To use the word "man" today reflects an insensitivity to sexism. Many women are getting up and walking out of the Church because of its insistence on the use of sexist language.

In 1965, the final document issued by the Second Vatican Council, *Gaudium et Spes: The Church in the Modern World*, had this to say about the relationship of the Church to movements for civil rights and equality in society: "... every type of discrimination... whether based on sex, race, color, social condition, language or religion is to be overcome and eradicated as contrary to God's interest."9 The Church stood shoulder to shoulder with movements for liberation in society. As I read the documents of the Second Vatican Council today, while I am struck by their prophetic and passionate power, I am also jarred by the sexist language. The movement for inclusive language postdated the Council. Would the contemporary movement toward the use of inclusive language in the Church have been within the spirit of the Council? In the light of this quote from *Gaudium et Spes*, it would seem so.

The Canadian Conference of Catholic Bishops, in a *Pastoral Message on Inclusive Language: To Speak as a Christian Community* (1989), reflects a direction toward inclusiveness as a natural evolution of this spirit.

As Christians we are called to witness to the fundamental equality and dignity of all people. This involves diverse actions for social justice which promote human life and dignity. One relatively simple but effective action is the use of inclusive language...[10]

Trying to head off the anticipated furor from reactionary Catholics who contend that inclusive language is part of the "secular" and demonic movement of feminism, the bishops continue:

Inclusive language was introduced into society by the contemporary women's movement. As a result, some people feel it may only be a cultural question. Vatican II, however, reminded us that the Church exists in the world and that Christians have a responsibility to read the "signs of the times" and interpret them in the light of the gospel. One of the signs of the times identified by Vatican II and recent popes is the changing role of women in society. There is, therefore, a special duty to listen to what women are saying about the need for inclusive language. Through listening and reflecting, it becomes apparent that there are significant theological reasons for using and promoting inclusive language.[11]

Sexism and the use of sexist language is a theological issue as well as a cultural development. The Canadian bishops go on to outline the theological reasons for the use of inclusive language. Language, they say, has constantly evolved in the Church as it has sought to express the Good News of salvation to every generation. Inclusive language is an expression of the God-given equality between men and women. The Church, they conclude, is called to be a sign to the world of the equality and the unity of humanity preached by Jesus Christ. Inclusive, nonsexist language is therefore closer to the spirit of Christ's teaching.

John Paul II's theology of fundamental difference between male and female stands in sharp contrast to the teaching of the Canadian bishops. Given the emphasis John Paul places on these differences rather than on the unity of the human race, and also the fact that the Vatican refuses to recognize "gender" as a social construction of masculinity and femininity, it might logically follow that the Vatican would be in favor of differentiating linguistically between male and female humanity. This is not the case.

In 1990, the U.S. National Conference of Catholic Bishops embarked on a new translation of the lectionary, the cycle of biblical texts used as daily readings during the Eucharist. One of the criteria they put forward was that the translations "should be as inclusive as a faithful translation permits." A year later they approved a new lectionary for Sundays that used inclusive language, as well as an inclusive-language revision of the Psalter. The Vatican's Congregation for the Sacraments, the office normally responsible for text used in the liturgy, approved the inclusive-language Psalter in 1992 but withheld approval of the lectionary. Two years later, an edict came down from Cardinal Ratzinger's office, the Congregation for the Doctrine of the Faith, which revoked the previous approval of the Psalter. A year later, this office issued new norms for biblical translations but kept them secret.[12]

In 1996, yet another secret committee of the Vatican—and because the membership was never revealed, it is by no means certain that the members were native English speakers—met to discuss and issue anonymous "observations" on the English translation of the lectionary. A journalist for the *National Catholic Reporter* eventually succeeded in breaching the wall of secrecy surrounding the membership of the Committee. Eleven men, two of whom were non-English speakers, discarded three decades of work by Scripture scholars and ignored the guidelines for inclusive language laid down by the U.S. bishops in 1990. Michael Waldstein, the sole Scripture scholar in the group, is German-speaking by birth though fluent in English. At least one member of the Committee, Father Mario Lessi-Ariosto, had only a "spotty command of the English language."[13] Several members of this committee had a history of objecting to the use of inclusive language. The Hebrew psalms, for example, have few masculine pronouns for God, but this committee rejected the use of inclusive language in the Psalter. In effect, they chose to translate the Bible inaccurately rather than appear to give in to demands for more inclusive language.

This flurry of activity concerning the use of inclusive language in the liturgy occurred just around the time of the 1995 papal statement which placed a ban on any discussion of women's ordination. Not only were women to be banned from officiating at the altar, but even the thought that God might speak directly to and through women as well as men was evidently becoming too threatening a proposition to be entertained.

In 1996, seven U.S. cardinals went to Rome to try and broker a resolution to the standoff on inclusive language. It was only in 1997, six years after the first draft had been sent to Rome, that an agreement was worked out which included "a moderate degree of horizontal [i.e., with reference to humans but not to God] inclusive language."[14] The Vatican vetoed altogether the substitution of plural nouns or pronouns for singular. This means that the translation "Let none of you deceive yourselves" proposed by the bishops for a sentence in Paul's First Letter to the Corinthians must revert by order from Rome to "Let no one delude himself." In 1998, six years after the Congregation for the Sacraments had initially given it the stamp of approval, Ratzinger vetoed the new translation of the Psalter. Any praying of the psalms in U.S. Catholic churches will henceforth conform to the male-only version of the 1970 translation.

These are just some examples of a concerted effort on the part of the Vatican to reverse progress made toward the use of inclusive language in the Church and to block any further attempts to bring the language of Catholic theology, ritual, and education in line with the universal movement taking place in our time to eliminate sexism in the world. It demonstrates that their "equal but different" definition of women, put forward in documents such as John Paul II's *Mulieris Dignitatem*, is hollow rhetoric masking an agenda of intransigent sexism. As with other areas which touch on women in the Church, the struggle waged by Rome to retain "man" as a collective noun for humanity reflects the relentless determination of the men in Rome to exorcise any influence of the feminist movement from Catholic circles and to retain male dominance in Church and family. The seriousness of this struggle also became evident in the recent battle over the English translation of the "Universal" Catechism.

THE TRANSLATION OF THE UNIVERSAL CATECHISM

In 1992, the Vatican published a compendium of Catholic belief titled *The Catechism of the Catholic Church*, commonly known as the Universal Catechism. This catechism project was proposed by Cardinal Bernard Law of Boston at the Synod of Bishops in 1985 and was eagerly adopted by Rome as a means to crack the whip of orthodoxy by issuing a compendium of the Catholic faith. The theological nuances of Vatican II were causing too much confusion, it was felt. Catholics, especially teachers, needed to be brought in line with Rome's new orthodoxy and back to the basics of Catholic doctrine.

Most Catholics, especially religion teachers, had been relieved when the Second Vatican Council moved the Church away from the simplistic, black-and-white, question-and-answer pedagogy of the Baltimore Catechism, which had been the textbook for Catholic education up to the 1960s. The mind-numbing experience of rote learning and reciting catechism answers had left many young Catholics ill prepared for the transition to adult faith.

In 1992, the updated catechism was published in French, and translations into all other major languages except English appeared in 1993. Why the delay in distribution to the English-speaking world? Because, lo and behold, the "demonic" influence of feminism had seeped into the ranks of the committee entrusted by Rome with the English translation.

In a meeting with the English translators in Rome in February 1993, Cardinal Ratzinger, Head of the Holy Office, told them that there was "too much inclusive language."[15] The Vatican then dismissed the committee chair, Father Douglas Clark, an American, and appointed Archbishop Joseph D'Arcy of Hobart, Australia, to revise and reverse Clark's inclusive-language version of the catechism. It should be noted that Clark's version had retained exclusively male language for God. It was the definition of the human race as normatively male which was at stake.

Like his counterparts in the Canadian hierarchy, D'Arcy also held that the use of inclusive language has theological implications but in a diametrically opposed direction. "The second divine person became man," stated D'Arcy in an interview with the London *Tablet* "... and one of the many teachings developed throughout the whole catechism is the relationship between God and man. If you use different words (i.e., inclusive language for humanity), you dilute the richness of that relationship."[16] Although D'Arcy never stated this in so many words, what he seems to be saying is that by admitting that women are fully and equally human, what might be diluted by inclusive language is the emphasis on the male gender of the second person of the Trinity and the "natural resemblance" which only men can have to God.

When the English translation finally appeared in the summer of 1994, D'Arcy had not only rendered all of the uses of the word "homme" as "man" (not even "mankind"), but extra male pronouns had been worked into the text. Right in the opening sentence, Clark's version read: "The Father created the human race to share in his blessed life." D'Arcy's amendment reads: "God created *man* to make *him* share in *his* own blessed life [emphasis mine]."[17] This latter is the English version now approved for use in Catholic schools in Australia, Canada, New Zealand, the UK, and the United States.

In 1994, the Congregation for the Doctrine of the Faith (Cardinal Ratzinger's Holy Office), also overturned the approval given by another Vatican department, the Congregation for Divine Worship, for the use of the inclusive-language text of the New Revised Standard Version (NRSV) of the Bible for Catholic worship and education. The Holy Office once again found fault with the use of "inclusive-language gender-sensitive terms" in the Bible which, Ratzinger stated, was "the result of ideology."[18] The U.S. bishops, who had overwhelmingly approved the NRSV, immediately entered into negotiations with Rome. After three years of effort, the bishops failed to prevail over Rome's intransigence and in June 1997, they were forced to back down.

In the meantime, Rome issued secret norms for the translation of all biblical texts and liturgical prayers. A copy of these norms, obtained by the *National Catholic Reporter*, reveals that the Vatican wants even the devil to remain male: "The grammatical gender of God, pagan deities, and angels and demons according to the original texts must not be changed." The Holy Spirit is no longer a spirit but definitively male: "... the feminine *and neuter* [emphasis mine] pronouns are not to be used to refer to the Holy Spirit." Hebrew and Greek words are also, in Ratzinger's lexicon, male rather than neutral. "The word 'man' in English should as a rule translate *adam* and *anthropos* because this is so important for the expression of Christian doctrine and anthropology."[19] This is the same man who accuses proponents of inclusive language of being motivated by ideology rather than scholarship.

The Vatican owns the copyright to the catechism and, according to a March 1997 report in the *National Catholic Reporter,* it has insisted that any book from anywhere in the world that uses more than five hundred words from the catechism must be submitted to Rome for permission to use the text. A Committee for the Catechism was set up by the U.S. bishops in 1995. Names of the members of the committee are not to be revealed. "The committee established to oversee the copyright approval has determined that any works submitted must also undergo a detailed review process to determine if they conform to the catechism."[20] But the entire process of review is confidential. Neither publisher nor author have any contact or dialogue with the anonymous review team. The Office of the Catechism in Washington, D.C., eventually relays the findings to the publisher.

Needless to say, this Kafkaesque situation has publishers and authors of Catholic educational materials perturbed. A liturgical booklet, *We Gather in Christ: Our Identity as an Assembly* (published by Liturgy Training Publications, Chicago), which contained about nine hundred words from the catechism, was denied copyright permission to use the quotes on the grounds that the text as a whole "was not consistent with the catechism."

The most significant omission, according to the Office of the Catechism, was "the absence of any indication of the role of the bishop or priest presider within the community in his specific and essentially distinct role as the leader of the worshipping community precisely because of his configuration to Christ as head of his body, the Church."[21] In other words, even such a small booklet, intended as a tool to help parish leaders develop better participation in Sunday liturgy, must hammer home the message to those in the pews that the priesthood is male and hierarchical.

The patriarchal ideology of the Vatican not only promotes the use of exclusively male language in its own documents, but insists on the reinstatement of sexist language and the scrutiny of even the smallest of resources for any trace of inclusiveness of women. What message does this convey for Catholic education? That despite all efforts to the contrary in English-speaking society at large, in the military, in universities, in government, and in the business world to convert structures and individuals away from sexism to a more equal and safe world for women, the highest authority in the Catholic Church remains unrepentantly sexist. Male chauvinists may rest easy within the sanctuary of the Catholic Church. According to the Vatican, the male God portrayed and prayed to on Catholic altars is on their side. In all dimensions of Catholic ritual and prayer, women are neither to be seen nor heard.

SEXUAL HARASSMENT IN THE CATHOLIC SCHOOL

One phenomenon which perpetuates an unequal balance in relationships between men and women in all environments, Catholic or not, is sexual harassment. In the workplace, the university, and the school, equal access for women—especially to traditionally male occupations such as construction or fields of study such as engineering—is often hampered by rampant sexual harassment, which can be the last resort of men threatened by female "invasion" of their turf.

Many men are still socialized to believe that masculinity must be demonstrated by male control over women. Any incursion of women into masculine territory is therefore an affront to all men and threatens to weaken and breach the controls men have established on the boundaries of masculinity. Women who have successfully challenged these boundaries are viewed as fair game for abuse and harassment: even, in Canada, for murder.

On December 6, 1989, a single gunman, Marc Lepine, massacred fourteen female students in the Faculty of Engineering at the Ecole Polytechnique in Montreal. Lepine separated the male and female students and specifically targeted the women as feminists who had invaded a traditionally male territory. "Women to one side!" Lepine shouted as he brandished the gun. "You are all feminists! I hate feminists!"[22]

Many media commentators tried to portray the Montreal Massacre as an isolated incident, the product of the rage of a single deranged individual. But why was Lepine angry at these women? What was it that drove him to want to kill women in the engineering faculty? The Quebec journalist Francine Pelletier commented in *La Presse*, "The murders were a reproach for feminist successes." Lepine was carrying a letter that contained a hit list with the names of fifteen other prominent Montreal women, including the first woman firefighter and the first woman police chief in Quebec. "The arrogance of male dominance," stated an editorial on the massacre in the *Globe and Mail*, "is to be found, naked and unashamed, at the heart of our democratic system and in centres of higher learning."[23]

Several women colleagues and friends who watched the funeral of these young women on television later told me that this was their first awakening to the "arrogance of male dominance" in the Church. There was not a single woman at the altar during the funeral. The sight of bishop and priests, robed in ceremonial vestments and wafting incense over the fourteen white coffins of the victims, was a particularly jarring reminder that male dominance is unashamedly practiced on the altars of the Catholic Church.

As the Pope taught in *Mulieris Dignitatem* a year before the Montreal Massacre occurred, and as Marc Lepine believed, women belong in the home and not in engineering faculties. Those fourteen students massacred at the Ecole Polytechnique were not engaged in preparing for what the Pope has decreed as their "supreme destiny" of motherhood. Perhaps the Catholic teachers in Montreal, like those criticized by the Archbishop in Toronto, had been negligent in not impressing upon these young women "the importance of motherhood."

This harrowing incident in Montreal brought to mind some of the frequent denigrations of women I had encountered in my classes. I recalled a "teachable moment" that had recently taken place in my grade 10 religion class. One Monday morning, I overheard the boys discussing their weekend. "I went to this great party," said one. "There were all these bitches there . . . some of them were real sluts. They were really spreadable!" I walked over to where this group of boys were sitting, surrounded by several girls. "Hey, Charles," I said, "it really upsets me when you refer to women in those terms because I'm a woman and it makes me wonder if you're thinking about me like that." "Don't worry, Miss," said Charles. "See all the girls here?" He swept his outstretched arm over the rows where the girls were sitting. "Look at them. They don't mind. They love it! None of *them* is saying anything."

Now Charles happened to be black. I decided to take an enormous risk. "OK," I replied, "then I guess by the same token it's all right for me to call you a nigger." The class erupted. "Listen," I said, "what Charles has just told me is that as a man he has the right to decide what women like and don't like. If they don't say anything, that means they consent. Up until a few years ago, most black people in this province would have kept silent in the same way if a white person, especially a teacher, called them by a name they hated. What's the connection here?"

A whole period of debate ensued. Racism and sexism. Racism versus sexism. Relations between the two. Differences between the two, but both sharing common experiences of oppression. The old adage of the "white man's burden" of civilizing the "black savages" compared to the male gender's right to teach these "hos and bitches" their place in life. "What you believe gives you the right to decide what women like to be called," I went on, "is the same thing my white ancestors thought gave them the right to decide how blacks should be referred to: the power to hurt them if they talk back. So the vast majority of people in that situation didn't and don't talk back."

The excuse, "But look, they love it!' which I have heard so often from the young men I have challenged about their sexist attitudes, is based on a whole series of presumptions which in the Catholic school are supported by religious beliefs. "They love it" in fact means "I have the power to decide what's good for them and what they should and shouldn't like. I have the right to define and control their lives. I will play God with impunity because the Church tells me I am made in the image of God and they are not." All true according to the Catholic Church. "They love it" can also mean "They had better like it or else I won't go out on a date with them" all the way to "They had better like it or else I'll beat it into them."

It is becoming ever more evident as a result of contemporary research in education that the level of sexual harassment directed toward young women in school classrooms amounts to a serious denial of their right to equality of education. A report published by the Ontario Secondary School Teachers' Federation in 1995 shows that by the time female students graduate from high school, 80 percent of them have experienced some form of sexual harassment.[24] Continuous sexual harassment can cause a slow death to the female spirit. In the Catholic school, sexual harassment has the added weight of divinely sanctioned approval of male privilege by the Church.

Young women adopt a variety of strategies to avoid sexual harassment in school. These strategies often hinder their efforts to obtain education. Most of the young women in my classes have adopted a policy of silence in the face of harassment in order to avoid the stigma of being called a "man hater" or "ball breaker." Young men who are not harassers will also keep silent when other male students harass females in order not to be labeled as "gay." The social life of adolescents revolves around friendships and dating. Girls in a co-ed situation, socialized at home and in their culture to please men and eventually find a husband, are so mortally afraid of ending up without a boyfriend that they will pay the price of keeping silent. This silence is then interpreted by male students as compliance.

When girls do speak out, they are swiftly slapped down. Even though these blows are verbal rather than physical, they still leave deep scars. One morning the chaplain used an inclusive-language version of the Sign of the Cross: "In the name of the Creator, Redeemer, and Sanctifying Spirit" instead of the traditional "Father, Son, and Holy Spirit" for the morning prayer, broadcast over the public address system. Jennifer, one of the brightest and most articulate students in grade 12 later told me that when the prayer was finished, a male student in her class had objected to this. "I thought it was really nice," responded Jennifer. "What do you know?" rejoined another male student. "You're just another stupid broad anyway." Several other men joined in with, "Yeah, leave us alone." The teacher did not intervene in this interchange. His silence was interpreted as support by the males and as disapproval of Jennifer's opinion. "I am never going to speak up in his class again," she told me. It is in this way that the "stupid broad" syndrome is perpetuated.

Girls walking in school hallways or cafeterias never know from what source the next sexual innuendo or put-down will issue. This forces all but the strongest young women into a posture of constant defensiveness. Several years of repeated put-downs can induce, at best, a state of numbed passivity or, at worst, an attempt to conceal intellectual prowess in order to avoid being labeled a threat to the fragile adolescent male ego.

John Paul II's anthropology divides male and female roles along lines of private and public domains. This division produces sexual stereotypes that fit within the paradigm of female passivity and male dominance, which is then replicated in the public sphere of the school. Women's concerns, because they have for so long been seen as "domestic issues," are dismissed as unimportant, even "stupid." Women have no right to bring minor domestic concerns such as sexual harassment out into the public domain. "Boys will be boys" has long been the dominant ethos of the public sphere, from the boardroom to the classroom. It is only in recent years that sexual harassment has emerged to face scrutiny, followed by preventive education and legislation.

In 1996 in Ontario, a tragic and prolonged story of sexual assault and harassment against girl students by a teacher employed by the Sault Ste. Marie Separate School Board came to light. During the course of twenty-one years of teaching, Kenneth DeLuca had routinely sexually abused girl students entrusted to his care. During what Michael Valpy, a columnist for the *Globe and Mail*, called "twenty-one years of wickedness,"[25]

DeLuca was transferred among four different schools. The girls and their parents who complained about DeLuca were told by Catholic school principals and trustees that they would face lawsuits if they made their complaints public.

On more than one occasion, the parish priest intervened, to support not the victims but the perpetrator, Kenneth DeLuca. The full weight of his religious authority was used to persuade the God-fearing Italian-Canadian community of the Sault that the girls' allegations of abuse should not be taken seriously. Worse still, the priest told the other students in one of the victim's classes that she was promiscuous and a liar, and would corrupt them if they continued to associate with her. One eleven-year-old victim, who reported to her principal that DeLuca had stripped her in the supply room at school and penetrated her with his finger, was not only expelled from that particular school but from the entire Catholic school system.

DeLuca was finally convicted of fourteen counts of sexual assault in 1996, but served only fourteen months of a twenty-six-month prison term before being released on parole in 1998. In the fall of 1996, more than ten thousand residents of Sault Ste. Marie, supported by the Ontario English Catholic Teachers' Association (OECTA), signed a petition requesting that the province conduct an inquiry into the Catholic School Board's handling of the DeLuca case. John Snobelen, then Ontario minister of education, refused. The mayor of Sault Ste. Marie, himself a former Catholic school principal, told the organizers to put the case behind them and move on with their lives.[26]

Sexual abuse and harassment is by no means a phenomenon confined to Catholic schools. But in the Catholic school, as the DeLuca case shows so vividly, the additional weight of religion is brought to bear against the female victims. Time and time again, God is used as a defense for male dominance. Young women, crushed by the initial experience of sexual abuse, are further reduced to complete silence by the patriarchal authority of the Church. It must be they themselves who are such flagrant temptresses that even a teacher placed in trust over them cannot resist these modern-day Eves.

More than 16 percent of the responses in the 1997 *Equity Report* published by the Toronto Secondary Unit of OECTA dealt with sexism in general, while a further 10 percent were concerned specifically with sexual harassment. That is a quarter of the total responses to the report. Men as well as women believe that sexism in the Catholic school system is a factor which continues to inhibit women. Sexual harassment affects women at all levels of the system, from principal to pupil.

One female respondent quoted in the OECTA report described a scene which took place at a staff Christmas party. "A female administrator who was fairly strict was given a gift of a mousetrap and a large screw. The gift card indicated that what she needed was "a good screw" and the mousetrap should be used to "pin her down."[27]

According to extensive research carried out at the Ontario Institute for Studies in Education in Toronto by June Larkin and others:

> Sexual harassment can be seen as the key to unlocking the whole debate on the inequality of education for girls because it is one of the most powerful forces acting against young women. Studies have shown that sexual harassment helps to shape the different ways in which women and men pursue and experience their education, and results in a diminished educational experience for women.[28]

As we have seen, girls will stay silent or keep their intellect reined in during class discussions. Larkin's investigation showed that girls will avoid certain parts of the school where boys hang out to avoid being "rated." They will drop classes to avoid the barrage of derogatory comments about women which may be initiated by male teachers as well as students, or subtle propositions which cast them as objects of sexual desire in an inappropriate context.

I recently counseled several young women enrolled in an Ontario Academic Credit (OAC) family studies class. OAC courses are a pre-university requirement in the Province of Ontario. The male teacher used the course material, which dealt with family, gender, sexuality, and other topics, to satisfy his prurient interest in the sex lives of female students. The OAC course includes independent research and compulsory individual consultations with the teacher. Students complained to me that the teacher would ask them during these conferences about the color scheme in their bedrooms, the size and shape of their mattresses, how comfortable their beds were, and whether or not they had a boyfriend with whom they had sex in their own bed. He would also relate to them how he would work out each morning and then walk around naked. "Do you like walking around naked?" he would ask them. "You are all so intelligent and beautiful," he would tell the mostly female class.

This teacher espoused traditional views about the role of women in marriage and refused to deal with any feminist perspectives on the family raised in the OAC course curriculum, "because," he told the class, "that's not part of the Catholic perspective on marriage, and this is a Catholic school."

The young women told me that they felt inhibited in class and forced to monitor their behavior carefully, "because we never knew where he was going to go next." Their attention, which should have been focused on the subject they were studying, was constantly distracted by the fear of being reduced to the level of a sexual object by the teacher. The young women had documented their concerns and eventually took them to the principal.

The principal seemed to take their concerns seriously, interviewed the teacher alone and then had the students express their concerns to the teacher in the presence of the principal. "But you know I didn't mean any harm" was his response. This is the common excuse of perpetrators who believe that sexual harassment is only what they perceive it to be and not what the victim experiences.

It happened that this teacher had applied for a promotion to head of his department. Two days after being called to account by these young women in the presence of the principal, he was appointed by the same principal as the new head. The students were devastated. "We never thought he would get promoted after what happened to us. The principal obviously didn't take us seriously." It had taken an enormous effort of mental and emotional preparation for them to voice their concerns to someone in the school who was in a position to do something about the situation. After all that, the students felt as if it had been useless. They also felt that the teacher's interpretation of the Catholicity of the school had directly undermined the one tool, feminist analysis, which would have empowered them to confront and attempt to change his behavior.

They were quite correct in this perspective. To the teacher in question, Catholicity in the school equaled traditional gender relationships: men dominate and women submit. Sexual harassment is woven into that power relationship. Women should take what is handed out to them and relax and enjoy it—after all, it's just a game the boys play, and they don't mean any real harm. If one refers to the U.S. bishops' *Pastoral on Women* discussed in Chapter 2, in particular the bishops' dismissal of the efforts of women's groups to get laws against sexual harassment enacted as "owing more to the tradition of the Enlightenment than to Catholic tradition," it becomes apparent how difficult it is to dislodge an environment of sexism from the Catholic school and from Catholic cultures.

SACRED STEREOTYPES

Pope John Paul II has elevated an unprecedented number of Catholics to sainthood. What beatification and then canonization into sainthood means is that certain people are held up to the contemporary Church as examples of faith and models of a life of discipleship which other Catholics should venerate and imitate. The making of saints is also, of course, a political statement to the world about where the Church stood at the time of the saint's life, and where it wishes to stand on current issues.

John Paul II's choice of women to elevate to sainthood has been particularly revealing. In 1994, at the time of the United Nations Conference on Population and Development in Cairo, the Pope wanted to send out a clear message to the whole world that the destiny of women had been defined by the Creator as essentially that of motherhood. That same year, he beatified two Italian women whom he said "would serve as models of Christian perfection for women."

One of these, Gianna Beretta Molla, died in 1962 at the age of thirty-nine. Molla, an Italian pediatrician, suffered from a malignant uterine cancer during her fourth pregnancy. She declined an operation that would have saved her life but cost that of the fetus, and died a week after giving birth. "We wish," said the Pope, "to pay homage to all those courageous mothers who devote themselves unreservedly to their families and suffer to bring their children into the world."[29]

The other woman, Elisabetta Canori Mora, died in 1825. The Pope praised her for remaining in an abusive marriage, where her husband physically and emotionally battered her. "Elisabetta Canori Mora," stated the Pope, "showed, in the midst of numerous conjugal difficulties, her total fidelity to the commitment assumed in the sacrament of marriage and the responsibilities deriving from it."[30]

What is an adolescent girl in a Catholic family to make of this message from the highest authority in the Church, an authority which claims a moral superiority that can ride roughshod over all "secular" values in the name of the "sacred"? In the case of these soon-to-be saints, the Pope sends out a clear message to women that the unborn child has a superior right to life than theirs. In the example of Mora, the Pope gives tacit approval to domestic violence by upholding as worthy of veneration a woman who stayed in an abusive marriage. That message is not lost on some young Catholic men, who feel exonerated of all responsibility in relationships and even imagine that they've been given the nod by the Pope to continue beating women: after all, the Pope seems to be suggesting that abuse will make their women holy.

In April 1998, reports of consternation over articles in one of Toronto's Portuguese-language newspapers surfaced in the *Toronto Star*. A series of articles entitled "Feminine Psychology" appeared in the weekly *Familia Portuguesa* starting in December 1997.[31] The paper is not endorsed by the Catholic Church in Toronto, but was founded by one of the archdiocese's parish priests, Father Alberto deCunha. Toronto's Portuguese community numbers about three hundred thousand, and the paper is widely distributed in Toronto churches with Portuguese congregations and in Portuguese businesses and community centers.

The series of anonymous articles in question contain such statements as "a woman's love is superficial, fickle, unstable" and warn husbands to be aware of women's tendencies to hold grudges and be indiscreet and vengeful. One article has this advice for men: "If you find your wife exhibiting any of these malicious defects, you should urge their correction with a strong hand."[32]

A group of Portuguese women and men, led by Tania Monteiro, a student at the University of Toronto, and her mother, Ermelinda, urged a boycott of the newspaper and complained to the Archdiocese of Toronto. The author of the offensive articles referred to the two women in the next edition of *Familia Portuguesa* as whores. The Archdiocese of Toronto attempted to distance itself from the views expressed in *Familia Portuguesa* and began an investigation of deCunha. In May 1998, he resigned from his parish, not on account of his misogynist statements but "because of his connection with the paper, he had been involved in commercial activity in violation of canon law." [33]

EDUCATION OF GIRLS, THE KEY TO THE FUTURE

The education of young women is the most effective tool recommended by the 1991 UN Report *Women: Challenges to the Year 2000* to ensure the survival of women and young girls in many parts of the world. From the experience of female students on the receiving end of sexual harassment in Catholic schools and communities in North America to that of young women in many parts of the world whose educational aspirations are limited by early pregnancy and childbirth, it is clear that equal access to education for women everywhere is limited.

For the present generation of Catholic teachers and for thousands of female students in denominational schools across the world, Catholic teaching on the nature and role of women presents a daily experience of educational dissonance. This was expressed by a participant in a workshop entitled "Equality in the Church: Practise What You Preach" which I presented at an OECTA conference in 1990. In her evaluation, she wrote:

> It is extremely ironic that so many of the issues in this workshop have been dealt with in the public context years ago—great progress has begun. But female sexuality, contraception, women in the workplace and so on are still only just being addressed—today—in the Catholic context. It is extremely difficult to balance this when you teach a class of young students. Do we say, Yes, boys and girls can be anything they want to be—except in the Church? Yet in Catholic education, the Church is integral. We are always at cross purposes.

This conflict between the philosophy of equal education and Church teachings has ramifications for women that extend well beyond the classroom. Nor are they confined to the internal controversy over the admission of women to ordination or to questions of Church discipline or doctrine. This struggle touches on issues which are at the heart of the very survival of the planet, a subject we will explore in the next chapter.

Chapter Five

The Vatican,
Global Politics, and Power

The present struggle within the Catholic Church over the nature and role of women is representative of the conflicting world views that face humankind today. We are living in the midst of change, challenge, and crisis at a level that touches every aspect of our lives, from the most intimate personal relationships to global corporate enterprise. The Catholic Church straddles the globe both through its religious institutions and through the diplomatic apparatus of the Vatican state. Because of the reactionary nature of its present leadership, the Church has become a symbol of contradiction in the world, often bolstering the forces of economic, religious, and political conservatism while continuing to espouse Catholic social teachings and ideals.

The personal is political and the political is personal. The Catholic Church in recent years has enthroned patriarchy at God's right hand in the Catholic family and in the Catholic school. The papacy of John Paul II has also supported an unprecedented and concerted effort to bolster patriarchal institutions around the world. John Paul II has traveled more than any other pope in history. He has ridden the white Popemobile down the streets of cities in every continent, dispensing blessings, advice, and admonition, often leaving behind a burden of debt for the host country. He has jockeyed for a place for the Vatican in world governance. And he has demanded a forum for his views whenever the global conversation touches on issues affecting women.

THE CATHOLIC CHURCH AT THE UN

The last thirty years have witnessed the phenomenon of women's issues being brought to the table at the United Nations. The Vatican has observer status at the UN, and it has used this to utmost advantage in recent years. The presence of Vatican "experts" at the UN conferences on women during the 1990s reminded me of an ancient Sufi parable, which goes like this:

I was once invited to the home of some acquaintances for dinner. When all the guests had arrived, the hostess invited us into the dining room. As I entered the room, I noticed with astonishment that there was a horse on the table. I caught my breath but didn't say a word.

I was the first to enter the room, so I was able to observe the other guests. They responded much as I had—they entered, saw the horse, gasped and stared, but said nothing.

It was cramped sitting at the table and trying to avoid the horse. Everyone was obviously ill at ease. We were all trying not to look at the horse, yet unable to keep our eyes off it.

I thought several times of saying, "Look, there's a horse on the table." But I didn't know the host and hostess well, and I didn't want to mention something that might embarrass them. After all, it was their house. Who was I to say they couldn't have a horse on the table?

I could have said that I didn't mind, but that would have been untrue— its presence upset me so much that I enjoyed neither the dinner nor the company. I excused myself early and went home.

I later learned that the host and hostess were hoping the dinner would be a success despite the horse. But both they and the other guests had thought about little else than the horse and how to avoid mentioning it.

There is a huge horse that sits with the Pope and his representatives at the world table. This horse steps off the plane with the Pope and his praetorian guard of all-male cardinals, bishops, and clergy. It leans over his shoulder when he speaks. It has sat with all the Vatican delegations to the UN conferences of this decade in full view of the whole world. This horse is the horse of sexism.

The very fact that under Pope John Paul II's rule, the Vatican has made women's issues so central to its teaching and practice has exposed its entrenched sexism to the light of greater critical scrutiny. John Paul II's views on the nature and role of women, which have alienated women from the Church, have also fueled the effort by successive Vatican delegations to block the progress of women everywhere, Catholic or not, toward controlling their own lives and the destinies of their daughters. And every time the Vatican delegates exhort the world on the topic of women's equality, the word "hypocrites" flashes on the back of the horse lying on the table in front of them.

THE STATE WITHIN THE CHURCH: CAESAR'S LEGACY

How has the Vatican, alone among other churches and religions, been able to gain direct access to the United Nations, and to exercise influence over its policy formation, processes, and debates? The Vatican, or, as it is officially referred to in UN protocol, the Holy See, has Permanent Observer Status at the United Nations. This protocol, one shared with Switzerland alone, allows the Vatican to participate in and vote at world conferences, to comment on UN documents, and to delay consensus on global issues. The only right it does not have is a vote in the General Assembly. But why is the Catholic Church accorded these privileges of statehood?

The Vatican delegation at the UN is the last relic of papal temporal power. The roots of papal temporal power can be traced back to the collapse of the Roman Empire in Europe and the upheaval and instability of the Dark Ages which followed. Menaced by marauding Lombard tribes to the north of Italy, Stephen III, Bishop of Rome, appealed to King Pepin of the Franks for help. In return for Pepin's military support in the defense of what would become the Papal States, Stephen journeyed north in 769 to anoint Pepin and his son Charlemagne as Patricians of the Romans. The Bishop of Rome took with him a document known as the *Donation of Constantine*, later exposed as forgery by the fifteenth-century scholar Lorenzo Valla. This document purported to be a bequest made by the Emperor Constantine on his deathbed. The newly baptized emperor bequeathed spiritual and temporal sovereignty "over all the churches in the world... and all palaces and districts of the city of Rome, Italy, and of the regions of the west" into the hands of the Pope.

The popes eventually lost control of the last remnant of temporal power, the Papal States in central Italy, in 1870. The sovereign state of Vatican City was re-established in the Lateran Treaty of 1929 as the result of a deal struck between Pope Pius XI and the Italian dictator Benito Mussolini. Vatican City now exists in law as a vassal state of the Holy See, which is the supreme governing power of the Catholic Church and the seat of the worldwide administration of the Catholic Church.[1]

It was as a result of this gift of Caesars, both ancient and modern, to the Church, that the Holy See was granted official status as a Permanent Observer at the UN in 1964. The Holy See is the smallest state at the UN, consisting of 0.44 square kilometers of territory, eight hundred residents, and four hundred citizens. All of this might be a matter of mere historical curiosity were it not for the fact that under John Paul II, the Holy See has used its status at the UN to weigh in on debates on women. Under this pope, the Vatican has behaved at the UN as if it bore the full political clout of an empire of 900 million Catholics. Surveys show that the majority of Catholics reject Pope John Paul II's views on women and sexuality. Now that only a minority of Catholics actually follow the Pope's teachings, some Catholics view his interventions at the UN as a desperate attempt to regain control inside the Church by expanding control over the rest of the world. But although the horse of sexism still dominates the Vatican table, the mare of Catholic subservience has long ago bolted from the Church stables.

In contrast to other nations represented at the UN which are required to submit annual reports on the state of their citizens, the Holy See never refers to the status and well-being of any person actually living within its borders. It offers no statistics on women in Vatican City—a minuscule population, all working in ancillary occupations such as cooking and cleaning—and still less information on women within the Church as a whole.

Despite the fact that the Vatican is a signatory to the 1945 UN Universal Declaration of Human Rights, which includes a clause on women's equality, the Holy See takes the view that the UN Charter does not apply within the borders of the Holy See or its global organization, the Catholic Church. Apartheid against women at the Church's altars and the lack of women's rights as employees of the Church are conveniently glossed over. The governing structure of the Holy See includes not a single woman, nor are women included in the Church's sole electoral body, the College of Cardinals. Yet the Holy See presents itself at the UN as an expert on the status and role of women around the world.

The Vatican has honed diplomacy and power-broking to a fine art. The 1980s and '90s have seen the evolution of its threefold strategy against the new "evil empire" of feminism. This strategy involves diplomatic alliances with other reactionary governments, placing a public relations spin of "cultural imperialism" on movements for women's rights, and presenting the Catholic Church as the natural champion of the world's poor nations against oppression by nations of the North and all their "monstrous regiments of women." These strategies first became apparent in the preparation for the United Nations Conference on Environment and Development (UNCED), known as the Earth Summit, in Rio de Janeiro in 1992.

THE RIO SUMMIT: VATICAN REDUCTIONISM

In the summer of 1992, some thirty thousand politicians, nongovernmental organizations (NGOs), and journalists assembled in Rio de Janeiro for a vital meeting on the state of the earth. An alternative conference, the Global Forum, drew about eighteen thousand activists from environmental and women's groups around the world. The Earth Summit was the largest and most complex international diplomatic gathering ever held in human history. About 24 million pages of documents were produced, but this prodigious effort accomplished very little in terms of changing global patterns of production and consumption to deal with global warming and other threats to the environment.

It did, however, mark the eruption of women's issues onto the world scene. The first UN World Conference on Women had been held in Mexico City in 1975. Two other conferences followed at five-year intervals (Copenhagen in 1980, Nairobi in 1985). In spite of this activity, women's concerns such as growing impoverishment, rape as an instrument of war, genital mutilation, and gender-based violence—issues that had been raised at these conferences—continued to be viewed at the UN as "domestic" issues and were not included in the mainstream agenda of international policy. Between 1990 and 1992, four preparatory meetings (PrepComs) were held for UNCED. Women made the agenda only at the third Prep-Com, and then only as a "minority" issue.

But as a result of the work of NGOs, women's groups, church activists, and environmentalists who lobbied intensively before the alternative summit at Rio, there emerged a draft platform known as *Agenda 21: Declaration of the Principles of Global Action Towards Sustainable and Equitable Development*. Women's groups from both North and South were also determined to put a discussion of population on the agenda of the Rio summit, a move fiercely resisted by the Holy See.

Chapter 24 of *Agenda 21* deals with objectives and programs of action to end discrimination based on gender. Women fought to ensure that women and women's concerns would be fully represented in all future international decision making. No longer would the world agenda be set *for* women by male-dominated UN committees but it would be directed *by* women themselves. *Agenda 21* was eventually ratified by the Plenary Assembly of the United Nations. The following clause in particular encountered sustained opposition from the Holy See:

> To implement, as a matter of urgency, in accordance with country-specific conditions, measures to ensure that women and men have the same right to decide freely and responsibly the number and spacing of their children and have access to information, education and means, as appropriate, to enable them to exercise this right in keeping with their freedom, dignity and personally held values.[2]

The Vatican delegation at Rio fought hard but unsuccessfully to remove any discussion of population in general and contraception in particular from the agenda of the Rio summit. They were supported in this by then U.S. president George Bush. This was not the first time that Vatican diplomats had found common ground with a Republican White House.

ALLIANCES WITH REACTIONARY GOVERNMENTS

Cordial relations had developed between the White House and the Vatican under the Republican administrations of Ronald Reagan and his successor, George Bush. In a move eerily reminiscent of the meeting in 769 between Pope Stephen and Pepin, King of the Franks, modern representatives of Stephen's successor in Rome had journeyed west to the new seat of empire in the White House to make a deal which would have wide repercussions in both the Northern and Southern Hemispheres. A 1992 a cover story in *Time* magazine revealed that John Paul II had orchestrated the assistance of Polish priests for undercover actions directed by the CIA which were aimed at the destabilization of the communist regime. In return, the Vatican agreed to crush liberation theology in Latin America which, with its emphasis on the preferential option for the poor, was threatening to destabilize U.S. control in that region. At home in America, the Reagan-Bush administration was fostering the right-wing agenda of "family values." This appealed to the Vatican because it included opposition to abortion and the cutting of federal funds to Planned Parenthood International under the pretext that such funds were being used to promote abortion.

Within the United States, conservative Catholics and evangelical Protestants had been holding discussions on the possibility of forming a common political front on the family values agenda which would help to elect Republicans to Congress. Opposition to abortion, gay rights, and feminism were the mainstays of the negotiations begun in 1992 among the Southern Baptist Convention, media mogul Pat Robertson, and representatives of the Catholic Church headed by Cardinal John O'Connor, Archbishop of New York. This alliance, officially recognized by the Vatican according to O'Connor, also included reactionary policies on welfare reform. The new Religious Right campaigned in the 1992 election to cut government assistance for single mothers based on the theory that this would discourage teenage promiscuity and bring America back to its Christian roots.

With the help of their new Catholic allies, Newt Gingrich and the Republican party won a resounding majority in the 1992 congressional elections. The "Contract with America," which Gingrich and the Republicans put in place, resulted in a widening gap between rich and poor and gave the United States one of the highest rates of child poverty in the world. Pax Americana at home and abroad was a goal partly achieved in the 1980s through the combined efforts of Ronald Reagan and John Paul II. The downfall of atheistic communism and the slashing of "socialist" welfare policies at home meant that the world would be made safe for capitalism with the blessing of the Catholic Church: the contemporary King of the Franks had his friend and ally in Rome. The Pope is also much admired by conservative evangelical Protestants because he is campaigning to return Catholicism to a new Pax Vaticana of obedience to the Pope, undoing Vatican II's tumultuous legacy of dissent over the issues of sexuality, gay rights, and women—issues that have been hotly debated in Protestant churches as well.

With their influence secured at the highest level of the world's new imperial order at the White House, Vatican diplomats set about cultivating their ancient enemies, the Islamic states in the Middle East. These might seem like strange bedfellows: Republicans in the United States, fundamentalist governments in the Arab world, and the promoters of a return to pure Christendom in the Vatican. What brings them together is at least in part their fear of the progress of women toward full equality, which threatens to break down the traditional boundaries of religious, cultural, and political authority.

In 1982, the Vatican convened the first of a series of secret top-level meetings with fundamentalist Islamic states, known as the Terra Mater seminars. Delegates from Saudi Arabia, Kuwait, Iran, Libya, and Sudan came together to forge a joint program of action to block the advance of the global movement for women's equality. In an attempt to discredit arguments for universal and equal rights for women, the representatives of these governments began to advance the notion of "cultural imperialism" masquerading in the guise of the Western feminist movement. It was at the time of the Earth Summit that Vatican speeches first began to make reference to the notion of "cultural imperialism" and its variant of "contraceptive imperialism" in order to discredit the efforts of women's groups to get reproductive rights placed on the global agenda.

The argument that feminism is a form of cultural imperialism proceeds something like this: feminism is a "white" phenomenon that arose in North America and Western Europe. North American feminists are now seeking to spread their ideas and "colonize" the women of the Third World. Feminism is a purely Western phenomenon, the product of suspect Western ideas which grew out of the sexual revolution of the sixties. The spread of feminism will replicate and reinforce old patterns of Western cultural colonialism in the Third World, and must be resisted. Feminism, so they say, is responsible for the promiscuity and hedonism which has weakened family values in the West. Men in the West woke up to this too late, but Third World men must guard their families from this impending invasion. What this argument does not mention is that it enables Third World men to continue to enjoy unchallenged all the privileges that have been their right for generations. It also ignores the fact that feminism has sprung to life on its own in the Southern Hemisphere, and is spreading rapidly in Third World nations as women confront their oppression.

The argument of cultural colonialism is a clever but specious manipulation of the truth. It is true that the philosophical structure of the first wave of the women's movement emerged from the human rights tradition in the West, which grew out of the French and American revolutions. This tradition is built on the notion that individual rights are inherent in the nature of the human person and not subject to the arbitrary whim of king or emperor. The concept of universal political and civil rights, granted initially only to property-owning white males, has been widened in this century to include, in theory at least, people of color, the poor, women, and, most recently, gays and lesbians. Freedom of speech, freedom of conscience, universal suffrage, the right to receive an education: all of these facets of Western democracy have been won or extended through a long series of political and legal battles. Beginning with the struggle for women's suffrage, in this century successive waves of feminists have fought for women's equality through both courts and legislatures.

These first feminist struggles took place in nations where, for the most part, women have not been chronically undernourished or displaced in large numbers as a result of war. In contrast, for many women in the Third World, the right to vote or to equal pay for equal work pales in comparison with the absence of basic social and economic rights, such as the right to shelter and nutrition for themselves and for their children. This became apparent at the second World Conference on Women in Nairobi, where Western women, who had so far taken it for granted that their issues and leadership would continue to prevail within the women's movement, were challenged by Third World women to broaden the agenda. By the time of the 1995 Conference on Women in Beijing, a greater diversity and also solidarity among different groups within the women's movement had become apparent.

The charge of cultural imperialism used against democracy or feminism is based on the premise that human rights are not universal. According to this premise, there can be no universal concepts such as justice or equality or freedom, but only local particularities which are determined by religion, ethnicity, and tradition. Such a view undermines the basic principle that human rights are inherent to every individual. It denies the principle of a shared or common humanity which transcends race, class, and gender. The argument advanced by the Vatican and its allies, that human rights for women are a form of Western cultural imperialism, assumes that non-Western cultures are somehow immutable and sacrosanct, and should not be changed to fit "alien" patterns that have arisen primarily in Western societies. It is ironic, then, that many of the same arbiters of their nations' destinies have been eager to accept the dominance of global capitalism over their economies.

If we examine the religious and cultural status quo in both Christian and Islamic countries in most of Latin America, Africa, and the Middle East, certain common patterns can be observed. The controllers of religious interpretation, whether it be for Islam or Christianity, are men. Decisions about the rules and rituals of religion are made by men. Those who claim to speak for the voice of God/Allah are all men. So naturally, this male God/Allah never impinges on men's rights, as these are sanctioned in the dominant religion or culture. Men who benefit from the religious and cultural norms, norms according to which their God has allotted women a separate and inferior nature and role, accept this without question. It is those men who benefit from the domestic and agricultural labor of women, and who claim the right to chastise any woman who steps out of the role prescribed for her by religion and culture, who are the most resistant to any threat to their privileges.

In recent years, I have provided housing for a number of men who have come to Canada as refugees from Third World countries. One of the most common complaints I have heard is that "their" women are now calling the police when their husbands or boyfriends abuse them. The need to conform to a culture where physical control of women is no longer the norm but regarded as a crime is considered a negative cultural adjustment by these men.

Genital mutilation is outlawed in Canada but there has been a large influx of refugees from Somalia, where this is a culturally accepted practice. According to some members of the Somali community, the new generation of Somali girls will be deprived of full participation in their culture because physicians in Canada are forbidden to practice genital mutilation. This challenge to patriarchal values has been labeled a form of cultural imperialism on the part of Canada.

Control of women's sexuality has always gone hand in hand with the constraints of patriarchal religion and culture. Women's groups at Rio and at other world conferences who attempted what appeared at first sight to be an eminently practical task—giving women information and access to the means to control the number and spacing of their children—have found themselves embroiled in religious controversy. To provide women with the basic right to education requires that they have some control over reproduction. Western experience has clearly shown that to educate women and girls is the first step on the journey to full personhood, which enables them to question and then undermine patriarchal structures. Hence no contraception, no education for women, no questions.

The Holy See and its allies latched on to divisions between the women's groups and exploited them. The Vatican, posing as a neutral observer at the Rio Summit, played on the fears of poorer nations that their lives were going to be controlled by nations in the North. Third World women, they argued, would be forced to accept compulsory sterilization or abortion under the guise of education about contraception. The central issue in reversing the global decline into ecological disaster, they stated, is consumption. Overpopulation is a myth propagated by Western feminists who have betrayed their motherly instincts.

Overconsumption does contribute massively to global poverty and environmental degradation, but so does the lack of access to reproductive health among women. The credibility of the Vatican's voice as an ally of the South's stern critique of the consumption and the affluent lifestyle of the North is undermined not a little by its own practices. The present incumbents of high office in the Holy See do not indulge in the flagrant debauchery of some of their predecessors, but Vatican palace life and the pomp of princely ceremony in St. Peter's somewhat belie the sincerity of this papal championship of a simpler lifestyle.

JOHN PAUL II AND CATHOLIC SOCIAL TEACHING

It is both paradoxical and painful for Catholics to see the Vatican allying the Catholic Church with the cultural imperialism camp of anti-Western ideals, because the principle of universal human rights has been a bedrock of Catholic social teaching, social teaching which is based on the belief that every human being is made in the image of God and bears inherent worth and dignity.

In 1979, the first year of his pontificate, John Paul II wrote an encyclical letter, *Redemptor Hominis*, in which he set forth the vision of the mission of the Church which would guide his pontificate. Section 17 of this document is titled "Human Rights: Letter or Spirit." John Paul II wrote:

> ... we cannot fail to recognize ... with esteem and profound hope for the future, the magnificent effort made to give life to the United Nations Organization, an effort conducive to the definition and establishment of man's objective and inviolable rights, with the member states obliging each other to observe them rigorously ... There is no need for the Church to confirm how closely this is linked with her mission in the modern world. Indeed it is at the very basis of social and international peace...[3]

The new Pope continued with a resounding affirmation of the universality of human rights:

> The Declaration of Human Rights linked with the setting up of the United Nations Organization certainly had as its aim not only to depart from the

horrible experiences of the last World War but also to create the basis for continual revision of programs, systems and regimes precisely from this single fundamental point of view, namely the welfare of man—or, let us say, of the person in the community—which must, as a fundamental factor in the common good, constitute the essential criterion for all programs, systems and regimes.[4]

Human rights, autonomy, and self-determination, the Pope argued at the time, are fundamental to the operation of the state.

The essential nature of the state, as a political community, consists in that the society and people composing it are master and sovereign of their own destiny. This sense remains unrealized if, instead of the exercise of power with the moral participation of the society or people, what we see is the imposition of power by a certain group upon all the other members of the society... The common good that authority in the state serves is brought to full realization only when all the citizens are sure of their rights... the principle of human rights is of profound concern to the area of social justice and is the measure by which it can be tested in the life of political bodies.[5]

Sadly, the history of John Paul's change of heart is recorded in his successive letters. Nine years after *Redemptor Hominis*, John Paul II wrote *Mulieris Dignitatem*, in which he put forward his concept of the "equal but different" humanity of men and women. Thirteen years later, the Vatican formed an alliance with states such as Saudi Arabia which deny the fundamental human rights of women. The "woman question" has become the irreducible policy position that has shaped Vatican teaching on human rights as well as the nature of God, a position which many Catholics now hold is in error.

If John Paul still believed what he wrote in 1979, that the human rights laid down in the UN Charter of Rights really are universal and that they are the measure against which all systems in the world must be judged, then the Vatican would not be obstructing the work of the UN world conferences on women, when attempts have been made to evolve the notion of human rights so that these include the rights of women to autonomy and self-direction. As well, if the recognition of the universality of human rights is to be a measure of the level of social justice in any given system, how can the Vatican continue to claim exemption from this principle, refusing women equality and autonomy within the Church? If the Church, as John Paul II also states in *Redemptor Hominis*, is to be a sacrament and sign of Christ's presence in the world, a light to the nations and arbiter of truth and right living, how can the Church justify having a worse record on human rights for women than many "secular" societies?

Questions such as these are the reason why the gigantic horse of sexism still lies upon the Vatican's table. The betrayal of the Church's teaching on universal human rights is only another facet of John Paul II's "apartheid" anthropology and distorted theology. An "equal but different" human nature for women and men means an "equal but different" human nature for the son of God, Jesus Christ. So Jesus is "different" from women. There are only six sacraments in the Church for women but seven for men. There is one set of universal human rights for men, but women are subject to cultural particularities determined by patriarchal religion. It all fits together. But is this the Good News preached by Jesus Christ? Certainly not.

As I described in Chapter 2, John Paul II not only believes that women are a separate and inferior type of human being, he also behaves according to that principle on the world stage. In order to maintain male control within the Church, he has led the Church into error on the gender of God and the humanity of Christ. It is evident from his words and actions at the UN that in order to curtail the progress of women toward full equality and autonomy, an autonomy which poses a grave threat to male dominance in the Church, he is prepared to halt and even reverse the evolution of the Church's social teaching. Far from being the light of the world, the Church as represented by the Vatican has taken the position at the UN world conferences on women that has been a travesty of the gospel.

THE GROWING INFLUENCE OF OPUS DEI

Joaquin Navarro-Valls, the Vatican spokesman personally appointed by John Paul II and the voice of the Vatican in the media, is an avowed member of the Catholic sect known as Opus Dei. The fact that he professes this membership openly is remarkable because members of this influential group are usually highly secretive about their allegiance. Opus Dei has been highly favored by John Paul II. In fact, the increase of Opus Dei's control within the Church is one of the distinguishing and alarming features of this papacy. Thus, the Pope has not only aligned the Vatican with reactionary governments but also fostered reactionary movements within the Church as well.

Opus Dei was founded in 1928 in Spain by an associate of General Francisco Franco, Monsignor (now "Blessed," courtesy of the fastest beatification process in Church history) Josemaria Escriva de Balaguer. Until John Paul II welcomed it into the corridors of power, it was an obscure and secretive movement.

In 1987, Opus Dei placed a request before the Canadian Parliament to be granted the status of corporation. This produced a rare moment of public scrutiny for Opus Dei. The movement had already been granted its own Personal Prelature, or worldwide self-governance, by John Paul II, and it was seeking to have an independent standing in Canadian civil law which would be equivalent to that of a bishop's diocese, a status Opus Dei already held in canon law. A full debate on this issue was held in the Canadian Senate, and thanks to the exposure of Opus Dei by senators Jacques Hébert and Jean Le Moyne of Montreal, the request was rejected. Material about Opus Dei came to light in this debate and can be found on the daily record of parliamentary debates in Hansard for those years.

Josemaria Escriva, who died in 1975, rejected the reforms of the Second Vatican Council and was so distressed by the path laid out for the Church by the Council that he began negotiating for a transfer to the Greek Orthodox Church. The Constitutions of Opus Dei state that:

The Church... has fallen away from the true path, and the destiny of Opus Dei is to spread itself throughout the world by every means... Opus Dei is holy, unchangeable, everlasting: it contains everything necessary for salvation. Opus Dei could never need reform... Msgr. Escriva anticipated the Second Vatican Council in his creation of Opus Dei, therefore Opus Dei has no need to turn to the council's decrees for guidance.[6]

The image of the Church as a Pilgrim People of God, engaged in dialogue with contemporary society and traveling a common path to God with the rest of society, is contrary to the ethos of Opus Dei, which is described in its constitution as a corps of elite fighting men.

Our institute is certainly a family, but it is also a militia... a militia with the strength of a very strict discipline, best suited to fighting ... Opus Dei includes a certain number of people of low origin who play the role which is held in other religious congregations by lay brothers; these examples, incessantly put forward, cannot hide the true nature of Opus Dei, which essentially recruits in the aristocracy and the upper middle-class.[7]

Opus Dei's association with fascism in Spain and its history of opposition to the Allende government in Chile made it a logical choice to lead John Paul II's campaign against liberation theology. In 1996 the Pope appointed an Opus Dei bishop from Spain, Saenz Lacalle, to what had been Archbishop Oscar Romero's see in San Salvador. There was widespread outrage in El Salvador, though not a word of criticism from the Pope or the Vatican, when Saenz Lacalle accepted the post of brigadier general in the very army alleged to be responsible for Romero's assassination.

Needless to say, although women are admitted to the lower ranks of this Opus Dei militia, their role and influence is minimal. The ethos of Opus Dei is highly clerical and highly masculine. "Like Noah's good sons," writes Escriva in number 75 of the 999 maxims of El Camino, or The Way, "spread the mantle of charity over the faults you see in your father, the priest."

Escriva made no secret of his contempt for women and for their claim to equality and equal human rights. "Do you not believe that equality for women, as it is understood, is synonymous with injustice!" And further on: "The plan of holiness which the Lord expects of us features these three points: holy intransigence, holy coercion, holy effrontery."[8] It's not surprising, then, that Joaquin Navarro-Valls, the head of the Vatican Press Office and chief spokesman for John Paul II's policies on women, should be an Opus Dei man.

CHAMPION OF THE THIRD WORLD

The Vatican positioned itself at the Rio conference and at subsequent UN conferences on women as the advocate of the poor nations of the South. As a state within a Church, the Vatican argued that it was well qualified to defend their interests against the depredations of economic and cultural imperialism. This was a shrewd diplomatic maneuver. And given that church attendance has declined more dramatically in the First World than in the Third, the Vatican was also working to protect its interests.

The rhetoric sounds good, but the facts tell another story. Take, for example, the Vatican's policy on Haiti, the poorest country in the Western Hemisphere. On December 16, 1990, Haiti held the first democratic elections in its history. The result was a decisive victory for presidential candidate Jean-Bertrand Aristide. This election, which was reported as free and fair by visiting teams of international observers, drew a record number of 75 percent of eligible voters; 67 percent of these voted for Aristide.

Jean-Bertrand Aristide is a former member of the Salesian order of Catholic priests. During the corrupt administration of Jean-Claude Duvalier, son of the infamous Papa Doc, Aristide had worked and preached in the poorest neighborhoods of the capital, Port-au-Prince. He had been a principal organizer of a movement known as Ti Legliz, short for Petite Eglise, or "little church." Ti Legliz was a loosely knit network of small faith communities modeled on the "base communities," which had flourished in the springtime of liberation theology in Latin America in the seventies.

A base community is an assembly of Christians from a small neighborhood, usually in the slums or barrios of a city, which is organized around putting Christian faith into action for justice. Base communities were often initially led by priests or nuns, but now more often than not they are led by laypeople. The key element of the base community is the linking of faith with the struggle for justice. "The reign of God is now," said Jesus. According to liberation theology, for the reign of God to become present, it must include the material as well as the spiritual liberation of the poor. The poor must be freed from oppression here on earth, not just told to be patient and wait for their heavenly reward. As they studied and prayed over the Scripture, members of base communities heard anew the radical message of Jesus that God made a preferential option for the poor.

This liberation of the poor involves moving beyond charity to an examination of the structures that keep the poor oppressed. Links were forged between socioeconomic analysis and the Catholic faith. This became a powerful tool which threatened, in Mary's words in the Magnificat, "to cast down the mighty from their thrones and send the rich away empty."[9] The threat that the spectacular growth of base communities in Latin America posed to the Pax Americana policy developed by the United States for control and influence in the region caught the attention of John Paul II's ally, Ronald Reagan. In 1980, Reagan's advisors put together a New Inter-American Policy, popularly known as the Santa Fe Document after the city in New Mexico where it was written. Liberation theology is singled out for comment by the White House as one of the forces hostile to American interests in the region.

If the poor come to believe that God is on their side, they might get out of hand. If the poor are convinced that it was not God's will for them to suffer poverty in silence and await their reward in heaven, they might make demands here on earth. And if the Catholic Church in Latin America were to shift its traditional base of support and influence from the rich to the poor, the region could become destabilized. Eight years after the Santa Fe document, when Reagan and John Paul II agreed to an alliance to deliver Poland from Soviet communism, it was the poor of Latin America who paid the price.

The Vatican crackdown on liberation theology in Latin America was in full swing when Jean-Bertrand Aristide's fiery oratory began to attract the attention of the Duvalier regime in Haiti.[10] The majority of Haiti's Catholics come from the French-speaking upper class, who had historically been supporters of the Duvaliers. It was from their ranks that Haiti's bishops were selected. A concordat with the Vatican in 1966 had given Papa Doc the power to appoint bishops, a power he used with the connivance of Rome to co-opt the Haitian episcopacy and thus silence the Church.

When John Paul II visited Haiti in 1983, he denounced poverty and was so moved by the wretched living conditions of the people that he took off his papal ring and waded into the crowd to present it to a group of poor people. The members of Ti Legliz, whose leader, Father Aristide, had recently been sent into exile in Montreal by the Haitian hierarchy, began to hope that the Church would have a change of heart.

Aristide returned to Haiti two years later, in 1985. The Ti Legliz movement increased and multiplied. In 1987, under pressure from the Duvalier government, the Haitian bishops denounced Ti Legliz. In 1988, when Aristide's church was attacked and burned by Duvalier thugs, and thirteen people died as a result of this failed assassination attempt on their pastor, not a single member of the Haitian hierarchy condemned the attack. Aristide's parishioners marched to the heavily guarded palace of the papal nuncio, high above the slums of Port-au-Prince, to seek help. Perhaps, they reasoned, the nuncio could appeal to the champion of the poor, John Paul II, to intervene on their behalf.

Instead, the poor of Port-au-Prince received a rude awakening to the power politics of Pax Vaticana. Acting on orders from the Pope, the papal nuncio ordered Aristide to leave Haiti by October 1988. But on the day he was due to fly, protesters blocked the road to the airport, and Aristide instead went into hiding. In the meantime, the Pope put pressure on the Superior General of the Salesian order to expel Aristide from its ranks. Aristide's political involvement was condemned by the Vatican spokesman,

Joaquin Navarro-Valls, on the pretext that it was contrary to his priestly vocation. He was given an ultimatum under his vow of obedience to his superior to renounce all involvement in politics. When Aristide did not comply, he was expelled from the Salesian order in December 1988.

This treatment of Aristide stands in sharp contrast with that meted out to another member of the Salesian order, Cardinal Miguel Obando y Bravo of Managua, Nicaragua. Obando y Bravo, with the full blessing of Rome, had openly worked with the Contras in Nicaragua to bring about the downfall of the Sandinista revolution in that country. For John Paul II, the application of the rule forbidding involvement in politics depends on which side of the political fence the priest stands. It is within a priest's vocation to work against communism, but not to work against fascism.

No longer a Salesian but still a priest, Aristide in 1990 announced his candidacy for president of Haiti. After an election campaign fought against the combined power of the Church, the upper class, and the Duvalier government, Aristide was elected in 1990. Immediately after the election, the poor of Haiti attacked and burned the residence of the papal nuncio. It is significant that despite years of exploitation by the government and its upper-class allies, the greatest betrayal in their eyes was that of a Pope whose lips spoke so eloquently of their plight but whose actions supported the individuals and structures which caused it. When a coup forced Aristide into exile in 1991, he fled not into the arms of Mother Church but to the Clinton administration in Washington. The Pope ordered the papal nuncio restored to his Port-au-Prince palace, and the Holy See became the only country in the world to give diplomatic recognition to the renegade government of Marc Bazin.

John Paul II speaks eloquently on the value of justice for the Third World, but his actions legitimize the continuation of oppression there. The same pope speaks glowingly of the equality of women, but his actions perpetuate their subjection. The poor of Haiti came face to face with the lie and set fire to the papal nuncio's palace. Women have not yet stormed the Vatican, but the anger of women delegates to the 1994 Cairo

Conference on Population and Development was about to force the Holy See to beat a hasty retreat behind closed doors.

THE CAIRO CONFERENCE ON POPULATION

On March 18, 1994, Dr. Nafis Sadik, the Egyptian scholar and undersecretary of the Cairo Conference on Population and Development walked up the steps of the papal residence in the Vatican. It was at the time when the PrepCom meetings for Cairo had entered their final stages, and severe divisions were emerging between the Vatican and the majority of other nations and groups who would be represented at Cairo.

According to a memorandum Sadik wrote following this meeting, she had hardly taken her seat in front of his desk when the Pope launched an attack on the conference. "You know this is the year of the family. It seems to me the disintegration of the family... a family is husband and wife and their children. Homosexuals and lesbians are not families."[11] The conversation then turned to family planning and the spread of AIDS. Sadik pointed out that natural family planning involves an equal and stable relationship between the two partners, a situation which is a pipe dream for the many women in the world who live in violent, patriarchal relationships, where they have no control over the frequency and timing of the sexual act. She also reminded John Paul II of the hundreds of thousands of women who die each year from self-induced abortions. "Don't you think," John Paul II interjected, to her astonishment, "that the irresponsible behavior of men is caused by women?"[12]

Just as, for the Vatican, feminism is responsible for the collapse of family values, individual feminists have no one to blame but themselves if they get hurt as a result of the backlash against feminism. If women become feminists, men will not be "tamed" by good women and they will revert to being beasts. It's not the fault of men; it's the way God made them. Women are responsible for the collapse of civilization, for pornography, rape, child abuse, and domestic violence. That's why, in the Pope's view, the Cairo conference was "the work of the devil" because its goal was to offer women a real choice, that of going beyond the domestic boundaries imposed by uncontrollable fertility.

In March 1994, the Vatican summoned its entire corps of ambassadors to the Holy See to a meeting at which they were lectured on the Vatican's position on population. "The Pope's war against the United Nations goes on nonstop," reported the Italian newspaper *La Repubblica* in April 1994. In April, the Pope's attack on the UN became more frenzied. "I am going back to the Vatican," he told the Sunday Mass congregation at a parish church in Rome, "to combat a project prepared by the United Nations which wants to destroy the family."[13] An extraordinary conclave of cardinals was summoned to Rome in June 1994 in order to strategize resistance to the "pervasive influence of feminism" at the Cairo conference. These fathers of the Church, their thrones, titles, and regalia lifted straight out of the Roman Empire, and seated on diplomatic territory granted to them at Caesar's bequest, had the temerity to use the argument of "cultural imperialism" once again to try to discredit the efforts of the UN PrepCom.

A month later, Cardinal Jaime Sin of Manila in the Philippines stated that the UN wanted to "brainwash our children into accepting as normal, attractive and even glamorous, certain unnatural, abnormal and perverse sexual relationships such as homosexuality, lesbianism, incest, sodomy, oral sex, contraception, sterilization and abortion." In August, he led a protest of Filipino schoolchildren through the streets of Manila. In scenes reminiscent of the Inquisition, they burned copies of the Cairo Program of Action and accused the conference of promoting a "global dictatorship to deluge the developing world with contraceptives."[14]

With the election of Bill Clinton in 1992 on a platform of pro-choice for women, the Vatican had lost its old ally, the United States. The White House itself had fallen under the evil influence of feminism. Clinton, who had declared that one objective of the Cairo conference should be to make abortion "safe and rare," and Vice-President Al Gore were subjected to intense private pressure and public denunciation. The Pope wrote to Clinton in March 1994, stating that the Cairo platform "promotes a lifestyle that is totally individualistic to such an extent that marriage seems out-moded," a lifestyle "typical of certain fringes within developed societies, societies which are materially rich and secularized." But while the Pope was saying that the Cairo document was too American, his conservative protégé in New York, Cardinal John O'Connor, was denouncing the Cairo document as un-American, stating that it "promoted concepts totally alien to what we've believed to be our American philosophy."[15]

In April, the Pope telephoned President Clinton to talk about the Cairo conference. Details of the conversation were not revealed, but the Vatican delegate to the PrepCom, Monsignor Diarmuid Martin, stated that the Pope had tried to raise his concerns that "the United States wants the question of abortion as a fundamental dimension of population policy throughout the world to be a major theme of the conference." In a face-to-face meeting with Clinton in June, the Pope attempted unsuccessfully to pressure the president to change the direction of U.S. policy on Cairo. In August, Vatican spokesman Joaquin Navarro-Valls attacked Vice-President Gore, accusing him of lying in a statement in which he denied that the United States wanted to establish an international right to abortion. The Vatican then tried a last-ditch effort to shift U.S. opinion in an op-ed article written by Navarro-Valls which was carried in the *Wall Street Journal* a few days before the opening of the conference. "The conference themes," wrote Navarro-Valls "include coerced family planning, abortion, homosexuality and versions of women's rights which are harmful to women."[16]

THE HOLY WAR AGAINST WOMEN

In the lead-up to the Cairo conference, the Vatican intensified the pressure on its Muslim allies to denounce the Cairo agenda. In August 1994, a papal envoy, Monsignor Romeo Panciroli, met with Iran's deputy foreign minister, Mohammed Hashemi Rafsanjani, to plan a joint strategy in opposition to the Cairo Program of Action. In a move that shocked the majority of moderate delegates to the conference, the same papal envoy visited Tripoli to court Libya's support in return for a pledge of Vatican assistance to broker a settlement over Libyan terrorists accused of the 1988 bombing of a Pan Am jet over Lockerbie, Scotland.

But the Vatican was frustrated in its attempt to court fundamentalist Muslim support because the conference was held in non-fundamentalist Muslim territory, Egypt, and was headed by a moderate Muslim woman, Dr. Sadik. Egypt's minister of population, Maher Muhran, issued a statement saying that the Draft Program of Action did not violate the Koran, and the Egyptian government rallied moderate Muslim groups in support of the conference. Secular and moderate Islamic delegates spoke out in favor of family planning and gender equity. The Terra Mater alliance crafted by the Vatican in the 1980s began to dissolve. At the last minute, fundamentalist Islamic dissidents in Cairo called for a cancellation of the conference and threatened terrorist action against the delegates. Tim Wirth, U.S. undersecretary of state for global affairs, confronted the Vatican over its negotiations with Libya and requested that the Holy See condemn threats of violence against the conference. That request went unheeded.

Earlier in 1994, President Carlos Menem of Argentina had sent a letter to heads of state in Latin America, Spain, and Portugal urging them to take a position based on the "right to life," that is, the right to life of the fetus. He failed to get support for this Hispanic-Vatican alliance. On the eve of the Cairo conference, despite its extraordinary efforts, the Vatican was bereft of major diplomatic partners and could count on only Malta, Iran, Honduras, Argentina, and at different times, Guatemala and Nicaragua.[17]

Distortion of the conference agenda was another strategy employed by the Vatican and its allies. The Vatican deliberately confused abortion and contraception, constantly referring to contraception as a form of abortion. The head of the Pontifical Council for the Family, Cardinal Alfonso Lopez Trujillo, said that the Cairo conference "could cause the most disastrous massacre in history."[18] "The Cairo conference," said John Paul in a speech in Rome, "is a snare of the devil, and promulgates a culture of death."[19]

The truth is that not a single women's group has a platform favoring the kind of coercive state-controlled family-planning programs that have fallen into disrepute, but the Vatican tried to imply that the Cairo conference was a ploy by the First World nations to impose new compulsive sterilization programs on the Third World. The word "sterilization" did not even appear in the draft Program of Action, which states that "Reproductive health-care programs should provide the widest range of services without any form of coercion... All couples and individuals should have the basic right to decide freely and responsibly the number and spacing of their children and to have the information, means and education to do so." Yet, "compulsory sterilization" is scattered throughout Vatican denunciations of the Cairo conference.

The Vatican claimed that the recognition of a diversity of family structures throughout the globe would lead not only to increased rights for gay and lesbian families but to pedophilia and bestiality being recognized as acceptable forms of sexual union. So exasperated by these Vatican antics were the delegates at the fourth and final PrepCom meeting that they booed the Vatican representative—an unheard-of breach of normal diplomatic protocol. But nothing could have prepared the delegates for the attack mounted by the Holy See in the first five days of the conference itself.

"The force of women," stated a report on Cairo published in the Toronto *Globe and Mail*, "has cut a deep swath of influence across international diplomacy."[20] Every morning as the conference opened, women's organizations met to strategize. The global networking of women's groups, which began as a result of previous UN conferences, was a key factor in focusing the agenda at Cairo and in challenging the Vatican agenda. As some women plugged into their e-mail connections across the world, others such as the redoubtable Frances Kissling of Catholics for a Free Choice, based in Washington, D.C., prepared to confront members of the Vatican delegation in the conference hall at Cairo. Kissling and other women continually drew world attention to the sexist principles behind the Vatican platform. They were so effective that within three days there were no further Vatican press conferences and the previously open door to the Holy See's delegation was tightly shut.

For five days, the Holy See held up the progress of the conference over the wording of a clause on access to abortion. As a result, the Vatican managed to get a provision on abortion modified to include a reference to acceptable religious and cultural norms which hold that "in no case should abortion be promoted as a method of family planning."[21] The Holy See in turn dropped its opposition to the use of the word "condoms" to combat the spread of AIDS. So strident were the Holy See's attempts to sabotage the work of the Cairo document that this strategy ultimately backfired. The Vatican may have succeeded in changing the wording of one sentence on abortion, but this was achieved at the cost of alienating the vast majority of the moderate world from the Catholic Church, leaving the Church even more isolated and lacking in credibility.

The men in the Vatican, whose lives are never touched by the intimate details of family life and sexuality, seem unable to grasp the logic that by improving women's education and access to contraception and striving to break down barriers to equality, the delegates to the Cairo conference were actually working to make the world a safer place for children by emphasizing mutually responsible motherhood and fatherhood. The aim was not to promote abortion, but to make it unnecessary.

John Paul II's virulent but unsuccessful campaign to sabotage the Cairo conference may have all but cost him the battle for the heart and soul of humankind. The Vatican has used its position at the world table to campaign against women's rights. Its failure to win support has strengthened the cause of women in the long run, and will hasten the end of patriarchal religion's domination over the destiny of women. As a result of Cairo, women's rights, not women's bodies and biology, have become the focus of debates on population, development, poverty, and social justice. This presented a greater threat than ever to male control over women's issues.

The 1994 Cairo conference further exposed the glaring inconsistencies between John Paul II's position and Catholic social teaching on universal human rights. The campaign for the recognition of women's rights as human rights, accepted at Rio and Cairo, had also been advanced at the Vienna Conference on Human Rights in 1993. This conference placed a further spotlight on the Vatican's Achilles heel: the lack of equal rights and rites for women within the Catholic Church. The Vatican has lost key ground in the crusade to defend its self-proclaimed, God-given right to tell the rest of the world how to maintain control over women. The subsequent global debate at the Beijing conference would focus on gender as the fundamental determinant of men's and women's roles. As the UN prepared for the fourth World Conference on Women in Beijing, the Pope's anthropology of "equal but different" was waiting to be blown apart.

THE VATICAN'S RETREAT

"The Cairo conference," said Nafis Sadik after it was over, "was an outstandingly successful conference. The participants crafted a Program of Action for the next twenty years which starts from the reality of the world we live in and shows us the path to a better reality... with highly specific goals for infant and maternal mortality, education, and reproductive health and family planning, but its effect will be far more wide ranging than that... There will be fewer abortions in the future because there will be less need for abortions. This Program of Action," she concluded, "has the potential to change the world."[22]

The Cairo conference may actually have marked the beginning of the end of Vatican influence at the UN. The Vatican delegates, who went to Cairo expecting acceptance of their views, had been forced to negotiate with outside, even "secular" groups, and to accept several compromises in key areas. The Cairo conference also marked the emergence of Catholic women and groups well versed in theology and Church history, who were prepared to challenge the Vatican in its own territory. As a result, the Vatican took a much more muted approach to the Beijing conference. Harvard professor Mary Ann Glendon was appointed as head of the Holy See's delegation. It was a new phenomenon to see Catholic women debating for and against the Vatican on all sides of the issues.

The Vatican's critique of the draft Program of Action centered this time on two issues: the use of the word "gender" and the advancement of equal rights for lesbian women, and by implication, gay men. The Vatican realized that it would not emerge unscathed from open interference with the agenda itself, so attempts were made to pre-empt the discussion by obstructive tactics at the PrepCom meetings.

In March 1995, the Vatican delegates tried unsuccessfully to delete the use of the word "gender" throughout the draft Program of Action. Why did they attempt to mount opposition to this term? Because the social and theological supports for maintaining patriarchal gender relationships within and outside the Catholic Church are breaking down. "Gender" implies that male dominance is a product of history and socialization, not God's eternal will as written into biological laws. In the Pope's anthropology, masculinity and femininity are the immutable human conditions which structure the patriarchal relationships between the sexes. The concept of "gender" carries the potential to challenge this closed and comfortable hierarchical world.

The use of the word "gender" as opposed to "sex" indicates that masculine and feminine roles are culturally defined and socially learned. Since both cultural conditioning and socialized learning can be changed, so concepts of masculinity and femininity can evolve and change. Women can be mechanics, and men can be kindergarten teachers. Little boys can wear pink, and little girls can wear blue. Women can be CEOs, presidents of countries, even priests.

This is anathema to the Pope's concept of the "eternal feminine." To acknowledge that the qualities assigned to masculinity and femininity can change undermines the Pope's concept of the God-given biological imperative of motherhood. Upon this cornerstone of the unchangeable nature of masculinity and femininity rests the division of male and female roles in society and the right of men to determine women's destiny. On this also rests the definition of the masculinity of God and the exclusion of women from the Catholic priesthood. If the weight of centuries of conditioning and socialization into subservience can be deconstructed and then reconstructed in liberating ways, women can start to interpret God's will for them anew, which will lead to change in the structure of both Church and society.

The Vatican tried to disguise its real agenda on gender by distorting the meaning of the term. All other delegations to the Beijing PrepCom were quite clear on the commonly accepted meaning of the word "gender" as distinguishing male and female, but the Vatican insisted it could mean masculine, feminine, lesbian, homosexual, or transsexual. The Holy See and its allies also objected to the use of such phrases as "gender-based violence," insisting that this was anti-male and placed marriage and family in a negative rather than a positive light. This kind of distortion has since become standard fare in right-wing Catholic journals and commentaries.

The Vatican's interventions also led to semantic games around the term "sexual orientation." Before the Beijing conference took place, the caucus of lesbian women had persuaded the delegates to insert the phrase "sexual orientation" into the section of the Program of Action that deals with discrimination against women. The Vatican delegates countered that since in their view gay or lesbian sexual orientation includes a propensity to pedophilia, necrophilia, and bestiality, these latter practices would be automatically sanctioned by any civil laws which would be passed to protect gays and lesbians.

The same prejudice against gays and lesbians had also surfaced that year in the Canadian Parliament in the debates over Bill c-41 on hate crimes. Proponents of this bill sought to include abuse of gays and lesbians as a category that could be prosecuted as a hate crime. Unsuccessful opposition to this provision was mounted by a group of right-wing Catholic Liberal MPs, who stated that Bill c-41 would lead to an acceptance of pedophilia, necrophilia, and bestiality as alternative lifestyles.

In early 1995, using the rule that the PrepCom meetings must reach consensus before forwarding the Program of Action to the conference itself, the Holy See had garnered support from Guatemala, Honduras, Sudan, Malta, Iran, and China to agree to question basic statements such as "universal human rights" and specifics such as "reproductive counseling." The objective of this maneuver, in the words of one right-wing Canadian journalist, Larry Rock, was to "render the Beijing conference virtually impotent."[23] Sections of the Beijing document taken from the Cairo

Program of Action, which had been accepted by the Vatican, were also bracketed (that is, set aside) for discussion, leading to the suspicion that the Holy See was going to use Beijing as an opportunity to fight the Cairo campaign all over again.

With the exception of Malta, this cabal of the Catholic Church's allies all have records of flagrant human rights abuses, "disappearances" of opposition members, and torture. The scandal of China's compulsory sterilization and abortion programs and its dumping of unwanted baby girls in "dying rooms" in state orphanages had been highlighted in the media in the months leading up to the Beijing conference. Several women's groups had declared a boycott of Beijing because they felt it was an outrage to women to hold the conference on Chinese soil. Even though Vatican rhetoric repeatedly condemns compulsory sterilization and abortion in the strongest terms, Vatican delegates to the Beijing conference did not show any squeamishness about operating on Chinese soil. In fact, they were more than willing to form an alliance with the Chinese government to try to bar certain women's groups from participating in the conference.

In the same way that moderate Muslims had played a part at Cairo in combating the vitriol of Islamic fundamentalists, women of faith from different Christian denominations strategized at Beijing in order to present feminist Christian perspectives that differed from the official Catholic one. A group of some forty North American Catholic feminist organizations, which goes by the name of Women-Church Convergence and which includes Catholics for a Free Choice, published its own commentary on the report issued by the Holy See in preparation for the Beijing conference.

This report dissected the Vatican's criticisms of the Beijing Program of Action, criticisms based on John Paul II's concept of women's "specificity," which attributes women's human dignity only to her reproductive capacities. "No such assumption is made with regard to men," the commentary states, "whose dignity is presumed to be simply conferred by their humanity." These Christian women critiqued the hostility to and caricature of feminism which informs the Vatican's platform, and the absence of any analysis of the way gender roles contribute to violence against women. They called for a "new vision of social justice" which would emphasize that women and men are basically equal, and that within that equality there is a great deal of diversity. They also stressed the fact that women's contributions to humanity are not always linked to home and family but rather to building the community. Only a renewed "discipleship of equals," modeled on the pattern of the early church, will promote this.[24]

Several Canadian ecumenical groups also issued statements which supported the equality of women from a Christian perspective. The Vatican's privileged position at the United Nations and its arrogation at the Cairo conference of the right to speak for all Catholics, even for all Christians, was forcefully challenged at Beijing. The Statement on Gender issued by Canadian Communities of Faith in June 1995 was in response to the Vatican's attempt to bracket the word "gender" and sabotage the New York PrepCom meeting. The communities of faith "affirm that gender has been used since the 1980s... to refer to the social organization of the relationship between women and men." They pointed out that churches must "bear in mind the role of religious communities in constructing and prescribing gender in ways that have often been particularly oppressive to women and men." In a direct challenge to the Vatican and its allies, they urged governments "to honor all agreements including the use of the term 'gender' and commitments made at previous United Nations conferences regarding the status of women. These include respect for the universal human rights of women, the right to reproductive freedom and health, and the right to be free of violence."[25]

A network of Canadian Churches that worked together from 1988 to 1998 on an Ecumenical Decade of Solidarity with Women also issued a Canadian Church Women's Affirmation in preparation for the Beijing conference. It opened with the statement:

We affirm that God created both women and men in God's own image and that each of us is marvelously made... Our faith demands that we defend women's rights as human rights and that we seek to be peacemakers and community builders throughout the world . . . we challenge all power relationships that fail to respect the equality and dignity of women... we celebrate the struggle of our sisters who refuse to be victims... we stand in solidarity and commit ourselves to a common path toward the transformation of the world.[26]

The Holy See's tactics at Cairo had cost it its credibility as the only true representative of God at the UN. Too many groups had begun to talk openly about the horse of sexism at the Vatican's table. So the Vatican adopted a two-pronged tactic: first, silence the "uppity" Catholic women who kept pointing out the horse on the table at Cairo and then try to hide the horse by sending several women in the Holy See's delegation.

In March 1995, the Vatican used its position at the UN to lobby against Catholics for a Free Choice (CFFC) and its affiliates in Mexico, Brazil, and Uruguay. Vatican spokesmen argued that these groups should not be given the necessary credentials to attend the NGO forum at the Beijing conference on the grounds that "they are not legitimately Catholic." The CFFC spokesperson, Frances Kissling, had been, in her own words, "a thorn in the side of the Vatican" at Cairo. The Vatican knows that surveys have shown that the majority of Catholic women reject the Pope's views on women, so it resorts to the tactic of trying to silence this opposition. China joined the Vatican's move against progressive women to bar women's groups from Tibet and Taiwan from attending the conference. A storm of protest within the United States forced the UN to reconsider its decision and endorse the participation of CFFC.

Conservative Catholic groups in the United States, including the Knights of Columbus and the Catholic Campaign for America, also networked with organizations from the Religious Right to attempt to challenge the participation of the U.S. itself on the grounds that it would implicitly condone the human rights abuses in China. Their arguments were heard and rejected at a July 18 hearing by the U.S. House of Representatives International Relations Subcommittee on International Operations and Human Rights. The fact that these Catholic groups did not put similar pressure on the Holy See to withdraw from the conference exposed their action as a hypocritical tactic to silence the most powerful international critics of Vatican sexism.

Feminist Catholic women also came under attack from the anti-feminist group REAL Women of Canada. The acronym REAL stands for "Realistic, Equal and Active for Life." REAL Women accused the Canadian delegation of being "obsessed with lesbian sexual orientation" and of trying to "internationalize lesbian rights." It is difficult to discern what REAL Women's fight for equality is based on since they believe that "women cannot be treated as totally autonomous persons."[27] According to REAL Women, there is a left-wing conspiracy to have the United Nations take over the world. In a statement reminiscent of the New Right and the militia movement in the United States, the REAL Women's newsletter, *Reality*, had this comment on the 1980 UN Convention for the Elimination of All Forms of Discrimination Against Women (CEDAW). "Soviet-aligned groups spearheaded this Soviet legislation on women's rights and used it as a model at the UN so as to have the nations of the free world bring their citizens in line with those of socialist countries."[28]

Like their counterparts in the U.S. Religious Right, REAL Women is a staunch defender of the neo-conservative revolution in economics and would like to see Canada strengthen its armed forces. It opposes "women's groups who have as their ultimate goal and objective the destruction of our free market economy, the limitation of a strong defense, and the radical change in traditional family structures and values."

In early November 1989, a group called the Northern Foundation held its inaugural conference in Ottawa. Delegates from REAL Women of Canada, the Christian Heritage Party, the Alliance for the Preservation of English in Canada, and the Fraser Institute met to form the platform for a new right-wing coalition. The joint agenda that emerged included opposition to the policy of bilingualism in Canada, more restrictive immigration policies, a return of the death penalty, opposition to abortion, a stronger military, and lower taxes. The vice-president of the Northern Foundation, Anne Hartmann, was also on the board of directors of REAL Women. The widow of Western Guard member Paul Hartmann, who died in June 1986 under mysterious circumstances, Hartmann had maintained connections with neo-Nazi groups across North America. Western Guard is a neo-Nazi white supremacist group with links to the Ku Klux Klan. It supports a "white Canada"; terms such as "the jewdicial system" of Canada and the "mongrelization" of Toronto are scattered through its publications.[29] Hartmann is a lawyer and continues to provide legal advice for REAL Women.

A platform of opposition to bilingualism and resistance to the recognition of special status for Quebec often conceals a covert racism in English Canada, a racism that pervades the platform of the Northern Foundation. It is strange, though, that a Catholic group such as REAL Women would be opposed to the protection of French-language programs in Canada, since the origins of Catholicism in Canada and the rights of Catholic schools in various Canadian provinces stem from the history of Quebec. It is also curious to note that in 1990, a year after it had called for a reduction in taxes, REAL women applied for $400,000 in government funding.

Such inconsistencies have marked this group's activities since its inception. But it is REAL Women's rabid homophobia that has earned the organization special notoriety in Canada. In 1990, REAL Women held their national convention in Vancouver, British Columbia. In preparation for the conference, the B.C. chair, Peggy Steacy, wrote a newsletter which was mailed out to delegates, using B.C. taxpayers' money, together with a letter of congratulations from then premier Bill van der Zalm.

"The thought of Vancouver being known as the 'San Francisco of the North,'" wrote Steacy, "or more accurately 'Sodom North' because we are accepting their lifestyle is sickening... I'm homonauseated. Most decent people don't know the disgusting, filthy activities indulged in by these people, homos and lesbians both ... we're paying a hundred thousand dollars a year to look after AIDS patients."

Steacy agrees with Pope John Paul II that "women are to blame for the irresponsible behavior of men." She offered the following speculative opinion to delegates as to the reason why Marc Lepine massacred fourteen women at the Ecole Polytechnique in 1989. "Speaking of Marc Lepine and the Montreal Massacre," she added, "who knows why he did it? The thought immediately occurred to me that he might just have been a man whose child had been aborted by a feminist and that might have been enough to trigger a terrible response to the abuse of his childhood."[30] When a storm of outrage broke out as a result of Steacy's remarks, neither she nor the national office of REAL Women rescinded a word of the newsletter. With their "homonauseated" minds made up, they set forth for Beijing to do battle for the Holy See.

When Mary Ann Glendon, head of the Vatican delegation, rose to address the delegates at Beijing she, unlike all previous Vatican heads of delegations, was not wearing a cassock or a clerical collar. Many saw this as a significant sign of progress, but her presence was purely symbolic. Real significance would have been to see a woman in clerical robes. The Vatican's agenda might have been clothed in a new wineskin but it was the same old wine which spilled out on the table. Her address marked an acknowledgment of the role of women in the workplace (she herself is a professor of law), but working women are collectively referred to as "working mothers." Glendon lacks, in the Pope's eyes, that "natural resemblance to Christ" which would qualify her for decision making within the Holy See. The rest of the world knows this. So even an intelligent and highly qualified woman such as Glendon failed to achieve credibility for the Vatican because she operates at the behest of men who legislate apartheid of gender behind the closed doors of decision-making structures to which she is not admitted.

One major issue at the Beijing Conference on Women centered on the application of universal human rights in the context of issues of national sovereignty and cultural traditions in theocratic states governed according to religious law. Conservative delegates tried unsuccessfully to use this debate to re-open the contentious discussion on abortion at Cairo and to accept punitive laws in some states against women who have had an abortion. The Vatican had voted to uphold the latter, since the Catholic Church applies an automatic penalty of excommunication for any woman who has had an abortion. The Vatican also failed in its attempt to remove a statement in the Program of Action which gives women "the right to control over and decide freely and responsibly on matters related to their sexuality, including sexual and reproductive health." It was not successful in getting a conscience clause to exempt Catholic hospitals universally from providing abortion and reproductive health services, even though it has negotiated these within individual countries.

The only area where the Vatican did succeed was in opposing the rights of lesbian women. The term "sexual orientation" was not included in the document's section on the prevention of discrimination and violence, but the decision was made on procedural rather than substantive grounds, and not without a full public debate on the issue of sexual orientation—a first in the history of the UN.

Also a first in the history of the UN was a petition that was circulated calling for the removal of the Vatican from accreditation as a member state. This was initiated by progressive Catholics and women's groups from Canada, the Caribbean, Europe, Latin America, and the United States. Titled "A Call to the United Nations to Consider the UN Status of the Holy See," the petition asks the question: "Should the Roman Catholic Church continue to be treated as a state?"[31]

A petition such as this would have been unthinkable even five years earlier, at the time of the 1990 World Conference on Women. But since 1990, the Holy See's opportunistic and bullying tactics at Rio, Cairo, and now Beijing had caused exasperation to turn into action. "Quite simply and sadly," said Daniel Maguire, professor of theology at Marquette University, in a speech to delegates at Cairo in September 1994, "I believe that the Vatican has squandered its moral authority on issues about which it has no privileged expertise."[32]

"The Holy See," states the 1995 petition, "overreaches—with increasing frequency—its observer status and obstructs action and development of consensus among member states... the Holy See uses the UN to advance the theological positions of the Catholic Church... In UN conferences from Rio de Janeiro to Beijing there has been increasing vehemence in Holy See diplomacy that sacrifices substantial consensus on matters of women's rights and reproduction to the theological agenda of the Church."[33] Furthermore, they might have added, this theological agenda is rejected by the majority of Catholics. The petition garnered much support and was widely reported in the international media. If and when there is another UN conference, if the Vatican has not rid itself of the horse of sexism, it may find there is no longer a place set for the Holy See at the table of world governance.

"There is no going back on this Program of Action," stated Gertrude Mongella, secretary general of the Beijing Conference on Women, in her concluding remarks. "Nairobi provided us with a compass," wrote the U.S. delegation in a report to President Clinton, "Beijing gives us a map."[34] The steps taken along the path of all the UN conferences which led up to Beijing placed women at the center of the world's agenda.

The policies on women orchestrated by John Paul II have marked a change in direction for Vatican participation at the UN. Gone are the paeans of praise for the UN's role in fostering world cooperation which are found in the landmark encyclicals of previous popes—*Pacem in Terris* of John XXIII or *Populorum Progressio* of Paul VI, even *Redemptor Hominis*, issued at the beginning of John Paul II's papacy. Rome now seems bent on a collision course with the rest of the world on women's issues.

It appears that the Vatican would ideally like to keep all of the world's women, Catholic or not, subject to Church teaching on women's health and reproductive issues. That this overarching claim to supreme authority over women's health can affect even a supposedly secular health system was recently evident in the forced hospital mergers in Toronto.

One of the items on the agenda of the Conservative government elected in Ontario in 1995 has been to drastically scale back the level of service in publicly funded health care in the province. Hospitals that serve the poor in the downtown area of Toronto have been particularly hard hit. One of these was the Wellesley Hospital, located at the corner of Wellesley and Sherbourne in one of the most densely populated low-income areas of the city, and on the eastern edge of the "gay ghetto." This neighborhood is also host to street people, drug addicts, and prostitutes for gay, straight, and transvestite clienteles. Staff at the Wellesley Hospital had worked long and hard to develop a creative and caring outreach to this local community.

As a result of the cutbacks to health care put into effect by the Harris government, in 1997 the Wellesley Hospital was ordered to close down and merge its programs with those at St. Michael's, a Catholic hospital in the downtown area. The Ontario government pledged that the hospital restructuring would not affect the programs at the Wellesley. The staff feared otherwise, and fought a long but unsuccessful battle to keep the hospital open.

St. Michael's promptly announced that it would continue to veto abortions, as well as vasectomies, tubal ligations, and other birth control methods, and also birth control counseling in the use of contraceptives by nurses and doctors for the general population formerly served by the Wellesley Hospital. "Our core values will not change," announced the hospital's director of services.[35]

There is an insidious hypocrisy in this statement, one that mimics the Vatican's stance at the United Nations. On the one hand, a Church institution welcomes the financial support of non-believers as well as believers by way of public taxes, and pays lip service to public democratic values. The Vatican pays nominal adherence to the democratic and egalitarian values of the United Nations Assembly in order to enjoy access to that Assembly, but rides roughshod over those values within the Catholic Church. In the same way, a Catholic hospital, funded by tax dollars and involved in the very delicate process of a forced merger with a highly successful public hospital, claims the right to impose Vatican policies which ride roughshod over the very public values it feigns to support in order to get access to the public purse. The same contradictions exist in the publicly supported Catholic school system in Ontario, as outlined in the previous chapter.

At the end of the gospel of Luke, there is a story that is a favorite with many Christians which is called the Walk to Emmaus.[36] Two disciples are leaving Jerusalem after the crucifixion. Many commentators now suggest that the pair could have been a man and a woman. They are returning to their village of Emmaus, sad and perplexed by the death of Jesus which seems to signal the end of a dream. Along the way they are joined by the risen Jesus, who walks and talks with them. They do not recognize him until he stops and breaks bread with them.

This story describes the route for the journey toward renewal marked out for the Catholic Church by the Second Vatican Council. The presence of the Church as a sign of Christ in the world is a mystery until it is translated into a structure. When the structure no longer serves the mystery, the Spirit of Christ finds a way to break out and walk away. The Church is a Pilgrim People of God, called to walk alongside humankind. Christ listened before he spoke. His words were not based on preconceived answers to preconceived questions, but on the real context of the disciples' lives. He neither sought nor accepted a privileged place nor extraordinary treatment. He sat and shared a bottle of wine. He touched their hearts, we are told, invited them to participate in the mystery of his presence, and then he was gone.

Women struggling to walk along the path toward a better world for themselves and their children will no longer take advice from men cracking the whip from their chariots of privilege or from knights in the shining armor of their own self-appointed expertise. The Catholic Church will be left behind while the rest of the world carries on historic debates on women and the family. Whatever happens within the Church in Rome, the Pilgrim People of God will continue to tread the path of history in the footsteps of the poor carpenter from Nazareth, who inspired us to dream of ever-new possibilities for transformation. The pontificate of John Paul II may have fostered patriarchal privilege within the sanctuary of the Catholic Church, but I believe that ultimately, like the triple crown worn by popes until very recently, patriarchy and all its trappings will one day be consigned to history and the Vatican Museum.

Chapter Six

The Catholic Church
in the Next Millennium

"Hope has two daughters," wrote St. Augustine, "anger and courage." It is paradoxical that a theologian who had such a difficult relationship with women, and whose theology is so remorselessly antipathetic toward women, should name hope, anger, and courage as female virtues. Augustine of Hippo bears much responsibility for the negative attitudes toward sexuality that have marred Christian thought; but despite my suspicion of Augustine's opinions on sexuality and the nature of women, I can still acknowledge that many of his other writings—his prayers and his discourses on the Trinity, for example—are inspirational. In fact, the *Confessions* of St. Augustine was one of the formative influences of my youth.

A recognition of the ambivalence within every human being—of the juxtaposition of good and evil, human and divine, dark and light, in the depths of our souls—lies at the heart of the renewed spirituality that is struggling to be heard around the world at the outset of this new millennium. The feminine principle, which has so often been viewed with suspicion as the shadow side of humanity, is now seen as a way forward out of the dualism of patriarchy, a philosophy that, in separating reality into antipathetic, polar opposites, now threatens to destroy the planet.

I have learned to recognize that there can also be a negative side to feminism. At times, women's anger at injustice can slide into bitterness and recrimination. As well, feminism is not without its high priestesses of righteousness. Much as the papacy of John Paul II has often come to resemble the totalitarian system of repression he so successfully resisted in Poland, feminism has sometimes reproduced the very hierarchies and dualism which it rejects.

"Men are the enemy" provided a neat but simplistic theme for some early feminist discourse and actions. This has been giving way to the more nuanced view that while patriarchy has oppressed women in general and while men in general have benefited from it and must be held accountable, individual men are not responsible for all the deleterious effects of patriarchy on individual women.

The Catholic spirituality which nurtured me provides a healthy counterbalance, one which undercuts any assumption of self-righteousness by acknowledging that "we hold our treasure, not in cups of gold, but in earthen vessels."[1] As we struggle to create a more just and balanced world for our children and grandchildren, we must constantly seek to heal and reunite the brokenness and divisions of humanity which we experience within ourselves and in society, and also in the planet we inhabit. In Jesus risen, all divisions are healed: body and spirit, earth and heaven, female and male—all are reunited within the inner life of God.

As tribute to the mystery of the uniting of opposites, Catholic spirituality has celebrated this divine-human union by using earthly and fleshly sacraments to "body forth" the mysterious essence of God. Catholics drink and dance at the altar as well as at the hearth. In its best moments, Catholicism has acknowledged that the Church is a human institution and therefore not perfect but *semper reformanda*—always in need of renewal and reform. As acknowledged in the final document of Vatican II, the Church itself has been responsible for the alienation of many from the gospel message. In discussing the rise and spread of atheism in the modern world, the Council accepted that "believers themselves often share some responsibility for this situation... [Atheism] arises from a variety of causes, among which must be included a critical reaction against religions ... and against the Christian religion in particular. Believers can thus have more than a little to do with the rise of atheism."[2]

The tragedy of John Paul II's papacy is that it has been false in so many respects to this insight into the need for humility and gracious generosity, qualities which have so often characterized the Catholic spirit in the past. The final years of John Paul's papacy have seen a retraction of the condemnation of Galileo as well as a formal apology to the Jewish people for the conduct of the Catholic Church during the Second World War. Although it fell short of acknowledging that Catholicism bore much responsibility for the long history of anti-Semitism in Europe, the apology demonstrates that the Pope is somewhat open to the need for repentance in high places in the Church. Perhaps a future pope will see fit to apologize to women for the Catholic witch hunts of early modern Europe and to retract the handbook of the Inquisition, the *Malleus Maleficarum: The Hammer of Witches* (1486),[3] which condemned thousands of girls and women to torture and death.

But under John Paul II's papacy, women's equality is considered to be at best a completely secular notion; at worst, feminism is imagined to be a corruption of God's design for women, and the ordination of women is considered a heresy. In this way, he has evoked the dangerous, shadow side of Catholicism, which has surfaced before in periods such as the Inquisition. With the ascendancy of Opus Dei in the Vatican, this papacy has witnessed the return of anonymous denunciations, secret trials with no right of appeal, and excommunication of theologians on a scale not experienced in the Catholic Church since the time of Pope Pius X and the anti-modernist crusade at the beginning of this century. The lightning rod for this spiritual oppression, especially in the latter half of his papacy, has been feminism.

Many Catholics have been struck by the ambivalence of the papacy of John Paul II. On the one hand, he undoubtedly sought to advance the cause of human rights in society, and has campaigned arduously for the advancement of universal human rights. On the other hand, he has ruthlessly and systematically denied any discussion of the advancement of these same rights within the Church. The United Nations Charter of Universal Human Rights, to which the Vatican is a signatory, has not been enforced within the borders of Vatican City, nor has it crossed the threshold of any Catholic Church worldwide. This hypocritical "Do as I say but not as I do" posture is one of the main factors alienating Catholic youth from the Church and has caused increasing numbers of older Catholics to seek elsewhere for the living God.

As outlined in Chapter 3, I believe that in its relentless and increasingly hysterical opposition to the ordination of women, the Roman Catholic hierarchy (as distinct from the People of God as a whole) has fallen into a dangerous delusion which has led it into serious distortions of some central Christian beliefs. This is not the first time this has happened in the history of the Church. During the time of the Aryan heresy in the fourth century, many bishops and even Pope Liberius fell prey to the heretical teaching that in the Trinity, God the Son ranks lower in divinity than God the Father. Pope Liberius forced Athanasius, one of the champions of orthodox belief in the Trinity, into exile and publicly condemned his teaching. But the People of God debated the Aryan controversy in the squares and marketplaces and their persistent resistance to the papal and episcopal heresy eventually set the bishops straight.

I believe that a similar situation is occurring in the Roman Catholic Church today. Despite the threat of excommunication, the People of God must continue to use all means possible to challenge the Vatican's heretical stance and to oppose their bishops on the issue of the ordination of women until the Vatican is either discredited or is released from the grip of this delusion. I believe that, to paraphrase the quotation from Augustine at the beginning of this chapter, the anger and courage of those who continue to resist this spiritual blindness bears within it the hope of a renewed Catholic Church.

THE DOMINANCE OF CORPORATE CULTURE

In a brilliant study of the spirituality of nonviolent resistance, *Engaging the Powers*, the American biblical scholar Walter Wink has described the spiritual anatomy of what he terms the "Domination System."[4] Modern institutions, including the Churches, are dominated by what the Bible calls the "Principalities and Powers." These Principalities and Powers are the spiritual forces at work within all systems and institutions, forming the inner direction of the institution. That patriarchal powers have come to dominate much of modern institutional life is a result of past human choices, not of some supernatural or demonic force. This means that the same powers can be resisted and rendered impotent as a result of human choices in the present and future.

Wink describes the Powers as "the inner and outer aspects of any given manifestation of power," and continues:

> As the inner aspect, they are the spirituality of institutions, the "within" of corporate structures and systems, the inner essence of outer organizations of power. They are at once personal and structural realities, the personal and political manifestations of the life of an institution. As the outer aspect they can be recognized at work in political systems, appointed officials, the chair of an organization, laws—in short, all the tangible manifestations which power takes.[5]

When a particular power—and the powers are named in various parts of the Scripture as diversely as kings and rulers, death itself, Pharisees and synagogues, angels and archangels—places itself above God's purposes for the good of the whole universe, it becomes idolatrous. "The Church's task," writes Wink, "is to unmask this idolatry and recall the Powers to their purpose in this world."[6] As described by Walter Brueggemann in *Hope Within History*, this is a process not unlike that of the awakening of Moses and the exodus of the people of Israel out of slavery.

But the call to the Churches to unmask the "Principalities and Powers" of this world is by no means a call for a return to the dualistic ideology that the Church is all good and the world is all bad, an ideology prevalent before the Second Vatican Council. The Churches, too, according to Wink, can fall prey to the influence of the Principalities and Powers. "The angel of a church [a symbol used at the beginning of the Book of Revelation] becomes demonic when the congregation turns its back on the specific tasks set before it by God and makes some other goal its idol . . . indeed, it is precisely those institutions that have the highest task that are capable of becoming the most demonic."[7] It then falls to other members of the Church to discern, unmask, and engage with the powers within the Church in order to exorcise the influence of their delusions.

In the various Christian denominations, this function has been fulfilled in history, often at great individual cost, by saints and other prophetic figures who have been rejected as heretical in their own time but vindicated as messengers of God by later generations. The medieval reformer Catherine of Siena comes to mind in this connection, or closer to our own context, the German theologian Dietrich Bonhoeffer, who unmasked and challenged the union of Church and State in Nazi Germany, as did Oscar Romero in El Salvador some thirty years later. I believe the same kind of courage is called for today to unmask the delusional patriarchal system which holds sway over the Catholic Church.

For a delusional system to achieve absolute power over the hearts and minds of its adherents, people must be made to believe that there is no other system: "There is no alternative." Following the collapse of Soviet communism, the free market capitalism of the 1990s, aided by a largely captive media, has had brilliant success in this regard. The well-being of society and its ability to function properly—or in the case of the Church, the eternal soul of the believer—is made dependent on his or her uncritical obedience to the rules of the dominant system, whether this be the code of free market capitalism or the code of canon law. One of the other strategies of this corporate culture is to convince everyone that the system is constantly under threat and must be defended against enemies, both internal and external; otherwise, their own future survival will be placed in peril. This feeds into the adversarial mentality of patriarchy, which fosters an "us and them" or a "win-lose" approach to reality. If I am right, you must be wrong. If I am stronger, I must always win.

Vatican II represented a significant attempt to unmask the ways in which authority and power have been misused in the Catholic Church. The Council made very tentative steps toward acknowledging that a hierarchical system modeled on the Roman system of government, and with it the whole apparatus of patriarchy, are not inherent to the Catholic Church. It was adopted to structure the Church as a result of historical circumstances and is therefore subject to change in the present or future. The Council called on the Church to return to its most ancient roots: back to a dream forged by a wandering Exodus people and carried forward in the life of a poor preacher from Nazareth.

But the corporate culture of clericalism within the Catholic Church was not rooted out after the Council, and it has reasserted itself with a vengeance during the papacy of John Paul II. This corporate culture in the Church is virulently opposed to the equal participation of women in the priesthood. Opposition to women's ordination has been carefully crafted by the powers that be in Rome to convince the "simple faithful" that so-called secular feminism poses a grave internal threat to the survival of the Church. The very fact that Rome's denunciations of feminism and women's ordination have in recent years grown so vehement is proof of the fact that these issues challenge the "Principalities and Powers" of the Vatican.

As Chapter 5 made clear, the reassertion of a patriarchal hierarchy within the Catholic Church and the increasingly stringent penalties attached to a denial of this have come at a time when the Pope has assumed a posture on the world stage as a champion of human rights, including the rights of women. This kind of cognitive dissonance in high places is evidence of a system caught in the depths of delusion while wearing a mask of benevolence and peace.

Even as John Paul fought so successfully to undo the grip of the totalitarian communist system in Poland, he has been bent on restoring totalitarian rule within the Catholic Church. Unquestioning obedience to authority is upheld by threat of exile—if not to a camp in Siberia, at least, in the case of Bishop Gaillot of Evreux, to the desert see of Mauritania. Bishop Jacques Gaillot was summarily removed from the French episcopate in January 1995 because he had spoken out in favor of married priests, the ordination of women, and the use of condoms for the prevention of AIDS.

In commenting on Rome's removal of Gaillot, Joseph Duval, president of the French bishops, stated:

> This is an authoritarian act which cannot be accepted by society, even if it is carried out by the Church. Authoritarian gestures on the part of Rome have multiplied in recent days. The Universal Catechism, the encyclical on morality, the ban on ordaining women. These acts make the Church look like a rigid, closed organization.[8]

The Catholic Church, for all the great encyclicals and pastoral letters on peace that it has produced in recent times, has seen Rome and its episcopal appointees of the past twenty years resort to increasingly extreme means of dealing with internal dissent. It seems clear that the corporate culture of clericalism demands the suppression of new ideas.

THE REALIGNMENT OF THE CHRISTIAN WORLD

Those who favor a Church of self-defined purity, free from contamination by what is regarded as the hostile influence of the world, have rejoiced that John Paul II refused to lend a sympathetic ear to questioning within the Church and moved to reimpose rigid conformity in Catholic belief and practice. This withdrawal into a fortress type of Christianity has also been occurring in other Christian denominations. Some of these Churches have found common cause with John Paul's version of a Catholicism firmly opposed to both the ordination of women and the acceptance of homosexuality as part of the human condition.

But increasing numbers of Christians today, in denominations hitherto divided by history, have been moving in a different direction. As Jesus showed so often with his paradoxical parables and his absolute refusal to be drawn into denunciations of those labeled by the Pharisees as sinners, each and every human being, from pope to peasant, lives in a world of ideals misdirected and energies misspent. The only certainty that we can trust in absolutely is the love of God. This does indeed call for fidelity to the past, but a creative fidelity which acknowledges that new wine cannot be forced into old wineskins or it will burst out, its flavor dissipated.

I believe that compassion, humility, and generosity must be the hallmarks of institutional Christianity if it is to survive into the next millennium. The cost of this will be high, because it will involve the constant re-evaluation of Christian history as well as the discernment of the ongoing movement of the Spirit within and outside the churches. It takes courage and hope to face up to this. The United Church of Canada, for example, caused a storm of controversy among its membership in 1998 when it formally apologized to native peoples for its part in the treatment meted out to them in the past in residential schools run by the United Church.

One of the reasons the delusional system within the Catholic Church is so hard to unmask is that the system socializes people from a very early age. The phrase "cradle Catholic" is an apt description of the pervasiveness of Catholic culture. The rewards offered by unquestioning obedience to the system seem to outweigh the penalties inflicted on those who dare to question. Wink quotes the words of Vaclav Havel, written when the communist regime was still in power in Czechoslovakia:

> Because the regime is captive to its own lies, it must falsify everything... past, present and future... It pretends to respect human rights. It pretends to persecute no one. It pretends to fear nothing... Individuals need not believe all these mystifications, but they must behave as though they did, or they must at least tolerate them in silence, or get along well with those who work with them. For this reason, however, they must *live within a lie*. They need not accept the lie. It is enough for them to have accepted their life with it and in it. For by this very fact, individuals confirm the system, make the system, *are* the system.[9]

Many Catholics, priests as well as laypeople, reject the Vatican's teaching on the place of women in the Church, on sexual orientation, on contraception, divorce, and remarriage. And yet they continue to make more and more accommodations to "live within the lie" because they have no faith in the possibility of change within the Church.

Feminism, as a movement based on nondualistic and nonhierarchical principles, is more at ease with ambiguities than absolutes. It is viewed by some as the most potent threat to the power of the Catholic Church today. I see it instead as one of the greatest hopes for the future. The age we live in has witnessed global shifts in the balance of equality and power between men and women in every sphere; yet during the late twentieth century there has been a backlash against the gains of the women's movement. While the churches on the one hand are called to be agents of conversion and transformation, and there are many recent examples of this, the Church as an institution is also, as Vatican II recognized, under the sway of a hierarchy of power.

This profound ambivalence calls for an abandonment of triumphalist spirituality in favor of profound humility and a willingness to accept that those who hold opposing views act in good faith as well. Resistance to the dominant stranglehold of patriarchal structures in all institutions has been part of the *Zeitgeist* of the second half of the twentieth century. I believe that we are witnessing a profound realignment of the Christian world which will continue into the future and will ultimately unmask and confront the system of patriarchy in all religious institutions. This process is already well under way in other Christian denominations.

THE CHURCH IN THE TWENTY-FIRST CENTURY

The fate of the historical phenomenon known as the Catholic Church will revolve around its response to three sets of issues which are at the heart of witnessing to the gospel in the contemporary world. These issues touch every Christian, indeed every person of faith, and will form either bridges or chasms between the historically separate denominations within

Christianity. In fact, what is now occurring is, I believe, a transformation of the world's religions around these three areas, namely: women, the poor, and the earth. These issues are distinct but linked. All of them demand an abandonment of hierarchies of power and dominance in favor of an ethic of mutuality and service.

Although the Vatican has highlighted sexuality and sexual practices as defining of Catholicism—indeed, sex before marriage has been subject to the penalty of excommunication since the 1998 revision of canon law under John Paul II—I would hazard the opinion that sexuality will gradually cease to be a defining issue for Catholicism. My generation of cradle Catholics, many of us grandparents as we move through our fifties, has already massively disobeyed the Church's teachings on premarital sex, contraception, and divorce, and there is little indication that this trend will be reversed in the future. The relaxation of clerical celibacy is but a matter of time. When clerical celibacy goes, the prohibition against homosexuality will ultimately follow, in part because a significant proportion of candidates for ordination now entering Catholic seminaries are gay.

I do still believe that there is hope for a renewed Catholicism in the next generation. It is a hope that I cling to because I believe in the unlimited power of the Spirit of God to bring forth life even in the midst of death. As a teacher of some thirty years, the latter half of which have been devoted to teaching religion to Catholic youth and young adults, and as the mother of two sons, I have often had occasion to ponder the fate of the Catholic Church in the generations to come.

In both my religion classroom and while conducting street walks for young people, I have experienced the inbreaking of the Spirit into the hearts and minds of young people in marvelous and unexpected ways. In the mid-eighties, before the contemporary wave of repression took hold in Catholic education, I would go into grade 12 religion classes with a newspaper in one hand and the Bible in the other. A student would be assigned to bring in a current video or song, to open the class.

Every day we would plunge into current issues, the issues of the students' lives now and in the future. I would guide them through experiences based on the principles of what the great educator Paolo Freire called a "pedagogy of critical conscientization"[10] as opposed to the "banking method of education."[11] We asked questions like: Who wrote this song, or story, or designed this video? For what purpose? Who stands to gain from it? Whose lives are placed at risk by it? Then I would challenge them to search the Scriptures to see if they could come up with either a critique of or a justification for that particular behavior or opinion.

I remember one particularly bright young woman who had taken a seat in the back row of the class because, she later told me, she had never found anything worth listening to in a religion class. It was not long before she was one of those who would stand upon their chairs in order to participate and be heard during the rambunctious debates that ensued in the classroom. A few years later I met her downtown while I was leading a street walk. She had graduated from university with a degree in biology and was working on contract in a health clinic for poor women, conducting an investigation into women's health as part of her research toward a master's degree. She had completely abandoned any hope of change on the part of the Catholic Church and had given up attending Mass.

My critics then and now would say that by encouraging students to question, I am leading them to leave the Church. Not at all—my classes were actually attracting students to an exciting and challenging way of living out their faith. I remember two young women who had not been to Mass regularly since their confirmation in grade 8. "This class is so exciting," they told me one day, "that we have decided to go back to Church." This they did the following Sunday. On Monday they returned to class with crestfallen faces. "Miss, it was terrible. The priest just lectured us about how bad young people are today... we're not going there again."

These grade 12 classes coincided with my first public involvement, described in Chapter 1, with the issue of the sexual abuse of children by Catholic priests. One day I was asked to be the guest on a popular lunchtime talk show. I had a spare period which coincided with the time of the program, and the radio station sent a cab to ensure I would not miss a minute of scheduled class time. Some students were listening to the show on a portable radio in the cafeteria, and when a particularly hostile listener called in to express her views, one of my students called in to the station from the cafeteria phone and went on the air in my defense.

Now it happened that the Director of Education of the Catholic School Board had also been listening to the show on his car radio. When this young woman came on the program and identified herself as a student of mine and named the school, the director picked up his car phone to call my principal—who had given me leave to appear on the program—and, in the latter's words, "He hit the roof." When I got back, the principal stopped me in the hall and told me I had been summoned for an interview at the Board the next morning. At that meeting, the director handed me a letter stating that I was denied permission, under pain of suspension from teaching, to ever leave the school in future to do media interviews.

When I returned to class, the students were proud that one of their peers had been on the program in what they considered to be a rare opportunity to hear the voice of youth in the Church. When I told them of my experience with the school authorities, they were dumbfounded. The repression and fear of their opinions served to reinforce all their previous cynicism and readiness to dismiss the Catholic Church as an anachronism, an impression that I was trying so hard to combat both inside and outside the classroom.

The effects of this repressive Church culture came into play in a similar incident I was involved in more recently. One of the first acts of the Conservative government of Mike Harris, elected premier of Ontario in 1995, was to drastically slash welfare rates and social services. In response to this attack on the poor, various religious groups customarily keep vigil on the steps of the legislature at Queen's Park to pray and protest the government's actions. One day when I was conducting a street retreat in the downtown area, I took a group of students to participate in one such gathering.

On this particular day, a larger than usual group had assembled, including spokespeople from the opposition parties, and microphones had been set up on a stage outside. After the speeches and formal prayers, the mikes were made available for anyone who wished to speak. Two of the students with me spoke movingly of their encounters with street people that day, and of their desire to respond to the call of Jesus to speak up on behalf of the "least" among us. I felt proud that they had found the courage to bear witness in such a public forum to the truth that is within them.

The teacher who was accompanying this particular group was the vice-principal of the school. She made no comment at the time, but the following day I received a phone call from the school chaplain, who had arranged the retreat. The chaplain had been called into the school office and reprimanded for allowing the students to participate in a "political protest" that had not been officially sanctioned in advance by either the Church or the school. Some of the parents, she was told, would be upset if they knew their children were being exposed to such one-sided political propaganda, and in future students from the school were forbidden to visit Queen's Park in the course of the retreats.

I hoped and prayed that the students would have the maturity to realize that this incident demonstrated how powerful their young voices could be as a contemporary expression of the call of the gospel. Just as it was in the time of Jesus, to identify with the poor today is a threat to the powers that be. Even within the walls of a Catholic school, the small sparks of enlightenment nudged into expression through the action of the Spirit can be prematurely snuffed out by a corporate culture of fear.

"Do not quench the Spirit and do not restrain inspired messages," wrote Paul in one of his earliest letters to the Thessalonians.[12] I wondered if the school administrators were aware that their suppression of even the mere threat of controversy could sow the seeds of disillusion in the hearts and minds of these young people. These and other experiences with young people led me to the conclusion that they feel themselves to be very much on the margins of the Church, but it is from these margins that future insights into the gospel will flow.

THE PREFERENTIAL OPTION FOR THE POOR

The Spirit *is* speaking at the margins in our time, in a diversity of tongues and through subversive narratives. This is leading to a deconstruction of patriarchal Church structures by the reading of Scripture through the eyes of those who have not been considered reliable interpreters of the Word of God—women, the poor, and non-whites, for example. These new movements catch the energy and imagination of the emerging generation of believers who are open to a rearticulation of Christian tradition. They engage the historical memories of disadvantaged groups and so revitalize and infuse the Christian tradition with new insights under the guidance of the ever-present and ever-creative Spirit of God.

The past fifty years have seen a massive shift in the Christian world toward theology, liturgy, and history from the perspective of the disadvantaged. The Latin American Church was the first to put into practice the insights of Vatican II. A revolutionary theology of the "preferential option for the poor" was articulated at the Latin American bishops' conferences at Medellin (1968) and Puebla (1979). The 1970s and early '80s saw a flowering of liberation theology from the perspective of the poor in Latin America. This Church of the Poor in Latin America continues to be baptized with the blood of martyrs: mostly lay women and men, some priests, and now two bishops, Oscar Romero of El Salvador in 1980 and Juan Girardi of Guatemala in 1998.

At the heart of liberation theology is Jesus' preaching of the coming of the Reign of God. The inbreaking of the Reign of God occurs at moments of conversion of individuals and structures away from the delusion of selfishness and toward the communal ethic expressed in the Beatitudes. The Reign of God does not wait for Heaven but is something concrete, to be realized in the here and now. Jesus showed humanity a way to live as if God reigned. Indeed, the heart of the gospel message lies within the preferential option for the poor that Jesus lived out. This does not imply that God dislikes the rich, but rather that those who follow Jesus are called to live as he did, in solidarity with the poor.

This call to solidarity with the marginalized is a call to conversion, a conversion that is both personal and collective. The theology of liberation includes a transformation of the notion of sin beyond the personal to the social. There is a structural element to the personal oppression suffered by the poor. European colonialism, for example, led to the destruction of the indigenous cultures of Latin America and the appropriation of its resources by dominant nations such as Spain, Portugal, and, in more recent times, the United States. Liberation theology unmasks the system of colonialism and the part played by Christianity in the oppression of indigenous peoples. It calls the Catholic Church to account for its part in supporting the conquest of that continent by Europeans, whose main goal was the acquisition of wealth and slaves, with forced baptism as part of the agreement between Church and State.

Liberation theology calls in question the notion that any individual Christian, or the Church collectively, can follow the gospel and remain politically or socially neutral. This call to participate actively in transforming the structures of society in favor of the poor is one that echoes the social teaching of the Catholic Church over the past hundred years. It is one which continues to encounter fierce resistance from conservative Christians, who prefer that the Church should focus on individual sexual morality rather than on corporate social ethics. Despite this resistance, a renewed Church of the Poor and the Latin American base communities dedicated to living the preferential option for the poor have spread like the fire of a new Pentecost in the aftermath of Vatican II.

The analysis of colonialism on the Latin American continent also brought under scrutiny the contemporary politics of the Vatican. At the time of Archbishop Romero's assassination, the Vatican was embarking on an alliance with the conservative Republican governments of Ronald Reagan and George Bush. As already mentioned in Chapter 5, the Catholic Church was restored to power in Poland in exchange for Vatican acquiescence to the U.S.-backed supression of the liberation movement in Latin America, and the discrediting of liberation theology within the Church as a whole.[13]

Despite this, the influence of liberation theology has by no means died out within the Catholic Church. Following its supression in South and Central America, liberation theology has attracted a broader audience worldwide. The question arises: if liberation theology preaches a message of freedom to the poor in the Southern Hemisphere, what is the call of the Spirit to the oppressors of the poor in the North? If liberation theology arises out of the experience of the poor, what are the repercussions of their experience for the wealthy, especially in those countries that continue to reap the rewards of colonialism in the South? What does it mean for a Church of the wealthy to live and act in solidarity with the poor? The simple answer is: to live as we are told the early Christian community did, "claiming no possession as their own, but holding all in common."[14]

Jesus' phrase, "Blessed are the poor for theirs is the kingdom of heaven,"[15] has often been used as an excuse for the Church not to do anything to combat the misery of the poor here on earth. But liberation theologians such as Gustavo Guttierez point out that neither Jesus nor the early Church promoted poverty as an ideal in and of itself, but instead formed a community whose ideal was to hold all goods in common so that there would be no poverty. "The meaning of the community of goods is clear: to eliminate poverty because of love for the poor person... only by rejecting poverty and making itself poor in order to protest against it can the Church preach something that is uniquely its own: 'spiritual poverty,' that is, the openness of humanity and history to the future promised by God."[16]

Wealthy North Americans and Europeans need to hear a different kind of call to conversion than do the poor of Africa or Latin America: not one of liberation from the structures of oppression, but freedom from the stifling effects of greed and materialism. As I experienced in the course of my visit to Africa, the material poverty of the South unmasks the spiritual poverty of so much of what passes for religion in the North. The poor themselves are instruments of this call to conversion. As global capitalism has become more dominant in the 1990s, the insights of liberation theology have in turn become more timely and provocative than ever.

The central theme of the street retreats that I have led over the past two years is the call to today's disciples to adopt the preferential option for the poor, not just by arm's-length donations to charity, but by "walking humbly, acting justly, and showing a tender love"[17] toward those whom the rest of society so often marginalizes. Poverty in a rich society such as Canada is not only a physical burden but also an emotional one. The poor are hidden away, almost as if they have a shameful and contagious disease.

The street walks that we conduct in downtown Toronto provide students with the opportunity to consciously live out the gospel for one day in solidarity with the poor, to go to the kinds of places where Jesus would spend time if he were in a modern city, and to let the poor be their teachers on the streets. After the experience, which takes the form of small group walks or visits to places where the marginalized in society gather, we ask participants to identify how the Holy Spirit has spoken to them through their encounter with the poor. If they experienced any strong emotions such as shock, anger, or delight, we ask them to pray over these reactions to discern if they may be indications that God is calling them to do work for transformation in their own lives and communities.

I remember one particular group of students from a suburban high school who were walking with me in Parkdale, one of the poorest neighborhoods in Toronto. We went into one of the local drop-ins for homeless people, and I told the students to sit at separate tables and try to melt into the crowd. I noticed that not a single one of them went to get a cup of coffee, and they sat at the tables with their arms folded. When I raised these observations about body language with them at the de-briefing later, they told me that they were afraid to drink out of "their" cups or to let their bodies touch the tables, even though the homeless people had all been very welcoming. Though they did not put it quite so bluntly, it turned out that they were afraid of contamination by contact with the poor.

When I asked them to identify where the fear which led to the creation of such barriers between human beings resides, they replied, "Within us." This led to a conversation about how the gospel calls us to renounce the prejudices inculcated in us by family, friends, and society. Through the life of Jesus, God challenges us to conversion and a recognition that the poor are actually our teachers in this process. The shame and uncleanness which the powers that be would have us believe resides in the poor actually comes from within ourselves. As Jesus said, "It is not what goes into your mouth from the cup outside that makes you unclean but the hatred and deceit which comes out of your own heart."[18]

To sit at a table with the homeless and share a cup of coffee from a common coffee urn becomes a small but significant act of solidarity with the poor. It demands that we allow God to break through our defenses to let the message of the gospel shake us out of complacency. Young people do not necessarily need to go to Latin America to experience the profound impact of adopting the option for the poor. Sadly, the opportunities are right here in our own backyard. In this way, the Churches of the North can become places where youth and adults work together toward a more just society.

On many occasions I have witnessed the grace of God at work on the streets of the city and in the lives of young people who are open to Vatican II's call to interpret the gospel in the light of contemporary society. This is often a painful process. Their spontaneous reactions to direct encounters with the poor can bring students face to face with Jesus' challenge that the fire he brought to earth "will divide fathers against sons, mothers against daughters."[19] A simple invitation to drink a cup of coffee in solidarity with the poor can also bring home the cost of Jesus' invitation to encounter him in the poor.

During the bitterly cold Canadian winter, some churches in Toronto have become part of the Out of the Cold movement. Volunteers undertake to provide food and warmth during the day to the increasing number of poor and homeless people out on the streets. Students on street walks will often help other volunteers to prepare and serve these meals. Sometimes we invite a few students to participate in the much more challenging experience of being on the receiving end of this charity and to actually line up incognito with the poor and eat lunch with them.

One day I was particularly struck by a girl's reaction after she and a friend had gone through the experience of lining up for an Out of the Cold lunch. She described in detail the conversations she had had with people ("I never knew that these people were so normal"), but then she suddenly became crestfallen. "You know," she said, "I don't think I'll be able to tell my mother what I did today. She would be in total shock." She pondered and prayed during the rest of the afternoon. Would she have the courage to continue the process she had begun, of seeing life in solidarity with the poor if this meant confronting some of the prejudices within her own family?

On another occasion I was trying to persuade the group of students I was with to buy lunch at a local café, but they balked at this and eventually, after a long search, found the one pizza franchise in the neighborhood. This search in itself was enlightening. When I asked the young people why it was that none of the familiar fast-food chains was readily available there, they realized that it was because none of these corporations thought that such a poor neighborhood was worth investing in. The tiny corner pizza outlet felt safe to them because it was closest to their experience of the shopping mall. I stayed outside while they ate inside in silence, all six of them squashed into a booth designed for four.

An old and destitute woman, a garbage bag slung over one shoulder, went into the pizza shop. She laboriously counted out some coins and then stuffed the slice of pizza she had bought into the garbage bag. As she came out, I approached her and asked if she was all right. She looked at me and nodded. She had a gnarled face with no teeth, framed by lank strands of mousy hair. She wore a blue polyester top which was undone, apart from one button, exposing her cleavage and a rolling belly underneath. I asked her if she would like a drink. "Oh yes, please," she replied. I went into the store and came out with a can of Sprite, which I gave her. She reached into the garbage bag and took out the pizza. "Here, take half," she said, and held it out to me. I took it, and we ate side by side. I asked her name. "Lois," she replied, and I told her mine. Then we shook hands solemnly and she shuffled away.

The students had watched everything through the window. "Do you know why I did that?" I asked them afterward. They shook their heads. "Well, when I saw Lois go in there, I said to myself: There goes Jesus in disguise. And sure enough, like Jesus on the road to Emmaus, she broke bread with me."

"That woman would never have been allowed inside our local shopping mall," one of them remarked.

"Would Jesus be welcome there, I wonder?" added another.

On other walks, we challenge students to examine the corporate values of consumerism that dominate so much of their lives. First, we study the labor practices and environmental ethics of some of the big-name brands. Then we invite them to go into the stores to examine the manufacturers' labels and ask questions of the sales staff about the labor and environmental codes of those companies. Before they go out, the students practice by reading the labels on each other's clothes. This exercise in analyzing some of the values of the multi-billion-dollar clothing industry can cause students to conclude that the clothes they wear come to them at the price of abusive labor practices. It is the kind of shock that Jesus gave people when he overturned the tables of moneychangers in the temple.

We encourage students not to throw up their hands in despair at this discovery but to begin to work to overturn the abuses of global capitalism by using their own power as consumers. Youth are the number-one target of manufacturers eager to capture and hold the loyalty of future buyers. Most students, once they are enlightened, are eager to see how they can use that power to work for a better world. The reactions of sales staff in clothing stores to direct questioning by students about the labor practices of their suppliers is often telling. Students will come back with statements like "They seemed so threatened by us" or "They were really rude." These reactions are indications to young people of their potential power to effect change on behalf of the poor.

We also send students, two by two like the first disciples, into the head offices of the big banks in the downtown core. As often as not, on the way into the bank they will have encountered a homeless person begging by the door. Once inside, they will ask about loan policies for youth. Then they will pose a question such as: "If a poor or homeless person came in and asked you for money or a loan, what would you do?" Responses from bank staff will vary from shock and disbelief to outright ridicule. "But surely you are making enormous profits," the students will respond, with all the innocence of doves. "Why can't your branch spare the odd five dollars for lunch for a homeless person on your doorstep?"

On their return, the students read the parable of Dives and Lazarus. It hits home, but they do not descend into mere guilt or helplessness. They have experienced firsthand how they can act as advocates for the poor in the halls and chambers of commerce. Many will have future aspirations to study law or business. Use your talents to the full, we tell them, and equip yourself to be a strong and credible voice for the voiceless in the corridors of power. This is one of the differences that having a Catholic education could mean when you get to university or college.

For many of these young people, this will be their first experience of the cost of what it means to be, as the theologian Gustavo Guttierez describes it, in solidarity with Jesus as revealed in the poor. "In the humiliation of Christ, his *kenosis*, he does not take on the human sinful condition and its consequences to idealize it. It is rather because of love for and solidarity with others who suffer in it . . . it is to struggle against human selfishness and everything that divides persons and allows that there be rich and poor, possessors and dispossessed, oppressors and oppressed."[20] For some students, a street walk will be a one-time experience, but for others it will sow the seeds of a lifetime's orientation to the gospel. Hard-hitting though many of these experiences are for students, they are nonetheless truly an example of the Spirit of God moving in the hearts and minds of this generation no less than in previous times.

THE PREFERENTIAL OPTION FOR WOMEN

Feminist theology, which interprets theology from the perspective of women, is another voice of the Spirit speaking to the Churches in our time. Previous chapters in this book have outlined some of the dimensions and dynamics of feminist analysis, and traced the intense war against the recognition of an equal place for women within the Catholic Church which has been waged during the pontificate of John Paul II. The will to persevere in this struggle has been strengthened by the groundbreaking work of feminist theologians who are reclaiming and articulating what are often ancient but hitherto hidden or censored facets of the truth.

A brief survey of the hope that feminist theology has inspired within my own life cannot do justice to more than a few of the treasures I have discovered. The recognition and honoring of the God beyond gender is certainly a central insight. The reinterpretation of biblical texts and the recovery of hidden or neglected Church traditions have played a major role as well.

One such treasure has been the recovery and reassessment of the biblical figure of Sophia, who appears late in the Hebrew Scriptures in the Book of Wisdom. The scriptural legacy of Sophia remains one of the most tantalizing mysteries recovered by scholars who are mining the treasury of the Scriptures today. Sophia is described as the companion of the Creator at the moment of Creation and the guiding spirit at key moments of Hebrew history such as the Exodus. She appears in Paul's letter to the Corinthians, where Christ is named as the "Sophia of God."[21] This elusive feminine metaphor of divine presence and action is portrayed in ways which highlight connectedness as contrasted with the dualistic transcendence of the patriarchal tradition. Sophia in the Book of Wisdom is the feminine spirit whose creative power was present within God from the beginning. She represents insight and discernment, but is also playful and free, not bound within the constraints of a nurturing or motherly role.

This and other contemporary insights into the neglected feminine presence of God in the Scriptures has been complemented by the study of the history of women in the Church and the unique contribution they have made. One example of this is the rediscovery of the women saints and prophets who have gone before us like a cloud of witnesses, and in whose memory we can strive toward the goal of a transformed creation. The history of women saints has been colored by patriarchal revisionism—the early martyr Perpetua, for example, who nursed her baby son in prison, appears later in the Church's calendar as a Virgin—but the miracle is that such a strong and diverse witness to women's holiness has survived in the Church's memory at all.

The rediscovery of this suppressed history has been an incentive to women in all Churches to struggle toward a greater contemporary recognition of their gifts. This is beginning to spill over into the consciousness of Catholic girls. As described in Chapter 2, the cult of the submissive and asexual Virgin Mary has long been a hallmark of the patriarchal Church and was revived under John Paul II. But Catholic girls today reject this meek and mild Mary.

I remember one group of students who had come to a retreat at the Centre for Justice, Peace and Creation and had visited a refugee intake shelter. They were using Matthew's story of the flight of Jesus, Mary, and Joseph into Egypt as the lead-in to their presentation. I have scripted a version of this story in a contemporary setting which portrays the Holy Family arriving at Pearson International Airport and claiming refugee status in Canada. The role of Mary is one of a wife and mother pleading for a new opportunity for her family. She is quite deferential toward the authorities. The girl who played Mary on this particular occasion introduced subtle changes in the text so that her Mary was more assertive and demanding. When I commented on this afterwards, she replied, "*This* Mary has brass knuckles!"

"Mary with brass knuckles" is an image I have often meditated on since then. That young girl, who may have herself come from a refugee family, articulated the gospel using a metaphor that captured the image of Mary for her generation. Uninhibited by the constraint of generations of patriarchal interpretation, she had illumined the gospel story with startlingly fresh insight. Here was the playful but profound spirit of Sophia moving over the waters, bringing new life to a familiar story. If we adults could put aside our need for control and instead open ourselves to trust in the Spirit of God, we would see that young people are indeed engaged in the process of reinterpreting the gospel for their generation.

The impact of feminist thought and theology has been what some theologians describe as a *kairos* moment in the lives of young Catholics today. *Kairos* means a moment of crisis in which there is both challenge and opportunity. Some of the street walks organized by the Centre for Justice, Peace and Creation around issues of gender and power have had just this effect. The Centre is located on the edge of what is locally known as the gay district, the strip of Church Street in downtown Toronto which runs south from Bloor Street to College. We use the opportunities presented by this proximity to raise issues of homophobia and gender relationships which are so central in the lives of young people. The "gender-bender walk," as the leaders call it, has become an occasion for some powerful moments of conversion.

It is quite fascinating to see the role reversals that take place when a mixed group of youth takes a walk into the heart of the gay district. Often a young man will grab the arm of one or even two young women. Why? "To protect myself" will be the response. I have never witnessed a single threatening gesture directed toward these students from anyone in the gay community, but because sizing up and rating the potential attractiveness of young women is so much a part of adolescent male culture, the young men assume that they will be the target of similar ogling on the part of gay men. "How does this make you feel?" we will ask them. "Like a piece of meat," they answer. Then we turn to the young women: "What's your response to that?" "Now they know how *we* feel twenty-four hours of the day," they will reply.

As part of this walk, we invite students to sit and drink a coffee in the Second Cup, a coffee shop in the heart of the gay district. Occasionally one or more will refuse to even go inside. "Where do you think Jesus would be? Who did Jesus identify with, and what does that mean for us today?" we ask them. The experience of being in a minority, and what they perceive as a threatened minority, can provide a powerful opportunity for the unmasking of the ugly face of domination which hides behind gender relationships. Fear of the feminine often also results in intense homophobia among adolescent males. I remember one casual though very dramatic incident which brought this into the open.

One day a group of students was sitting somewhat nervously drinking coffee in the Second Cup on Church Street when one young man said, "Can you believe we're actually in a gay bar?" To which another replied, "Oh, don't be such a fag!" A moment of shocked silence was all it took for the group to realize the context in which they were using this offensive term, one which has become a common put-down in adolescent culture today. The students expected a reaction, retribution even. They were, after all, in the minority in what was unknown and perhaps hostile territory for them. A gay couple at the next table rolled their eyes, but no one returned the insult.

As they related this incident to the rest of the group later that afternoon, one of the young men broke down in tears. "This has made me realize just how much homophobia is all around me ... in my house, my community, my school. My father told me he would throw me out of the house if I even got an earring," he said. "People at school call each other fag or dyke all the time. Next time I hear it, I'm going to say something." His confession and tears of repentance were followed by several minutes of silence. This was a sacramental moment, where the presence of God was palpable.

And what was the vehicle God used for this inpouring of grace? A community of gay men. Their nonviolent reaction to insult was a key element in this moment of conversion for the students. If the gay men had reacted with a return of insults or an exchange of threats, the likelihood is that this would have reinforced the homophobia of the students. Instead, their nonviolent response to evil reduced it to impotence. It struck me again that if Christianity could revert once more to its peripatetic and provocative roots—the Pilgrim People of God—it would be a powerful antidote to the watered-down version of the gospel preached in so many Churches today.

THE PREFERENTIAL OPTION FOR CREATION

The movement that looks at theology and spirituality from the perspective of the earth itself is the most recent work of the Spirit within the Churches, although its roots are perhaps the most ancient. It has arisen from a variety of sources and, like the other two movements of the Spirit outlined above, it is still in the process of evolution.

There are two fundamental orientations within which creation theology, as it is known, places the revelation of the divine. First, that the initial revelation of God in the Scriptures is through moments of original blessing (Creation) and liberation (Exodus). This presents a significant shift from Christian spirituality, which has traditionally been oriented along a Sin-Fall-Redemption axis. Secondly, creation theology emphasizes the interconnectedness and interdependence of all life, including animal, plant, and inanimate life.

In 1967, the historian Lynn White wrote an article in *Science* titled "The Historical Roots of Our Ecological Crisis."[22] White had worked in Sri Lanka, and was prompted to write the article by his observations of the contrast between Buddhist and Christian approaches to the relationship between nature and technology. Christianity had always operated under assumptions of a hierarchical separation of humanity and nature, with the latter being regarded as soul-less and therefore inferior. In the commonly accepted Judeo-Christian interpretation of Genesis, God places all creation at the disposal of humanity. In contrast, Buddhism views all life as interdependent. White cites examples where, in Buddhist culture, the demands of technological progress are considered secondary to the rhythms of nature. On one occasion, for example, he witnessed a delay in the completion of roadwork in Sri Lanka to accommodate the passage of a colony of snakes.

The controversy provoked by articles such as these, coupled with the pressing need to respond to the deepening global ecological crisis, have caused a re-examination and re-evaluation of the androcentric nature of Christian beliefs and ethics. The biblical injunction in the Book of Genesis to "subdue the earth" has often been used as a license for unbridled exploitation of the earth's resources in the name of a humanity exalted by God over and above creation.

While creation-centered theology has unmasked some of these delusions, it has also uncovered alternative voices within the Judeo-Christian tradition. The biblical figure of Sophia, the creative and playful energy of God present at moments of creation and liberation, provides a link between liberation, feminist, and creation-centered theology. So much of the imagery of the teaching of Jesus is also rooted in the earth: seeds, flowers, trees, birds, weather—all are vehicles for the revelation of God. As a healer, Jesus used physical touch and had an intuitive grasp of the connection between mind, body, and spirit. Jesus challenged those who would hoard or squander the goods of the earth: its riches are not to be exploited or sold for exorbitant profits but are to be used sparingly and held in common.

The ethic of environmental conservation is a contemporary expression of the ancient Christian practice of asceticism. One of the challenges we place before groups on street walks is to forgo the usual fast-food diet and go out into downtown Toronto in search of a vegetarian restaurant. If they are open to it, we suggest that they begin to raise questions about the food supplied in their school cafeteria, the disposal of waste, the use of paper, and other myriad ways of befriending creation within their own contexts.

In one way or another, all three developments in contemporary theology and spirituality have challenged some of the presumptions of patriarchal religion. In my experience, all three provide rich means of preaching the gospel in the language of today's society.

The spirit of the gospel must be caught, not taught in a vacuum. While many teachers in Catholic schools dread being assigned to teach religion, I revel in it. Too often, students are presented with an arid and lifeless set of truths culled from the pages of a catechism, with no context or meaning in their own lives, and couched in language that is unreachable and unrecognizable. They are forbidden to question or open up any debate. Then they are told to go and put the gospel into practice.

This is so contrary to the way Jesus taught, and it is crucial to remember that the one title Jesus preferred was "teacher." Jesus took hold of life, and only then started to ask questions and teach about it. His teaching arose out of real life stories and situations, not vice versa. By contrast, the present rulers of the Church expect real life to fit what is set out in preordained and eternally unchanging text. True joy, exuberance, and creativity have been stifled in favor of a stuffy pomposity and contrived celebration. The fierce feminine spirit of Sophia has been fenced into carefully guarded areas labeled chastity, motherhood, and meekness, while the Vatican's response to the spiritual yearnings of our age has been to constrain the Catholic people within a "Universal Catechism."

PILGRIM CATHOLICS IN EXILE

This present period of repression in the Catholic Church may yet bear fruit at a much deeper level. The Second Vatican Council in the 1960s seemed to open the way for the Catholic Church to renew and transform itself into a means of transmitting the message of God's love within the contemporary world. Yet looking back from the vantage of some thirty-five years since the Council ended, we can see that in some ways the changes introduced by the Council were too easily adopted and the language of *aggiornamento* (bringing the Church up to date) was too superficial. The Second Vatican Council was only the beginning of what has become a seismic shift in outlook and priorities at the foundation of the Catholic Church. Also, at that time the new work of the Spirit in the Church and in the world had not yet been tested and strengthened in the fire of opposition.

Many Catholics who began to implement the work of the Council with joy and enthusiasm, and who sought to carry forward and develop the impetus toward renewal, have been forced into exile during the papacy of John Paul II. Still, the latter half of the twentieth century, since the end of the Second World War, has witnessed an enormous outpouring of the Spirit of God into the modern world. This is too fiery, fierce, and feminine to be contained within the boundaries set by the excommunicators and inquisitors of the present Vatican. God has new revelations for her people which transcend even the scope of the Second Vatican Council. Catholics who experienced the changes in the way the Mass was celebrated which followed immediately in the wake of the Council did not realize at the time that changing the altar around to face the people was just the harbinger of radical upheavals in the way the Church understood itself and its mission.

Catholics in exile have found that the God of life has accompanied us on our pilgrim way, though we have often lacked the confidence to articulate this intuition. The living God has deserted the temple in Rome and pitched a tent once more with the people in exile. This Church of the People must travel light, and tread with care upon the earth. It will not look for the living God in houses of stone or golden tabernacles, but deep within the pulse of the life of the planet. The Catholic Church cannot return to its former worship of power. In this time of transition, Catholics in exile need not become fixated on rebellion or submission but can confidently move forward to complete the process of renewal begun by Vatican II, and so grow into full stature as adult believers. The anger that so many have felt at the reversals of the Council's insights during the pontificate of John Paul II has given birth to new signs of courage and hope.

Increasing numbers of Catholics are creating and discovering new life in small faith communities, and building alternatives outside the walls of the temple. These small faith communities are both autonomous and connected, as well as inclusive and ecumenical. This movement is now beyond the control of the Vatican; its authority comes directly from the Spirit and does not seek the blessing of a centralized power.

New developments have emerged within these small faith communities. One is the naming and celebrating of the feminine in God; another is the emphasis on social justice; and the third is the reaching across denominational boundaries toward the worldwide movement of Christians who are beginning to define themselves by what unites them rather than what divides. A new Christian Church "from below" is in the making, and its dimensions reach beyond the boundaries of denomination. God's Spirit is being dispersed in our age in a new Pentecost, similar to the first one. The gifts of the first Pentecost came without strings labeled "gender" or "race" or "class." Following in the footsteps of Jesus, men and women, married couples, single people, Jews and gentiles, set out in the footsteps of Jesus to risk their lives to break new ground under the shadow of empire and temple.

In the very earliest days of the Church, Priscilla and Aquila, friends of Paul in Rome, were a married couple united in ministry. There is no record that they asked permission to serve the Church in that capacity— they just did it. The apostle Philip baptized a non-Jewish Ethiopian without permission, but he checked in with the community after the fact. Lydia ran her own household church. Phoebe traveled and preached as an apostle. The early Church was unencumbered by prejudices around gender or material assets. Catholics now must act with the same confidence. The Church is being renewed again at its very foundations by a faith nurtured by the compassion which results from becoming directly involved with the marginalized in society.

The key to the discovery of the Spirit of God at work in our age is to walk the earth, as Jesus and the earliest Christians did, among its most marginalized peoples and creatures. It is there that we will hear the voice of the Spirit speaking "from below." The way forward—especially for those of us who in one way or another have been banished from the hierarchies of power bestowed by race, gender, or class—lies in acknowledging our personal and collective darkness and uncertainty and in total reliance on the grace of God. We must learn to make a home for the darkness within ourselves and our institutions, not to wallow in victimhood but to be aware of our ongoing need for personal and collective conversion. This is especially hard for Catholics, raised as we have been for centuries in a system of hierarchical power and certitude.

In August 1995, I spent a week on a pilgrimage that had been organized to mark the fiftieth year since the bombing of Hiroshima and Nagasaki. Participants from many faiths and from all across North America, some from beyond, gathered at the University of Nevada on the outskirts of Las

Vegas. After some days of study, discussion, and prayer, we prepared to travel to the site of the U.S. nuclear testing range, still restricted by the military, deep in the Nevada desert, for a commemoration of the fiftieth anniversary. This day was to weave many threads of my past experience and my hopes for the future into a rich tapestry of courage and hope.

We gathered before dawn on the grounds of the university. A Buddhist monk tolled a bell which had been cast from the remains of used and unused bombs taken from B-52 bombers. Similar bells had tolled in 1945 as the Japanese survivors of the atomic blasts in Hiroshima and Nagasaki searched for the remains of bodies; the bell had summoned them to mindfulness as they went about their gruesome task. Then a fire was lit, and two members of the Shishone tribe, on whose ancient lands the test sites are located, began to sound a drumbeat which was a call to prayer and dance. As they danced a circle around the fire, the Shishone chief sang out a prayer, a prayer for the rocks, the rivers, the plants, and the sun. Gradually the sky lightened, and a fire lit up the rim of the clouds to the east. The sky turned from green to pink, then orange and yellow, and the blinding edge of the sun rose from behind the clouds. The fire we had built was extinguished.

We traveled for over an hour, deeper and deeper into the desert and into the silence. Only the mountains kept vigil over our journey. Once we arrived at the test site, the service began. An altar had been set up at the barbed-wire fence which surrounds the test site. A procession of dancers blessed the altar and laid garlands of origami cranes, symbols of the post-Hiroshima dream of peace, all along the wire fence. A male and a female rabbi came to the altar and together began a great lament. A lament for the two thousand years since the burning of the Temple in Jerusalem, and for the fifty years since the Holocaust. They brought prayers written by Jewish children in Israel to be burned here, at what they called "the Wailing Wall of the West."

I started to weep as I listened to these ancient melodies and gazed out onto the scorched circles etched by the bomb blasts into the desert terrain. I remembered my uncle Frank, killed during the Second World War. I thought of Grace, of Assumpta, and other men and women at Anne Frank House, victims of contemporary violence and wars. I felt the sheer vastness of the blue sky: not a cloud, not a whisper of an airplane. The highway, too, was silent. Only the wind carried the sound of our prayer and anguish. The Christian chant "Veni Sancte Spiritus" began, again accompanied by a most beautiful dance. We raised our hands in invocation to the Spirit of God to bring fire once more into our hearts.

Then Bishop Leontine, one of the first black female bishops ordained in the Methodist Church in the United States, rose to speak. Her words indeed brought fire to our hearts. She spoke of visiting U.S. Army bases and talking to black recruits there. They spoke to her of their good life in the military—of health care and education for their children, who, in their words, "would otherwise be diseased, drugged, or dead." But the irony was that these black soldiers risked their lives for a democracy which at home denies them basic human rights. She spoke of Martin Luther King, and as her great golden episcopal robe billowed behind her in the wind, she began to chant the song "We Shall Overcome." She reminded us of how that same song had been sung in German at the fall of the Berlin Wall, in Mandarin at Tiananmen Square, in Czech as the city of Prague was liberated, and in English in South Africa as Nelson Mandela walked out of jail.

This woman afire with hope in the midst of despair inspired us to link arms and march to the entrance of the test site, led by the Shishone drummers and singing "We Shall Overcome." We formed a huge circle at the entrance and then, in small groups, some of us went through the barrier to be arrested and placed in holding pens in the desert. I went back to the fence to touch the origami cranes. In the deep desert silence, I thought of the shattering of the earth below and on the surface by the terrible rage of the bomb.

On the way home from the test site, we saw a sign, "Women's Temple," and decided to investigate. A stone pathway bordered by green plants led to a small clearing in which there was a cream-colored adobe building, open at the roof and on all four sides. A woman came out to welcome us, as though we had been expected. She laid out a soup made of blackberries and different fruits, cups of cider and plates of sponge cakes. She introduced herself as the guardian of the temple. The Women's Temple had been constructed a few years earlier by a woman who had been unable to bear children. She had prayed to the Egyptian goddess Sekhmet, and became pregnant not just once, but three times. Three daughters were born. In thanksgiving, she had bought twenty-two acres of land near the test site and returned it to the Shishone, having secured their permission to construct the temple.

Inside the temple were four large statues in the corner niches. Two were from Latin America, the Madre del Mundo and Our Lady of Guadalupe. The Egyptian goddess Sekhmet and Aphrodite filled the other two niches. A small statue of Artemis stood at the doorway. I sat in silence for a while. The dome above was a perfect circle open to the sky. Inside the temple it was peaceful and shady. I felt a powerful and strengthening presence, beyond categorization or description. "O Sacred One," I prayed, "lift me up to you." At that moment, I knew that the feminine divine presence which I could feel within that sacred place would heal our world, shattered as it was by war, racism, sexism, and environmental destruction. All my experience of God, illuminated by the personal and political events of my life, came together in that still point in the desert. The utter sacredness and all-consuming love of God can somehow accept ambiguities. A dualistic world in which male and female, black and white, rich and poor, nature and humanity are held to be mutually exclusive and irreconcilable opposites is false to the nature of God. The Sacred One is beyond gender: "neither male nor female, Jew nor Greek, rich nor poor,"[23] but in both and all at the same time—in glorious diversity.

It has been my experience, over fifty-something years of life, that I have found God present in new and unexpected ways whenever I have exhausted the resources of whatever outer and inner strength I could summon of my own volition and let myself fall into the arms of God. This was my early experience of descending into a dark well during the Spiritual Exercises and, on a more recent occasion, in the silence of the Nevada desert. As all mystics have experienced, God is reached and reaches out from darkness: God is found in obscurity, in the struggles of faith and the dark nights of hope. The rich ambiguity of the mystic and the fierce fire of the prophet are the most reliable guides for the future. We must watch and pray in order to be ready when the moments of breakdown and then breakthrough appear.

My dog and I still walk in the park at the dawn of each day. Women still sit in the early morning light on the steps of the shelter at Dundas and Bathurst. These are survivors who have endured long nights of terror and abuse, and are now living in exile from home and family. Their struggle to cling to life and sanity has inspired me to persevere and to complete this book. Theirs is the true courage and sheer tenacity that has kept me clinging to the hope for a better future for women in the Catholic Church and in the world. The Sacred One who moved a great stone from the entrance to the tomb and sent women out into the Easter dawn can yet change stony hearts into hearts of flesh. For all women, whoever and wherever we are, this long time of exile will come to an end.

Que es la tenebrosa nube   *How dark is the cloud*
Que a la noche esclarecia   *Which lights up the night*

—St. John of the Cross (Juan de la Cruz)
*Stanzas Concerning an Ecstasy of Experience
in High Contemplation*, 1584[24]

Notes

INTRODUCTION

1. The encyclical letter *Ordinatio Sacerdotalis* was dated May 22, 1994, and published a few days later.
2. The apostolic letter *Ad Tuendam Fidem* was dated May 18, 1998, and made public on June 30, 1998.
3. I use *The Spiritual Exercises of St. Ignatius: A Literal Translation and a Contemporary Reading* by David L. Fleming, S.J. (St. Louis: The Institute of Jesuit Sources, 1978), as well as *Orientations* by John Veltri, S.J. (Guelph, Ontario: Loyola House, 1981), which is designed for Annotation 19, a program for following the Exercises over a period of twenty-nine weeks.

CHAPTER I: A SPIRITUAL JOURNEY

1. John 16:12–13, *Good News Bible: Today's English Version* (American Bible Society, 1992). This translation of the Bible uses mostly inclusive language when referring to humanity and yet carries the 1994 imprimatur of the Canadian Conference of Catholic Bishops. All subsequent biblical references are quoted from this version of the Bible.

2. Francis Xavier Durwell, *The Resurrection* (London: Sheed and Ward, 1960), p. 1.

3. The theology of the Church as the Pilgrim People of God is found in Chapters 2 and 7 of *Lumen Gentium: The Church as the Light of Humanity,* issued by the Vatican Council on November 21, 1964. It is developed in more detail in the document *Gaudium et Spes: The Church in the Modern World,* issued by the Council on September 7, 1965.

4. The statement that the Church is *semper reformanda,* or in need of continual reform, is found in *Lumen Gentium* (par. 6 and 8) and in *Unitatis Redintigratio: Decree on Ecumenism* (par. 4 and 6), issued on November 21, 1964.

5. Pierre Teilhard de Chardin, *The Hymn of the Universe* (London: Collins, 1965), pp. 23, 28.

6. Peter Hebblethwaite, *John XXIII: Pope of the Council* (London: Geoffrey Chapman, 1984), p. 498.

7. Jean Shinoda Bolen, *Goddesses in Everywoman: A New Psychology of Women* (New York: Harper & Row, 1984), pp. 71, 79.

8. Luke 12:49–53.

9. The Winter Commission report was produced by the Commission of Enquiry into Sexual Abuse of Children set up by Archbishop Alphonsus L. Penney of St. John's. Members: Gordon A. Winter, O.C.; Frances O'Flaherty, M.S.W.; Sister Nuala P. Kenny, M.D.; Rev. Everett MacNeil; and John A. Scott, Ph.D. Published by the Archdiocese of Newfoundland in June 1990. The analysis of the causes of sexual abuse by clergy is found in Chapter 5 of Volume I, "Why It Happened."

10. This interview with Archbishop Ambrozic was conducted by Michael McAteer and published in the *Toronto Star* on April 28, 1990, A1.

11. Walter Brueggemann, *Hope Within History* (Atlanta: John Knox Press, 1987). The outline of the stages of faith from which the quotations are derived is found in Chapter 1, "The Exodus Narrative as Israel's Articulation of Faith Development."

12. Ibid., pp. 19–20, 24.

13. *Challenge* magazine is published by St. Bernard Charities, Winnipeg; *Catholic Insight* is published by Alphonse de Valk, C.S.B., Life Ethics Information Centre, Toronto.

14. The "Just Cause" clause is found in Article 10 of the Toronto Secondary Unit's

Collective Agreement with the Metropolitan Separate School Board. The full text of the judgment in my grievance arbitration runs to seventy-five pages. The members of the Board of Arbitration were Gerald Q. Charney, Q.C., chair; Mary Cornish, union nominee; and Eleanor Cronk, employer nominee.

15. 1 Corinthians 13:1

CHAPTER 2: WHAT IS A WOMAN'S WORTH?

1. *Mulieris Dignitatem*: *The Dignity and Vocation of Women* (Sherbrooke, Quebec: Editions Paulines, 1988).

2. For the history and partial texts of various drafts of the U.S. bishops' *Pastoral Letter on Women*, see *National Catholic Reporter* (September 11, 1992), p. 3; and *Origins*, Catholic News Service documentary service, 21:46 (April 23, 1992), pp. 762–776.

3. "U.S. Pastoral on Women: The Debate Goes On," *Catholic New Times* (June 23, 1991), pp. 1, 12.

4. For information on the childhood and early years of John Paul II, see Carl Bernstein and Mario Politi, *His Holiness: John Paul II and the Hidden History of Our Time* (New York: Doubleday, 1996), Part I, "Lolek."

5. The quotation from Dr. Kenneth Zucker is from "Gender Bendable, New Reasearch Hints," *The Globe and Mail* (July 7, 1998), A1.

6. *Mulieris Dignitatem*, par. 10.

7. Ibid.

8. For the Pope's views on the two life choices open to women, see Chapter 6 of *Mulieris Dignitatem*: "Motherhood-Virginity."

9. *Mulieris Dignitatem*, par. 8.

10. Ibid.

11. For a development of the theme of God as "wholly other," see Gustavo Guttierez, *The God of Life* (Maryknoll, NY: Orbis Books, English translation, 1991), pp. 26–27.

12. Ephesians 3:14–15.

13. *Mulieris Dignitatem*, par. 8.

14. Isaiah 42:14.

15. Encyclical letter of John Paul II, *Laborem Exercens: Human Work*, September 14, 1981 (Boston: St. Paul Editions, 1981), par. 19.

16. United States Conference of Catholic Bishops, fourth draft of *Pastoral Letter on Women* (1992).

17. "Violence Killing Millions of Women," *The Toronto Star* (July 22, 1997), p. 1.

18. "Little Progress in UNICEF Report," *The Globe and Mail* (July 23, 1997), A12.

19. Ibid.

20. Assembly of Quebec Bishops, *A Heritage of Violence: A Pastoral Reflection on Conjugal Violence* (Montreal: Assembly of Quebec Bishops, 1989), Part 1, sec. 2.

21. Ibid., Part 2, sec. 3.1.2.

22. Ibid., Part 3, recommendation 3.4.3.

23. Ibid.

24. *Mulieris Dignitatem*, par. 10.

25. Ibid.

26. Ibid.

27. Encyclical letter of Pope John XXIII, *Pacem in Terris* (April 11, 1963), Part 1, par. 15.

28. Ibid., par. 41.

29. Peter de Rosa, *Vicars of Christ: The Dark Side of the Papacy* (London: Bantam, 1988). Quotations from *The Syllabus of Errors* are taken from pp. 245–246 of de Rosa's book.

30. That the Vatican believes the devil is still very much at work in the world is evident in the decision to update the ritual for exorcism, issued from Rome in January 1999. Like its predecessor, issued in 1614, this text is only available in Latin. No problem, according to Cardinal Medina Estevez, "because the devil understands Latin." Philip Pullella, "Devil's Still on the Job, Vatican Warns," *The Globe and Mail* (January 27, 1999), A9.

31. Matthew 6:28.

CHAPTER 3: GOD IS MALE

1. Hebblethwaite, *John XXIII*, p. 431.

2. *Love Kindness: The Social Teaching of the Canadian Catholic Bishops*, ed. E.F. Sheridan (Sherbrooke, Quebec: Editions Paulines, and Toronto: Jesuit Centre for Social Justice, 1991). For Cardinal Flahiff's speech (October 11, 1971), see pp. 496–499.

3. Ibid., Bishop Robert Lebel's speech (October 14, 1980), pp. 536–538.

4. Ibid., Archbishop Vachon's speech on "male-female reconciliation in the Church," pp. 539–542.

5. The text of the Pontifical Biblical Commission's 1976 report was never made public. It was published in the July 1, 1976, edition of *Origins*, the documentary service of the Catholic News Service. See James R. Roberts, "Women Priests: Reflections on Papal Teaching and Church Response" (Langara College, 1994, photocopy), p. 1, n. 2.

6. Roberts, "Women Priests," p. 3.

7. "Vatican Says Jesus Didn't Want Women Priests," *The Globe and Mail* (January 25, 1997), pp. 1, 11.

8. "Diaconate Just for Men, Vatican Says," *National Catholic Reporter* (March 20, 1997), p. 1.

9. *The Catholic Register* (June 7, 1998), p. 1.

10. Cardinal Joseph Ratzinger, commentary on *Ad Tuendam Fidem* in *National Catholic Reporter* (July 17, 1998), pp. 14–15.

11. For an analysis of Aquinas's views on the ordination of women (*Summa Theologica* I, 92), see Rosemary Radford Ruether, "Women's Difference and Equal Rights in the Church" in *Concilium* (1996:6), pp. 11–18.

12. Romans 6:4–5.

13. Hebrews 4, 5.

14. Revelation 21:14.

15. Matthew 10:1–15; Mark 16:14–18; Luke 24:48–49.

16. Luke 10:1–12, 17–20.

17. Ephesians 5:21–33.

18. See John Paul II's explanation of the "spousal" love of God in *Mulieris Dignitatem*, Chapter 7.

19. *Mulieris Dignitatem*, par. 26.

20. Acts 10:28

21. Galatians 2:11–14.

22. Acts 8.

23. Acts 10:24.

24. Letter to the gentile believers from the Council of Jerusalem, Acts 15:23–29.

25. For the Church as *semper reformanda*, see Chapter 1, note 4.

26. Carter Heyward, *Touching Our Strength: The Erotic as Power and the Love of God* (San Francisco, Harper & Row, 1989), p. 102.

CHAPTER 4: GIRLS IN THE CATHOLIC SCHOOL SYSTEM

1. *Women: Challenges to the Year 2000* (New York: United Nations Publications, 1991), p. 7.
2. Winter Commission report, Vol. I, pp. 94–97.
3. British North America Act, sec. 93 (1).
4. Catholic High School Commission of the Archdiocese of Toronto, *Report of the Pastoral Visitation of the High Schools of the Archdiocese by Archbishop Ambrozic, 1984–85.*
5. Ibid.
6. Toronto Secondary Unit of the Ontario English Catholic Teachers' Association, *Equity Report* (Toronto: OECTA, 1997), p. 40.
7. Dorothy Vidulich and Thomas Fox, "Women's Letter Draft Moves Sharply to Right," *National Catholic Reporter* (September 11, 1992), pp. 3–5. See also news article, p. 16.
8. John Paul II, *Sollicitudo Rei Socialis: Concern for the Social Order* (Sherbrooke, Quebec: Editions Paulines, 1987), par. 42.
9. Vatican Council II, *Gaudium et Spes: The Church in the Modern World* (December 7, 1965), par. 29.
10. Canadian Conference of Catholic Bishops, *To Speak as a Christian Community* (Ottawa: CCCB, 1989), Introduction, p. 20.
11. Ibid.
12. Robert McLory, "Vatican Agreement 'Moderately' Inclusive," *National Catholic Reporter* (May 9, 1997), pp. 3–4.
13. *National Catholic Reporter* (September 25, 1998), pp. 3–5.
14. McLory, op. cit., pp. 3–4.
15. *National Catholic Reporter* (March 26, 1993), p. 8.
16. "Doctoring the Catechism: Chris McGillion Interviews Eric D'Arcy," *The Tablet* (March 19, 1994), pp. 7–8.
17. Ibid.
18. Tom Roberts, "Vatican Rescinds Inclusive-Language Approval," *National Catholic Reporter* (November 4, 1994), pp. 8–9.
19. Pamela Schaeffer, "Debate Over Language Lingers: Lectionary Vote Is Inconclusive," *National Catholic Reporter* (July 4, 1997), pp. 3–4.
20. Robert McLory, "Publishers Afraid to Risk Infidelity to New Catechism," *National Catholic Reporter* (March 21, 1997), pp. 3–5.

21. Ibid.

22. Barry Came, "Montreal Massacre," *Maclean's* (December 18, 1989), p. 14.

23. "Why Were Women in the Gunsight," *The Globe and Mail* (December 8, 1989), A6.

24. Ontario Secondary School Teachers' Federation, *The Joke's Over: Sexual Harassment in High Schools* (Toronto, OSSTF, 1996).

25. *The Globe and Mail* (September 21, 1996), A1.

26. Catherine Dunphy, "Why Wasn't I Worth Protecting?" *The Toronto Star* (December 10, 1998), H9.

27. *Equity Report*, p. 99.

28. June Larkin, *Sexual Harassment: High School Girls Speak Out* (Toronto: Second Story Press, 1994), p. 67.

29. Frances Kissling, "Holy Role Models: The Vatican's Beatifications Send a Message to Girls," *Conscience* 15:3, p. 41.

30. Ibid., p. 42.

31. "Feminine Psychology," *Familia Portuguesa* (April 1998), as quoted in Dale Brazao, "Tirades on Women Upset City's Portuguese," *The Toronto Star* (April 22, 1998), A1.

32. *The Catholic Register* (May 11, 1998), p. 1.

33. *The Catholic Register* (May 25, 1998), p. 9.

CHAPTER 5: THE VATICAN, GLOBAL POLITICS, AND POWER

1. For a discussion on the status and role of the Holy See at the United Nations, see *Church or State? The Holy See at the United Nations* (New York: Center for Reproductive Law and Policy, 1995).

2. United Nations Conference on Environment and Development, June 1992, *Rio Declaration, Agenda 21 Guide to International Action*, Chap. 24:2(g).

3. John Paul II, *Redemptor Hominis: The Redeemer of Man*, March 4, 1979 (Boston: St. Paul Editions, 1979), sec. 17, p. 35.

4. Ibid., p. 37.

5. Ibid., p. 38.

6. References to the Constitutions of Opus Dei are from Hansard, *Debates of the Senate of Canada*, 33rd session of Parliament, Vols. I–IV (September 30, 1986, to October 1, 1988), *An Act to Incorporate the Regional Vicar for Canada of the Prelature of the Holy Cross and Opus Dei* (June 2, 1987).

7. Ibid. (June 2, 1987), p. 1,152.

8. Ibid. See also "Escriva's Inopportune Beatification," editorial in *The Tablet* (February 29, 1992), pp. 267–268.

9. Luke 1:46–55.

10. See news reports in *National Catholic Reporter* (January 24, 1992; January 31, 1992; August 14, 1992).

11. Bernstein and Politi, *His Holiness,* p. 521.

12. Ibid.

13. For John Paul II's remarks and the commentary in *La Repubblica* (April 1994), see Denise Shannon, "All Roads Led to Cairo," *Conscience* (Winter 1994), p. 6.

14. Christopher Gould, "Hellfire and Deplomacy," *Conscience* (Winter 1994), p. 17.

15. Shannon, op. cit., p. 6.

16. Joaquin Navarro-Valls, "The Courage to Speak Bluntly," *The Wall Street Journal* (September 1, 1994), quoted in Shannon article (see n. 13), p. 8.

17. Rosemary Radford Ruether, "The Vatican and Islam: The Alliance That Fizzled," *Conscience* (Winter 1994), p. 5.

18. Gould, op. cit., p. 17.

19. Shannon, op. cit., p. 6.

20. John Stackhouse, "A Victory for Women's Rights," *The Globe and Mail* (September 12, 1994), A8.

21. *The Toronto Star* (September 4, 1994), D2.

22. See Frances Kissling, "From Cairo to Beijing and Beyond," *Conscience* (Winter 1995), pp. 16–22.

23. Larry Rock, "Radicals Again Fail to Take Over UN Conference," *The Interim* (April 1995), p. 19.

24. The Women–Church Convergence, "Equal Is as Equal Does," *Conscience* (Spring 1995), pp. 3–4.

25. Statement on gender endorsed by Canadian Communities of Faith and circulated by the Ecumenical Decade in Solidarity with Women Coordinating Group (Toronto: July 1995).

26. Canadian Church Women's Affirmation (Toronto: Ecumenical Decade in Solidarity with Women Coordinating Group, 1995).

27. REAL Women's brief to the federal government, 1988, as quoted in Penny Kome, "REAL Women's Moral Morass," *NOW* (July 2, 1987), pp. 7–8.

28. Ibid.

29. W.P. Kinsella, *Web of Hate: Inside Canada's Far Right Network* (Toronto, HarperCollins, 1994), pp. 260, 245; Carol Goar, "Protest Alliances Develop on Tenuous Links," *The Toronto Star* (November 7, 1989), A21; Howard Goldenthal and Wayne Roberts, "Francophobia," *NOW* (March 17, 1990), pp. 10–12.

30. Kathleen Kenna, "B.C. Blasted for Mailout of REAL Women Hate Literature," *The Toronto Star* (April 27, 1990), A18.

31. *A Call to the United Nations to Consider the UN Status of the Holy See*, initiated by: Carribean Association for Feminist Research, Trinidad and Tobago; Catholics for a Free Choice, Washington, DC; Center for Women's Global Leadership, New Brunswick, NJ; Development Alternatives for Women for a New Era, St. Michael, Barbados; International Women's Health Coalition, New York; Latin American and Caribbean Women's Health Network, Santiago, Chile; National Coalition of American Nuns, Chicago; Stichting Onderzoek en Voorlichting Bevolkingspolitiek, Amsterdam; Women in Development in Europe, Brussels; Women's Global Network for Reproductive Rights, Amsterdam.

32. Daniel Maguire, "Good Religion, Good Politics," speech to UN delegates at Cairo (September 8, 1994), reprinted in *Conscience* (Winter 1994), pp. 11–12.

33. *A Call to the United Nations.*

34. Frances Kissling, "From Cairo to Beijing and Beyond," *Conscience* (Winter 1995), pp. 16–22.

35. *The Toronto Star* (May 30, 1998), L14.

36. Luke 24: 13–53.

CHAPTER 6: THE CATHOLIC CHURCH
IN THE NEXT MILLENNIUM

1. 2 Corinthians 4:7.

2. Vatican Council II, *Gaudium et Spes*, par. 19.

3. Robin Briggs, *Witches and Neighbors: The Social and Cultural Context of European Witchcraft* (New York: Viking, 1996), p. 259.

4. Walter Wink, *Engaging the Powers: Discernment and Resistance in a World of Domination* (Minneapolis: Fortress Press, 1992), p. 3.

5. Ibid., p. 5.

6. Ibid., p. 164.

7. Walter Wink, *Unmasking the Powers: The Invisible Forces That Determine Human Existence* (Minneapolis: Fortress Press, 1986), p. 78.

8. Bernstein and Politi, *His Holiness*, p. 509.

9. Walter Wink, *Engaging the Powers*, p. 98.

10. Paolo Freire, *Pedagogy of the Oppressed*, trans. Myra Bergman (New York: Continuum, 1988), pp. 104–113. "Conscientization refers to learning to perceive social, political and economic contradictions, and to take action against the oppressive elements of reality." (Translator's note, p. 19).

11. Ibid., pp. 57–65.

12. 1 Thessalonians 5:19.

13. Carl Bernstein, "The Holy Alliance," *Time* (February 24, 1992), pp. 14–21.

14. Acts 2:45.

15. Luke 6:20.

16. Gustavo Guttierez, *A Theology of Liberation* (Maryknoll, NY: Orbis, 1988; revised edition), p. 173.

17. Micah 6:8.

18. Matthew 15:16.

19. Luke 12:50-53.

20. Guttierez, *A Theology of Liberation*, p. 172.

21. 1 Corinthians 1:22.

22. Lynn White, "The Religious Roots of Our Ecological Crisis," *Science* 155 (1967), pp. 1,203–1,207.

23. Galatians 3:28.

24. Kieran Kavanaugh and Otilio Rodriguez, *The Collected Works of St. John of the Cross* (Washington, DC: Institute of Carmelite Studies, 1979), p. 719.

Bibliography

Alsdurf, James, and Phyllis. *Battered into Submission: The Tragedy of Wife Abuse in the Christian Home*. Downers Grove, IL: InterVarsity Press, 1989.

Archdiocese of Newfoundland. *Report of the Archdiocesan Commission of Enquiry into the Sexual Abuse of Children by Members of the Clergy* (Winter Commission report). Vols. I and II. St. John's: Archdiocese of Newfoundland, 1990.

Assembly of Quebec Bishops. *A Heritage of Violence: A Pastoral Reflection on Conjugal Violence*. Montreal: Assembly of Quebec Bishops, 1989.

Belenky, Mary Field, Blythe McVicker Clinchy, Nancy Rule Goldberger, and Jill Mattuck Tarule. *Women's Ways of Knowing*. New York: Basic Books, 1990.

Bernstein, Carl, and Mario Politi. *His Holiness: John Paul II and the Hidden History of Our Time*. New York: Doubleday, 1996.

Bolen, Jean Shinoda. *Goddesses in Everywoman: A New Psychology of Women*. New York: Harper & Row, 1984.

Briggs, Robin. *Witches and Neighbors: The Social and Cultural Context of European Witchcraft*. New York: Viking, 1996.

Brueggemann, Walter. *Hope Within History*. Atlanta: John Knox Press, 1987.

Brueggemann, Walter, Sharon Parks, and Thomas Groome. *To Act Justly, Love Tenderly and Walk Humbly*. New York: Paulist Press, 1986.

Canadian Conference of Catholic Bishops. *To Speak as a Christian Community*. Ottawa: CCCB, 1989.

Canadian Research Council for the Advancement of Women. *Speaking from the Shadows: An Introduction to Feminist Thinking in Anthropology*. Vancouver: CRCAW, University of British Columbia, 1989.

Canadian Teachers' Federation. *A Cappella: A Report on the Realities, Concerns, Expectations and Barriers Experienced by Adolescent Women in Canada*. Ottawa: CTF, 1991.

Church Council on Justice and Corrections and Canadian Council on Social Development. *Family Violence in a Patriarchal Culture*. Ottawa: Church Council on Justice and Corrections and Canadian Council on Social Development, 1988.

Carr, Anne, and Elisabeth Schüssler Fiorenza, eds. *Motherhood: Experience, Institution, Theology. Concilium 1989/6*. Edinburgh: T&T Clark, 1989.

———, eds. *The Special Nature of Women? Concilium 1991/6*. London: SCM Press, 1991.

de Rosa, Peter. *Vicars of Christ: The Dark Side of the Papacy*. London: Bantam, 1988.

Dulles, Avery. *Vatican II and the Extraordinary Synod: An Overview*. Collegeville, MN: Liturgical Press, 1986.

Durwell, Francis Xavier. *The Resurrection*. London: Sheed and Ward, 1960.

Flannery, Austin O.P., ed. *Vatican Council II: The Conciliar and Post Conciliar Documents*. Boston: St. Paul Editions, 1975.

Freire, Paolo. *Pedagogy of the Oppressed*. Trans. Myra Bregman. New York: Continuum, 1988.

Gaskell, Jane, Arlene McLaren, and Myra Novogrodsky. *Claiming an Education: Feminism and Canadian Schools*. Toronto: Our Schools/Ourselves Education Foundation, 1989.

Guttierez, Gustavo. *A Theology of Liberation*. Revised edition. Maryknoll, NY: Orbis Books, 1988.

———. *The God of Life*. Maryknoll, NY: Orbis Books, 1991.

Hamington, Maurice. *Hail Mary?: The Struggle for Ultimate Womanhood in Roman Catholicism*. New York: Routledge, 1995.

Bibliography

Hansard. *Debates of the Senate of Canada*, 33rd session of Parliament (September 30, 1986 to October 1, 1988). Vols. I–IV.

Harris, Michael. *Unholy Orders: Tragedy at Mount Cashel.* Toronto: Penguin Books, 1990.

Hebblethwaite, Peter. *John XXIII: Pope of the Council.* London: Geoffrey Chapman, 1984.

Heyward, Carter. *Touching Our Strength: The Erotic as Power and the Love of God.* San Francisco: Harper & Row, 1989.

Jewett, Paul K. *The Ordination of Women.* Grand Rapids, MI: William B. Eerdmans, 1980.

John XXIII. *Pacem in Terris: Peace on Earth.* Boston: St. Paul Editions, 1963.

John Paul II. *Redemptor Hominis: The Redeemer of Man.* Boston: St. Paul Editions, 1979.

———. *Laborem Exercens: Human Work.* Boston: St. Paul Editions, 1981.

———. *Mulieris Dignitatem: The Dignity and Vocation of Women.* Sherbrooke, Quebec: Editions Pauline, 1988.

———. *Sollicitudo Rei Socialis: Concern for the Social Order.* Sherbrooke, Quebec: Editions Paulines, 1987.

———. *Ad Tuendam Fidem.* Apostolic letter. Vatican City: Vatican, 1998.

Johnson, Elizabeth A. *She Who Is: The Mystery of God in Feminist Theological Discourse.* New York: Crossroad, 1994.

———. *Friends of God and Prophets: A Feminist Theological Reading of the Communion of Saints.* New York: Continuum, 1998.

Johnson, Paul. *A History of Christianity.* New York: Atheneum, 1980.

Kinsella, W.P. *Web of Hate: Inside Canada's Far Right Network.* Toronto: HarperCollins, 1994.

Larkin, June. *Sexual Harassment: High School Girls Speak Out.* Toronto: Second Story Press, 1994.

Lernoux, Penny. *Cry of the People: The Struggle for Human Rights in Latin America—the Catholic Church in Conflict with U.S. Policy.* Harmondsworth: Penguin Books, 1984.

———. *People of God: The Struggle for World Catholicism.* New York: Viking, 1991.

Ludwig, Robert A. *Reconstructing Catholicism for a New Generation.* New York: Crossroad, 1992.

239

Myers, Ched. *Binding the Strong Man: A Political Reading of Mark's Story of Jesus*. Maryknoll, NY: Orbis, 1988.

———. *Who Will Roll Away the Stone?: Discipleship Queries for First World Christians*. Maryknoll, NY: Orbis, 1994.

Ontario Secondary School Teachers' Federation. *The Joke's Over: Sexual Harassment in High Schools*. Toronto: OSSTF, 1996.

Ontario English Catholic Teachers' Association, Toronto Secondary Unit. *Equity Report*. Toronto: OECTA, 1997.

Paul VI. *Ad Pascendam: Apostolic Letter Containing Norms for the Order of Diaconate* (August 15, 1972; Vatican Council II) in *The Conciliar and Post Conciliar Documents*. Edited by Austin Flannery. Boston: St. Paul Editions, 1975.

———. *Inter Insigniores: Declaration on the Question of the Admission of Women to the Ministerial Priesthood*. Apostolic letter. Vatican City: Vatican, October 15, 1976.

Pipher, Mary. *Reviving Ophelia: Saving the Selves of Adolescent Girls*. New York: Ballantine, 1994.

Reese, Thomas J. *Inside the Vatican: The Politics and Organization of the Catholic Church*. Cambridge, MA: Harvard University Press, 1996.

Roberts, James R. *Women Priests: Reflections on Papal Teaching and Church Response*. Langara College, Vancouver, 1994.

Schipani, Daniel S. *Religious Education Encounters Liberation Theology*. Birmingham: Religious Education Press, 1988.

Sheridan, E.F., ed. *Do Justice: The Social Teaching of the Canadian Bishops (1945–1986)*. Sherbrooke, Quebec: Editions Paulines and Toronto: Jesuit Centre for Social Justice, 1987.

———. *Love Kindness: The Social Teaching of the Canadian Bishops. A Second Collection (1958–1989)*. Sherbrooke, Quebec: Editions Paulines, and Toronto: The Jesuit Centre for Social Justice, 1991.

Schüssler Fiorenza, Elisabeth. *In Memory of Her: A Feminist Theological Reconstruction of Christian Origins*. New York: Crossroad, 1987.

———. *Discipleship of Equals: A Critical Feminist Ecclesiology of Liberation*. New York: Crossroad, 1993.

———, ed. *Searching the Scriptures: A Feminist Commentary*. New York: Crossroad, 1994.

Bibliography

Sheridan, E.F., ed. *The Social Teaching of the Canadian Bishops.* Toronto: Jesuit Centre for Social Faith and Justice, 1991.

Stacpoole, Dom Alberic O.S.B., ed. *Vatican II Revisited by Those Who Were There.* Minneapolis: Winston Press, 1986.

Task Force of the Women's Unit of the Anglican Church of Canada. *Violence Against Women.* Toronto: Anglican Book Centre, 1987.

Task Force on the Feminine Face of Poverty. *Women Liberating Economics.* Toronto: Ecumenical Decade in Solidarity with Women Coordinating Group, 1995.

Toriesen, Karen Jo. *When Women Were Priests.* San Francisco: HarperCollins, 1995.

United Nations. *Women: Challenges to the Year 2000.* New York: United Nations Publications, 1991.

Waring, Marilyn. *Three Masquerades: Essays on Equality, Work and Human Rights.* Auckland: Auckland University Press, 1996.

Wijngaards, John. *Did Christ Rule Out Women Priests?* Great Wakering, Essex: McCrimmon Publishing Company, 1986.

Wink, Walter. *Unmasking the Powers: The Invisible Forces That Determine Human Existence.* Minneapolis: Fortress Press, 1986.

———. *Engaging the Powers: Discernment and Resistance in a World of Domination.* Minneapolis: Fortress Press, 1992.

Women's Interchurch Council of Canada. *Hands to End Violence Against Women.* Toronto: WICC, 1988.

World Bank. *Toward Gender Equality: The Role of Public Policy.* Ed. by Kei Kawabata. Washington, DC: World Bank Publications, 1995.

Index

Abortion, 46, 159, 173, 174, 175, 176, 178, 179, 182, 187

Abuse: of children, 36-41, 43, 48-50, 55, 97-98, 122, 203-204; of power, 40, 42-43, 60, 97, 130-31; of women, 57, 149; *see also* Sexism; Sexual harassment

Ad Pascendam (apostolic letter, Paul VI), 30

Africa, 50-54, 56, 58

Aggiornamento, 220

Alienation from Church, 127, 129-32, 193-94, 195, 203, 204

Ambrozic, Cardinal Aloysius, 42-43, 44, 114, 124-25

Anne Frank House (Toronto), 6, 56-59

Apostles, 108-111

Aquinas, St. Thomas, 104-106, 121

Aristide, Jean-Bertrand, 169, 171-72

Aristotle, 105

"Artemis" and "Athena" archetypes, 34; Jesus, and Artemis archetype, 36

Aryan heresy, 195

Augustine, 82-83, 85, 192

Baptism, 100; of gentiles, 115-17; and women, 104-107

Base communities, 170

Beijing Conference, 9, 12, 13, 63, 121, 161, 179, 187

Bible: inclusive language in, 138 ; masculine and feminine qualities of God, 69-70; *see also* individual books

Birth control (contraception), 46, 158; in Africa, 50-51; Vatican's opposition, 51, 55, 173-78

Bishops: *Pastoral Letter on Women* (U.S. bishops), 64-66, 67; Quebec bishops on violence, 78-79; see also Canadian Conference of Catholic Bishops; National Conference of Catholic Bishops

Bonhoeffer, Dietrich, 197

Brueggemann, Walter, 47-48, 49, 100, 117, 196

Bush, George, 158

Cairo Conference, 9, 12, 13, 121, 173-79

Canadian Church Women's Affirmation, 183-84

Canadian Communities of Faith, 183

Canadian Conference of Catholic Bishops: debate ordination of women (1970), 93-94; recommend inclusive language, 133-34; resist discussion of sexual abuse (1989), 37, 38

Canadian Constitution and separate schools, 123-24

Canon law, 97, 202

Carter, Emmett, Cardinal of Toronto, 49, 50

Yellow-Wolf & Other Tales

of the Saint Lawrence

Philippe-Joseph Aubert de Gaspé had become a well-known figure by the time this engraving was published in Benjamin Sulte's *Histoire des Canadiens-Français* (1882; vol. VI, p. 56). The engraving was based on a photograph of the author taken by Ellison & Co. of Quebec City at some time between 1863 and his death in 1871. C14256. *Public Archives of Canada.*

YELLOW-WOLF
& Other Tales of
the Saint Lawrence

BY

PHILIPPE-JOSEPH AUBERT DE GASPÉ

AUTHOR OF

Canadians of Old

and

A Man of Sentiment: Memoirs

Translated from the French and
Annotated by Jane Brierley

MONTREAL

Véhicule Press

1990

DOSSIER QUEBEC

Published with the assistance of the Canada Council.

Dossier Québec Series Editor: Simon Dardick
Cover design: J.W. Stewart
Cover painting: Self-portrait by Huron artist Zacharie Vincent courtesy of
the Musée du Château Ramezay
Cover background map is a detail from "Carte du Cours du Fleuve de
Saint Laurent" (1761) by Jacques-Nicolas Bellin, courtesy of the Joe C.W.
Armstrong Canadiana Collection.
Imaging: ECW Type & Art
Printing: Les Editions Marquis Ltée

First published in French as *Divers* (Montreal: C.O. Beauchemin et fils,
Bookseller-Printer, 256 and 258, Rue Saint-Paul, 1893)

CANADIAN CATALOGUING IN PUBLICATION DATA

Aubert de Gaspé, Philippe, 1786-1871
[Divers. English]
    Yellow Wolf & other tales of the Saint Lawrence

(Dossier Québec series ; 19)
Translation of: Divers.
ISBN 1-55065-002-5

I. Title. II. Title: Divers. English.

PS8401.U2D5131 1990   C843'.3   C90-090320-1
PQ3919.G3D513 1990

Canadian distribution
University of Toronto Press, 5201 Dufferin Street,
Downsview, Ontario M3H 5T8

U.S. distribution
Bookslinger, 502 North Prior Avenue, St. Paul, MN 55104

University of Toronto Press, 340 Nagel Drive, Buffalo, NY 14225-4731

Printed in Canada

Contents

Foreword to the First French Edition (1893)

In making this work public, it is perhaps appropriate to preface it with the following remarks:

I discovered the author's manuscript among family papers. Having read it to a few friends, I was advised by them to print it.

I hope that the reader will be kind enough to take into consideration the fact that these are the last writings of an octogenarian, who died before having had the opportunity to look them over.

The Editor

Preface

Divers is a collection of writings found by my great-uncle Alfred Aubert de Gaspé among the papers of his late father, my great-grandfather, Philippe Aubert de Gaspé.

In all four stories there is a sentiment which may appear exaggerated to modern ears but which was quite natural to de Gaspé's contemporaries and even more so to him, the gentlest of all men. His treatment of the Indian is more sensitive than might be expected from a man of his time: the Canadian of the eighteenth and nineteenth centuries, whatever his language, was clearly inclined to condemn or scorn the Indian — or, indeed, anyone else — for no good reason other than the hope thereby to pull himself up by his own bootstraps into a position of prominence to which his entitlement was doubtful. To de Gaspé, the last of our indigenous aristocrats and an instinctively tolerant man, such thoughts were quite alien.

Throughout *Divers* we see the gentle old man at the end of his life, a man no longer with ambitions to satisfy, one who knows only affection for his fellow man rather than rivalry. *Divers* is the unpolished work of a man of old age, one buffeted by life but who remains without resentment where another would be bitter. Though it is a collection of unrevised papers probably devised for use in other writings, it sheds a gentle light on a man who was himself a gentleman in much more than the mere social sense of the word.

Louis de la Chesnaye Audette, O.C., Q.C.
Ottawa, 1989

Acknowledgments

———

I wish to express my gratitude for help in preparing this work to all those who so willingly provided assistance, and especially to the following: Louis de la Chesnaye Audette, O.C., Q.C., great-grandson of the author, for his kindness in writing a preface to this work; the Château Ramezay Museum and especially archivist Monique Laliberté for her assistance in researching illustrations and supplying photographs for publication; Mrs. Cynthia Dooley, librarian of the Literary and Historical Society of Quebec, for her help in locating the diaries of James Thompson and the Cholet brothers' statue of General Wolfe, as well as arranging for a photograph of the statue; the W.B. Edwards Studio of Quebec for the photo of Wolfe's statue; Major R. Girard, curator of the Museum of the Royal 22nd Regiment in the Citadel of Quebec, for the material on the second statue of General Wolfe; Joe C.W. Armstrong for permission to reproduce a map from his collection; Susanne Breen, archivist, Nathalie Thibault, archives technician, and the archives librarian, all of the Quebec Museum, for assistance in finding illustrations; Daniel Olivier and Mario Tessier of the Salle Gagnon of the Bibliothèque de la Ville de Montréal for help in locating references and illustrations; the librarians of the McLennan Library, the Lande Room, and the Rare Book Room of McGill University; and the Westmount Public Library for special Canadiana material.

J.B.

Introduction

———

This collection of pieces by Philippe-Joseph Aubert de Gaspé (1786–1871) was published posthumously under the title *Divers* (Montreal: C.O. Beauchemin et fils, 1893). De Gaspé had become well known in old age as a result of his novel, *Les Anciens Canadiens* (1864) and his *Mémoires* (1866).

The author's son, Alfred-Patrice (1831–1907), tells us that he found these pieces among his father's papers. "Yellow-Wolf, Malecite Chieftain of Old" and "The Woman of the Foxes" appeared for the first time in *Divers*. Alfred noted that the other two, "General Wolfe's Statue" and "Big Louis and the Legend of Indian Lorette," had appeared previously in *Le Foyer Canadien*, a literary magazine published monthly between 1863 and 1866, and less regularly until 1879. The magazine and the people concerned with it were important factors in encouraging de Gaspé's late-blooming gift for writing.[A]

Although Alfred de Gaspé pleaded his father's advanced age and the fact that the author had not revised the work for publication, the Montreal *Le Monde* commented in 1893 that, "We read these last works of an octogenarian in one sitting, and such as they are, more than one of our young fin-de-siècle writers would be happy to sign his name to them."[B]

Concerning posthumous publication of works, there appears to have been something of a tug of war between the historian, Abbé Henri-Raymond-Casgrain, and certain members of the family, particularly Alfred, with regard to the abbé's proprietary attitude toward de Gaspé's *oeuvre*. Casgrain seemed inclined to ascribe to himself the rôle of literary mentor and promoter of de Gaspé and his work, although the actual extent of his contribution is problematical. Queries as to his right to bring out posthumous editions of *Les Anciens Canadiens* were met with an evasive letter to "dear cousin" Alfred in October 1885. Perhaps as a result of this, the first edition of *Divers* pointedly included "first edition" in bold type on the title page, and overleaf the prominently displayed information that the work had been "REGISTERED in conformity to the Act of Parliament of Canada, in the year eighteen hundred and eighty-three, by ALFRED AUBERT DE GASPÉ at the office of the Minister of Agriculture, at Ottawa."[C]

In editing his father's work, Alfred seems to have taken a custodial approach, preferring to let the text and author's footnotes stand as they were, with the insertion of a minimum of editorial footnotes, including one by the Abbé Cyprien Tanguay — possibly one of the friends to whom Alfred mentions showing the work.

Three of these pieces concern Amerindians, the remnants of a proud lineage, an aspect that de Gaspé emphasizes. Is there a parallel with his own situation as the last seigneur of Saint-Jean Port-Joli? De Gaspé's Canadian forebears included the intrepid entrepreneur, Charles Aubert de la Chesnaye, ennobled by Louis XIV for his services to the Canadian community, and the soldier-seigneur, Philippe-Ignace Aubert de Gaspé, Chevalier of the Royal and Military Order of Saint-Louis and a veteran of both the Indian Wars and the Seven Years' War in North America. The author's best-

known work, the novel *Les Anciens Canadiens*,
evoked among other things the social watershed of
the Conquest and the passing of the old order.
Writing in the middle of the nineteenth century,
although essentially an eighteenth-century man in
spirit, he harkened back to what might well appear
a more dignified age in comparison with the hus-
tling industrial expansionism of the time. One can
get a sense of the difference from popular engrav-
ings of "views" of Quebec City and the Saint
Lawrence River between 1800 and 1870. The later
scenes bristle with smokestacks instead of the
graceful sailing craft and pensive Indians of an
earlier day.

One of the most valuable aspects of de Gaspé's
writing is his creative eye and ear, and his talent
for imaginatively describing events and encounters
in a way that makes them live for us once more. In
the pieces included in this book, the author proves
his ability to capture the ceremonial, almost biblical
cadences of his Amerindian interlocutors. In a few
places his Indians speak a broken French, but de
Gaspé is careful not to labour this device. In
translating these works, I have used the simple
formality employed, for example, in John Richard-

son's rendition of Pontiac's speech in *Wacousta*
(1832).

These pieces give us a sympathetic and sometimes rueful look at the Amerindian living in fairly
close proximity to the white man. Interestingly
enough, the author makes a point of portraying
something of their spiritual heritage, and has his
Indians protest at the incursion of the white man's
values — Christianity, money, and brandy. Perhaps
he is echoing the attitude of Abbé J.-B.-A. Ferland,
a historian he knew and admired. Ferland's ethno-
logical study of the Amerindians in his *Cours
d'histoire du Canada* spoke of Indian "philos-
ophers" and "theology," a quite unusual approach
for a nineteenth-century historian.[D]

The piece entitled "General Wolfe's Statue" is
odd man out in this collection. Nevertheless it gives
us one last chance to enjoy de Gaspé's easy,
discursive prose, much as we might if we happened
to spend an evening in his company. It is written
in the spirit of the Club des Anciens, an informal
group whose members used to meet in Quebec City
in the 1850s to discuss, record, and substantiate
details about the Quebec of their youth.

In preparing this translation, I have taken a few

(but only a few) liberties with the text, bearing in mind that the author had no opportunity to proof-read the contents before publication in book form. As with my translation of de Gaspé's memoirs (*A Man of Sentiment*), I have adopted a dual system of endnotes indicated in the text by numbers and letters respectively.

Jane Brierley
Montreal, 1990

"Yellow-Wolf"

There is a passage early in James Fenimore Cooper's *The Last of the Mohicans or a Narrative of 1757* (1826) where Hawkeye, the white scout, tells Chingachgook that Palefaces are not in the habit of handing down their history orally to the young men of their communities, but of committing it to writing. Those who have no chance to read this writing are therefore ignorant of their people's history.

It is only in fairly recent times that oral history, as told by native peoples themselves, has been committed to writing in a systematic way. As an author in the mid-nineteenth century, de Gaspé was acutely conscious of the importance of recording traditions and impressions that would otherwise be lost forever. In "Yellow-Wolf" he gives us the portrait and memories of a lonely old Indian, severed by the weight of years and his ancient beliefs from his Christianized fellow Malecites. Paradoxically, it is to the eighteen-year-old Paleface that the Indian entrusts his story, and de Gaspé tells it again for posterity.

One notable thing about de Gaspé is the conversational tone he adopts in his recital and the disarming simplicity of his style in comparison with that of the period. Even as the territories and traditions of the native peoples of northeastern North America were shrinking and fading, the romanticization of the Indian as a heroic figure in literature was moving into high gear, later to peter out in a spate of historical romances. The incorporation of native people as characters in fiction was fairly well established by the time de Gaspé began writing. In Canada, John Richardson's *Wacousta; Or, The Prophecy* (1832) contributed to the genre, portraying the gravely noble Ottawa chief, Pontiac, in a story otherwise rich in melodrama.

We know from de Gaspé's memoirs that he read with pleasure the novels of Sir Walter Scott and Captain Frederick Marryat, and it would be surprising if the historical novels of the immensely popular Cooper ("the American Scott") were not equally appreciated, particularly one such as *The Last of the Mohicans*, which deals with an episode during the fighting between the French under Montcalm and British forces in the Lake Champlain area. Such novels abound in detailed description of the characters' appearance, and de Gaspé does the same in the opening paragraphs of Yellow-Wolf, but with a humorous twist that is at once a sardonic reference to the overly-romantic style of literary predecessors and a look forward to the realism of late nineteenth-century writers. Let no one be offended: the joke is on the Paleface as much as the Indian.

YELLOW-WOLF
Malecite Chieftain of Old

Among the Indians who camped each year on our
beach during my childhood was an old Malecite[A]
by the name of Yellow-Wolf. According to my
father's calculations, taking into account this
Indian's acquaintance with the men of yesteryear
and the events he had witnessed, he must have been
a hundred years old at the time. Yellow-Wolf was
a great favourite with my family, and my father
loved to get him talking about the adventures of
his long career.

The old Indian was in the habit of pitching his
wigwam at some distance from his fellows. He
seemed to have little in common with them,
exchanging but a few brief words with those he met.
For their part, they seemed to feel more fear than
friendship for him. He led a solitary life in their

midst, his only companion being a small, distinctly
foxy-looking dog.

Ever sombre and meditative, Yellow-Wolf
treated my childish advances with discouraging
reserve. Witnessing my mischievous antics, he no
doubt considered me a frivolous being, incapable
of conducting a serious conversation. It wasn't until
I reached the age of eighteen that I succeeded in
overcoming his distaste for my company and gain-
ing his friendship.

Yellow-Wolf presented a most imposing ruin —
what was left of him after days of captivity and
hours of horrible suffering at the stake, at the hands
of enemies as versed in the art of torture as the
Iroquois. He had lost none of his tall stature, and
still walked, shoulders thrown back, with the fine
bearing of a man of forty. True, he had one blind
eye, but the eagle orb that remained still blazed
forth when he became animated. He might have
been a disciple of Molière's Toinette, who pro-
pounded the philosophy that having one eye
plucked out only made you see more clearly with
the other. His left hand had just the index finger
and thumb left, but these two digits, separated
though they might be from their brothers, were no

less prompt in their unfailing obedience to his behests.

As for Yellow-Wolf's lower regions, I had no way of assessing the damage. He tended to limp, despite efforts to hide it, and I am obliged to conclude that this infirmity was the result of his Iroquois enemies eating a few of his toes, after first smoking the nails in their *calumets* to pass the time.

The joys of indolence were dear to this savage of ancient lineage and noble race, and the rich gifts of the Crown to a great chief allowed him to indulge himself at will. One day I remarked how surprised I was that he didn't drink rum like his fellow Indians, and he told me that until the age of thirty he had been a drunkard. After he had gone on a two-week binge, his ancestor, the first Yellow-Wolf, had appeared to him in his sleep and forbidden him to taste firewater, which was poison to Redskins.

"The time had come," said the old chief. "I'd drunk up a hundred francs' worth of pelts, my gun, my canoe, and even my wife. I sold her to a Frenchman for a bottle of rum."

"You sold your wife, my brother? What a low thing to do!"

"It was the best deal I ever made," retorted the

Indian. "She was a no-good thief and an even bigger drunkard than myself. Ha! That Frenchman got more than he bargained for!"

"*Ma foi*, in that case I think you did well to let your friend the Paleface have her, my brother," said I. "But you married again to console yourself."

"Yes, and this time I was lucky. I married a good woman who gave me two fine boys, brave warriors. They were both killed at my side in a great battle against the English and their allies the Foxes. I revenged their deaths, but not enough. I still hear the voices of my children in the still of the night, in the raging storm and the waves lapping on the shore. Always I hear, 'Vengeance! Vengeance, my father!' "

There was a long pause, then the old man added, "*Hoa!* My heart is very heavy. To think I will never see my children again! Their mother made them Christians and they are with her in her heaven. I will hunt without them in my grandfather's paradise. He has never abandoned his grandson. When those dogs of Iroquois were torturing me, I called on him and he always came to my aid. But come and sit with me this evening and I'll tell you all about it."

A magnificent night greeted my arrival. Moon
and stars seemed to dance in the waters of the Saint
Lawrence, and I could hear the waves faintly
breaking on the sandy beach only a few feet from
the old Indian's wigwam. Some larks, disturbed in
their sleep, stretched their wings and hopped about,
uttering little cries as the water invaded the shore.

Yellow-Wolf was smoking meditatively at the
door of his wigwam. At my approach his dog started
up and barked, ears perked like steel blades. "*Que
ci! Céna* — Come here, hound!" shouted the Indian
without turning his head. The dog lay down obedi-
ently a few yards from his master, keeping a wild
and malevolent eye firmly fixed on me. I sat down
beside my aged friend. He said nothing for a few
minutes, then commenced the story that follows.

"Long, long ago, before the Paleface had passed
over the great lake in his giant ship to visit the
Redskins, my grandfather Areskoueh[1] took the
form of a yellow wolf. As he passed by a Malecite
village he saw a young Indian girl, daughter of the
voice of the woodlands, lakes, and mountains, and
carried her off to a cave far, far away. He made her
his wife, and she gave him a fine boy whom he
named Yellow-Wolf. By the time the boy was six,

he was stronger than the men of our day and those who will come after us.

"Areskoueh said to his wife, 'Show our son how to make the voice of the woodlands, lakes, and mountains speak, and I will make him a great hunter and warrior.' And the child learned to make the voice of the woods, lakes, and mountains speak, and his father taught him to be a great hunter and a fearsome warrior.

"When Yellow-Wolf became a man, Areskoueh said to his wife, 'Go and take your son to the Malecites and he will become a great chief. When he digs up the hatchet, the earth and trees of the forest will tremble beneath the feet of the warriors who run to answer his call! At each new moon he will drink from the skull of one of the twelve enemy chiefs to die by his hand and whose scalps hang in his wigwam. But before going on the warpath² he will pray to his father, and Areskoueh will come to him in his sleep and say, "Go!" Yellow-Wolf will then set forth, and enemies will fall beneath his hatchet like dry leaves before the storm! My son Yellow-Wolf will burn many prisoners to thank Areskoueh.' "

What did he mean, said I, interrupting the

narrator, by the voice of the woodlands, lakes, and mountains?

"When you speak aloud on a calm evening, standing in front of your house, what do you hear?" was his reply.[B]

"*Parbleu!*" I exclaimed. "I hear the echo of the cape."

"Good!" retorted the old man. "Well, all the descendants of Yellow-Wolf know how to make the echo speak whenever they wish, day or night."

"Then make it speak now," was my rejoinder.

"No, no, Areskoueh would be angry. He has forbidden his children to make the echo speak except in moments of great peril."

Yellow-Wolf was a ventriloquist, as will be borne out by what follows.

"But it seems to me," I started to say, "you were in considerable peril when your enemies . . ."

"Let me speak," said the Indian. "Yellow-Wolf is very old, and clouds pass through his head. Things suddenly go dark, and he has difficulty finding the trail of his memories." I had to be content with this. Yellow-Wolf passed a hand over his brow two or three times, and continued his story.

Malecite hunting and fishing territory once stretched from
the coastal and inland waterways of the Maritimes to the
Lower Saint Lawrence opposite Tadoussac. Indians
camped each year on the beach at the end of the de Gaspé
seigneurie in Saint-Jean Port-Joli. Yellow-Wolf's wigwam
would have looked much like those depicted in this
watercolour of Malecite dwellings. William Robert
Herries (1818–1845), "Indian Camp, New Brunswick,"
L:36.5; W:24.4. Beaverbrook Art Gallery, Fredericton,
New Brunswick.

"The sun was sinking when Yellow-Wolf and his mother came to a large Malecite village after a week of walking. In the old days, the wigwam of the Malecite was always open to the stranger, as it is today. The men of old used to say, 'Come, my brother, rest from your labours in my wigwam, and my squaw will make a fine stew to satisfy your hunger.' But today the poor Malecite often has nothing to offer travellers but the shelter of his wigwam. In order to sell pelts, the Palefaces have seized our forests and destroyed the game that the Great Spirit put there to feed his children.

"Several Malecites offered the strangers the hospitality of their wigwams," continued the old man after this digression, "but mother and son thanked them and asked first to speak to the chiefs, warriors, and old men of the village.

"The council fire was lit, and the chiefs, warriors, and old men took their places, waiting silently for the strangers to deliver their message.

"Yellow-Wolf stayed by the entrance while his mother, being the one to speak, went in alone. 'Let the heart of the Malecite rejoice, for your sister brings you good news,' said she. 'Let the old men search their memories, and they will recall that a young Malecite girl, the orphan of a great chief, was carried off by a wolf near this village.'

" 'My sister has spoken truly,' replied several old men of the council.

" 'My brothers remember well,' said the woman. 'Their sister who now speaks to them was the one carried off by the wolf.'

"The wise men of the council shook their heads at this and a great chief spoke these words: 'Wolves carry off young girls to eat them. My sister is lying.'

" 'My brother Malecites are easily amazed,' retorted the woman. 'Let them listen and then judge whether they are right in disbelieving the words of their sister.' The chiefs, old men, and warriors remained silent.

" 'The wolf carried the young squaw in his jaws a long way off,' continued the woman, pointing to the north. 'He said to the squaw, "Yellow-Wolf is Areskoueh, god of war. He has kidnapped you to be his wife, for you are the daughter of a great chief whom he loved, and you will be the mother of a race of formidable warriors!" '

"Then spoke Porcupine, a young Malecite and a great chief. 'My sister has fine words, but the words of a woman are as light as a feather on the wind.'

" 'Your sister will speak to Areskoueh,' replied Yellow-Wolf's mother, 'and he will answer her beneath the earth, in the sky, and under the water. Porcupine will open his ears and then he will believe his sister's words.' She stretched a hand toward the council fire, and a voice came forth crying, 'The wife of Areskoueh has spoken truly!' Then she lifted her hand toward heaven, and a voice descended crying, 'The wife of Areskoueh has spoken truly!' And she lowered her hand toward the river, where a voice arose crying, 'The wife of Areskoueh has spoken truly!' And all the chiefs, the old men, and the warriors cried, '*Hoa!* My sister has not lied.'

" 'Now that the chiefs, the old men, and the warriors believe their sister's word, will they let her bring in her son?' asked the woman. The men bowed their heads in assent.

"When Yellow-Wolf entered the council wigwam, the warriors cried out, '*Hoa!* Our brother is indeed the son of Areskoueh. Let him take his place in the council with his brother Malecites.'

" 'My brothers have spoken well and Yellow-Wolf thanks them,' replied the young man, 'but he will not sit in the Malecite council except as their great chief. When Areskoueh bade his son farewell, he said, "Go, tell the Malecites, 'I am Yellow-Wolf, son of Areskoueh and grandson on my mother's side of Arena, great chief of the Malecites. By this double heritage I am your great chief.'

" 'My brother speaks as though to command, but Porcupine will not give up his place to any warrior,' retorted the great Malecite chief. 'Let Yellow-Wolf take second place, and he will still be a great chief.'

" 'My brother Porcupine has a great heart and has spoken like a warrior,' replied the young man. 'Yellow-Wolf would have scorned him had he given up his place like a coward. But Yellow-Wolf, too, has a great heart. He loves the Malecites and asks only to pitch his wigwam near his brothers and live in peace with them.'

"And so Yellow-Wolf set up his wigwam in the village of his brothers. The Malecites had never seen such a formidable hunter. His arrow could pierce the eagle in the clouds. He could crush the black bear's skull with his hatchet and carry the animal back to the village on his shoulder as though it were a young badger.

"Six moons did Yellow-Wolf live among the Malecites. Then early one morning he rose and said to Porcupine, 'Let the great chief light the council fire, for his brother has solemn words.'

"The council assembled. 'Let my brother speak,' said the great chief.

" 'Areskoueh has visited his sleeping son,' said Yellow-Wolf, 'and has told him, "The Iroquois are advancing at great speed and their warriors are so many that the forest trembles beneath their feet! Before the sun has set three times, their war cry will be heard in the village of the Malecites." '

"The warriors smoked in silence, their hearts filled with sadness, for they knew the weakness of their tribe.

" 'Let my brothers open their ears and listen to the words of Yellow-Wolf, that their hearts may rejoice. Areskoueh has said to his son, "Go, and the dogs of Iroquois will fall beneath Yellow-Wolf's hatchet like dry leaves before the tempest!" Let the great chief strike the stake, call his warriors, and await the enemy a day's march from the Malecite village.'

"A great battle took place. The Iroquois, although taken by surprise, were so numerous that one would have thought the earth, trees, and rocks were spewing them forth like waves breaking upon

VIEW OF QUEBEC FROM POINT LEVI—1832.

Indian summer encampments were a common sight along the Saint Lawrence below Quebec. De Gaspé was impressed by the strict but efficient economy of migrant Indians with their birchbark canoes. "A gun, a powder horn, a pouch of lead, a small kettle, a dog about the size of a fox, and a roll of birchbark made up the cargo." In little over an hour, the roll of birchbark had been turned into a comfortable wigwam, and the small Indian family had settled in to hunt and fish the forests and waterways. R.A. Sproule (C.G. Crehen, Chromo.), "View of Quebec from Point Levi — 1832." A.57.526.E. Musée du Québec. Photo: Neuville Bazin.

the shore when the Great Spirit is angry and makes the storm blow. Porcupine was soon killed, and the Malecites, losing heart after the death of their great chief, were about to flee when Yellow-Wolf revived their courage with a terrible shout that shook the forest. He fell upon the enemy, splitting their skulls with a crunch that could be heard above the ghastly yells on both sides. The old people named this battle the feast of the Iroquois dogs' split skulls.

"After the enemy's defeat, Yellow-Wolf was named great chief of the Malecite tribe. His children and grandchildren succeeded him, and the old man who now speaks to you is the last chief of this family of fearsome warriors, and also the last of his line."

"When you cut me off just now, my brother," I interposed at this juncture, "I was about to ask why you didn't make the echo speak when your enemies tortured you so cruelly."

"When moon and stars shine in the night," the old man retorted, "they light the steps of the wanderer. The blood runs fast in the veins of the young man and clears his mind, but in the head of the old man who has seen a hundred winters it is often dark, and he needs rest. Let my brother come back tomorrow when Yellow-Wolf can speak once more."

I arrived punctually at our rendez-vous the next day.

"Yesterday evening," said the old man, "you asked me why I had not made the echo speak when my enemies tortured me. But Yellow-Wolf is a great warrior, you see, and he wanted to show those dogs of Iroquois that he cared nothing for their tortures. Listen, and I shall tell you of all this.

"For two weeks I had been hunting in the forest, and after a long tramp was very tired. Having seen no trace of the enemy, I went to sleep at the foot of a tree. I felt a blow and opened my eyes to find nearly a dozen Iroquois standing around me. They had taken my gun, hatchet, and knife.

" 'The Iroquois are great warriors!' I said, smiling scornfully. 'They are ten against one, yet they tremble at the sight of a sleeping Malecite and quickly seize his weapons. The Iroquois deserves the name "Fox," for he has its cunning and cowardice!'

" 'Yellow-Wolf would do well to call upon his grandfather Areskoueh before his enemies scalp him, burn him at the stake, and throw his bones to their village dogs,' replied Timakai, the Iroquois chief.

" 'Yellow-Wolf has no need of his grandfather's aid,' I retorted. 'The knife that will scalp him is still in the Paleface's stores, and the wood that will burn him at the stake has not yet come out of the earth.'

"The Iroquois enemies shrugged and bound my hands. We set off and walked until nightfall, when they tied me to a tree and built a campfire. While they prepared supper Timakai lit his pipe and smoked the little fingernail of my left hand, biting the finger off at the knuckle and spitting it in my face. A second Indian did the same to the next finger and put it in my mouth."[C]

"That must have been very painful, my brother," said I. "Your face must have twisted in agony. Why didn't you make the echo speak?"

The old man drew himself up with great dignity. "Yellow-Wolf is a great warrior! If he had grimaced as much as a Paleface with a finger-scratch, his enemy would have been delighted."

Hoist on your own petard, Paleface! thought I.

"We set out again next day and walked until nightfall without stopping. They built a fire near a

little spring while I sat on the ground. While the
meat cooked, another Iroquois smoked my third
finger, chopped it up and laughed as he threw it to
his dog. Now I had only two fingers on my left
hand, and I needed them to support my gun. It was
time to put an end to their games."

"I should think so, my brother," I remarked. "I
admire your patience, but I swear I'd have put an
end to their games from the moment they began
smoking my first fingernail."

The old man looked at me pityingly. There was
a moment of silence. "The Great Spirit created both
Redskins and Palefaces, but he gave them different
ideas," he said at last, and continued his account.

"I behaved just like a man about to fall sick —
struggling to get up, heaving sighs, gasping and
rolling on the ground, then lying perfectly still as
though I'd lost consciousness. The Iroquois threw
water in my face and I sighed like a man coming
out of a fainting spell. 'Where am I?' I cried. My
enemies burst out laughing. '*Hoa!* Yellow-Wolf
boasted of being a man, yet he fainted like a young
girl with a finger-bite.'

"I looked about me with a dazed expression and
replied weakly, 'Yellow-Wolf was sick when the

enemy ambushed him. He had not eaten for three days, being unable to hunt, and he has had no food since being taken prisoner two days ago. His enemies have allowed him no water to quench his fever. If Yellow-Wolf dies, his only regret will be his failure to show the Iroquois they were nothing but women who didn't know how to torture a warrior.' And I pretended to faint again.

"The Iroquois threw water in my face once more, then untied me and gave me something to eat and drink. When I had finished, I imitated the sound of indistinct voices on the trail behind us, calling, 'Iroquois! Malecites! Malecites! Iroquois!' As my captors reached for their weapons in fear of an enemy attack, I let out a Malecite warhoop, grabbed the tomahawk hanging from Timakai's belt, and split his skull with a shout of triumph before disappearing in the direction of the voices. The night was dark, and I quickly hid behind a tree until the Iroquois had fled in the opposite direction. Then I went back for the weapons Timakai had taken. But before bidding him farewell, I also took his scalp. *Hoa!* Yellow-Wolf is a great warrior."

"Indeed you are, my brother," said I, "and a warrior with little regard for his own skin."

"In time of war we must always be on the watch for ambush when hunting in the forest," the old man went on. "Each nation has war parties continually on the prowl. During the day the hunters spread out but they agree on a meeting place for the evening. I had been hunting for several days with four young braves. One morning, as we separated, I told them not to light a fire at our camp that evening, for I had just seen a wounded deer go by. But when I joined them at nightfall, they had started a fire to cook supper. 'My brothers have done wrong,' said I, 'for I have seen signs of the Iroquois. I climbed a tree and thought I saw a puff of smoke rising beyond the nearby hillside to the south.' We ate our supper and I cautioned them. 'Keep watch, my brothers. Yellow-Wolf senses the enemy's presence and is going on the warpath. If he yells, let my brothers be ready to flee or to fight.'

"It was very dark. Fearing an ambush I took a great many precautions, sometimes walking on all fours or slithering along on my stomach like a snake and frequently putting my ear to the ground. I heard nothing and kept moving forward. As I rounded a small rock five men jumped on me, but I let out a terrible yell before they could gag me.

Although I was their prisoner, my heart rejoiced at having warned my brothers. They made the most of it, too. A dozen Iroquois ran in their direction and we heard four gunshots. The Malecites had wounded two and killed a third before getting away. My captors returned bearing the body of the Iroquois dog.

"Although I was a prisoner, my heart was glad because my young braves were safe. The Iroquois led me off to their camp and tied me to a tree. Karakoua said to me, 'Let Yellow-Wolf call upon his Malecite brothers, who run away like cowards, to rescue him. Before the sun has set three times he will be burned.'

" 'When Yellow-Wolf is tied to the stake he will sing his death-song like a warrior,' I retorted. 'He will not shed tears as did the father of Karakoua when Yellow-Wolf, after tearing the skin from his skull, threw red-hot cinders on his head. Let Karakoua go to the wigwam of Yellow-Wolf and there he will find his father's scalp in the bed of Yellow-Wolf's dog.'

"After five days' walk we came to their village on the edge of a river. Next day they bound me to the stake and I sang my death-song like a warrior.

My torturers began by tearing off three of my toenails and sticking thorns and burning brands into my toes. That explains why I limp a little with my left foot. They branded my thighs with red-hot irons. 'My eyes look everywhere for men, but I see only *matchiotes*,'D said I. *Hoa!* This last insult cost me dear, for that dog Karakoua drank one of my eyes."3

"Drank one of your eyes?" said I. "How does an Indian manage that, my brother?"

The old man snorted. "You are not very bright. Karakoua said to me, 'Your eye looks good, Malecite!' Then he gouged it out with his knife and swallowed it. 'Karakoua does well to drink the eyes of Yellow-Wolf,' I told him, 'since he is too cowardly to meet the gaze of a Malecite warrior, even when tied to a stake.' "

I froze with horror at this account. "My brother," said I, "it seems to me that it was more than time to make the echo speak while there was still something left of you."

A little smile appeared on the old man's lips. "You are right, my brother. I thought so too, for if Karakoua had drunk my other eye, I could not have escaped. I made a voice come out of the sky, crying 'Untie the prisoner. He has the smallpox. If he dies in your village none of you will survive, from the old man who cannot leave his wigwam to the new-born *baboujine!*'

"The whole village fled in panic.[4] I believe I would still be tied to the stake if they had not sent back an old slave to cut my bonds, beating her soundly by way of encouragement. Once freed, I had no trouble finding weapons in the deserted village. I crossed the river in one of their birchbark canoes and camped on the opposite shore to taunt them. After two weeks I was well enough to return to my village, where my Malecite brothers received me with great joy, for they had never expected to see me again.

"A hundred winters have passed over the head of Yellow-Wolf," concluded the old man. "Now he lives alone in the midst of his tribe, for his brothers enter their wigwams at the sight of him, like little animals of the forest who hide beneath the ground when they hear the owl's mournful hooting. Micmacs and Malecites forget that when the enemy digs up the hatchet, Yellow-Wolf will strike the stake with his tomahawk and their fathers will hasten to answer the voice of the grandson of Areskoueh, who led them to victory!" And the centenarian's head fell on his breast.

"Listen, my brother," said I. "If I have understood your words aright, you do not worship the same God as your brother Micmacs and Malecites. They are Christians, but you worship heathen gods and that is why they shun you."

"When the eagle falls upon the marten that is about to devour the timid and defenceless hare, the hare — when he is safe in his burrow — will shout to the eagle, 'Go away! I owe you nothing. You worship the sun, and I the earth that feeds me!'" The old Indian paused for a moment, then added, "When Yellow-Wolf's hooded coat is old and worn, he throws it away and puts on another. But he cannot say to his beliefs, 'You are old and worn. I shall now toss you to the back of my wigwam for my dog to sleep on.'

"Good night, young man. Remember my words well."

"Woman of the Foxes"

De Gaspé's gift for setting a scene and bringing characters to life is epitomized in this little-known piece. Ostensibly about an Indian slave, "Woman of the Foxes" is in fact a delightful example of de Gaspé's discursive, rambling style, with the *raconteur* speaking directly to us and digressing as the fancy takes him. There is a mingling of fiction and fact in this tale that spans French and English régimes, with sprinklings of humour, whimsy, and pathos that reflect styles and themes of such favourite authors as Dickens and Scott.

Apart from his interest in things of yesteryear, de Gaspé may have been moved to write of a slave because the topic was very much in the air in the years leading up to the American Civil War, when he appears to have written most of his material. Institutionalized slavery had only been abolished in

Britain and its colonies in 1833. The acquisition of slaves in Canada had become relatively rare even before 1800, but the presence of Indian and black slaves and servants was fairly common in the late French and early British régimes. In *Les Anciens Canadiens* and in his memoirs, de Gaspé writes of his parents' perfect cook, the exuberant mulatto Lisette, who "was only a little afraid of her master" and obeyed her mistress's orders pretty well as she pleased. Slaves tended to be house servants, with the French reportedly preferring the tractable *panis* (from "Pawnee"), whereas the British were more likely to have slaves of African origin.

Whatever de Gaspé's initial intention may have been, the most significant literary element in the tale revolves around the ceremonious interchange between Seigneur Couillard and the old Abenaki, Katoueh. The scholarly seigneur exemplifies an eighteenth-century ideal, and one should note the humanistic little homily to his boatmen on the true meaning of the word aboriginal. Katoueh, while dispensing dignified hospitality to his brother Frenchman, strikes a wily bargain on his son's behalf. The Christian gentleman saves a soul, and all are satisfied.

Remember, little child, heaven sometimes
Revenges th'oppressed upon the heads of kings.
Beautiful Virgin, surely a goddess's offspring,
Fear lest the stranger perish in distress:
For the nameless beggar is the envoy of the gods.
                                        André Chénier[A]

WOMAN OF THE FOXES[1]

Before recounting the story of this slave[B] whom I
knew from my earliest childhood until her death,
I feel I must preface it with the following two
certificates. I owe these to the kindness of the Abbé
Tanguay.[C]

EXTRACT from the Register of Baptisms, Marriages and
Burials of the Parish of Saint-Thomas[D] for the year
seventeen hundred and sixty-one. The ninth of May, in
the year seventeen hundred and sixty-one, I, the undersigned, parish priest of Saint-Thomas, baptized with the
usual ceremonies an Indian woman aged about twenty-six,
belonging to Madame Couillard. The woman was named

Geneviève. The godfather was Monsieur André Couillard, ecclesiastic, the godmother Madame Couillard, mistress of the said Indian woman, who signed with the godfather and myself.

(Signed)

> [Marie-Geneviève] Alliés Widow COUILLARD
>
> A. THOMAS COUILLARD, ecclesiastic
>
> MAISONBASSE, priest

On the twelfth of October, eighteen hundred and eight, I, priest of this parish, did bury in the cemetery of this parish the body of Marie Geneviève, an Indian woman, a native of the land of the Foxes brought up from her youth in the house of Monsieur Couillard, *seigneur primitif*, where she was baptized, received a Christian and Catholic upbringing and her First Communion, and thereafter lived as a good Christian. She died at about seventy-five years of age, and was unable to receive the Last Sacraments and Extreme Unction because of the suddenness of her death, although she had received the Sacrament of Penance a few days previously. Present at the said burial were Monsieur Antoine Gaspard Couillard, undersigned, Pierre Fournier, C. Etienne Churet and several other witnesses who were unable to sign.

(Signed)

ANTOINE GASPARD COUILLARD

J. M. VERREAU, priest

Although this Indian woman was not baptized until her twenties, she was only about eleven or twelve when Monsieur Jean-Baptiste Couillard purchased her from an Abenaki Indian. I can only suppose that the curé of Saint-Thomas thought it his duty to instruct the neophyte before giving her the sacraments of baptism and penance, and that the young girl's slow intellect was the cause of this delay. La Grosse (I never knew her by any other name) had in fact a very limited intelligence, although she was by no means an imbecile. She spoke haltingly, using a patois of her own invention.

About the year 1746, Captain Jean-Baptiste Couillard de l'Épinay, seigneur of Saint-Thomas and Saint-Pierre,[2, E] left Quebec in the afternoon of a fine August day. As luck would have it, he was

forced to camp for the night in the parish of
Saint-Valier at the southwest end of Bellechasse
Bay.[3] At first he felt rather put out at being
prevented by wind and tide from reaching his home
in Saint-Thomas that same evening. However, it
being an ill wind that blows no good, he could only
be thankful in retrospect. The small boat[F] in which
he had taken passage was level with the parish
church of Saint-Valier when, upon a sudden drop
in the south wind, Captain Couillard gave the
following order:

"Lower the sails, grab the oars, and heave-ho
m'hearties!"

The two young boatmen obeyed. But sculling
against wind and tide is an arduous task, and
Joncas, one of the oarsmen, did not relish the
prospect of rowing five leagues before reaching the
manor house of Saint-Thomas. As they drew abreast
of the charming stand of maples that crowns the
headland west of Bellechasse Bay, he remarked to
Captain Couillard, who held the rudder in one hand
and a volume of Horace in the other, "Captain,
you're such a scholar: can you tell us who invented
sails?"

Monsieur Couillard,[4] pleased to be consulted on

so important a point of history, pocketed his book and drew out his snuff box to clear his brain. After blowing his nose and coughing, as must any learned man when consulted upon a weighty question, he said, "Noah's Ark had no sails, of that we can be sure, *primo* because, not being bound for any port, Noah cared little for the course his vessel took. *Secundo* . . ."

"As for *secundo*," said Joncas, "I think, Captain — begging your pardon — that I can give you the reason. Captain Noah and his crew couldn't see to steer because they were shut up in the ship's hold."

"Well, that settles the second point!" laughed Monsieur Couillard. "You're a bright fellow, Joncas, and with a little study you'd be a scholar. I know what I'm talking about, mark my words." The learned captain flicked the Spanish tobacco from his lace shirtfrill. "Did the ancients, who wore no shirts, use sails on their vessels? I must look into it some time," he muttered, then continued his lecture.

"Nevertheless, the divine Homer, who — as you know, my children — lived two thousand years before the Christian era, speaks of the Greek fleet that carried Agamemnon's countless battalions.

These vessels must have had sails, because
Agamemnon wished to sacrifice his daughter
Iphegenia to obtain a favourable wind from the
gods. The Argonauts, twelve hundred years before
Christ — the Argonauts, named for the good ship
Argo . . ."

"Excuse me for interrupting, Captain, but I
believe the good Lord invented sails," asserted
Joncas.

"Right you are, my son," replied Monsieur
Couillard. "God gave man intelligence and the
genius for invention, just as he gave animals their
admirable instinct." And forthwith the scholar
launched into a long-winded dissertation on things
physiological, theological, and metaphysical.

Joncas, taking advantage of a momentary pause
while the scholar produced his snuff box for another
pinch of tobacco, said hurriedly, "Since we agree
the good Lord invented sails, would you be kind
enough to tell me who invented oars?"

"Oars, my son, are as old as the art of navigating
in tiny boats or even on a piece of floating wood.
Homer tells us in his *Odyssey* — with which you're
no doubt familiar — that the wise Ulysses used
plenty of oars to escape the huge chunks of stone

hurled at his fleet by the Cyclops. I could quote numerous authors who talk of biremes, triremes, and so on. But Homer and Virgil being poets, they generally give Jason credit for inventing navigation, although it seems to me the credit, as with the invention of writing, belongs to the Phoenicians, already a powerful and flourishing nation when the Argonauts set sail from Greece to Colchis in the vessel *Argo* to capture the Golden Fleece. And even before Dido — *Sidonia Dido*, as Virgil calls her, you know — landed in Africa to found Carthage, the Phoenicians already possessed several long-established colonies on that continent — or so said Strabo and Diodorus of Sicily, whose views are not to be taken lightly. Personally, I think the origins of this art are lost in the mists of time."

"Just now, Captain," spoke up Lebrun, the second sailor, "you talked of Cyclops throwing huge chunks of stone. Those fellows must have had pretty remarkable wrists!"

"The Cyclops, my son, were giants with only one eye in the middle of their forehead."

"Well in that case I'm not surprised their aim was so bad," remarked Joncas, "even though the target was an entire fleet! Men with two eyes, like

An Abenaki man and woman of the mid eighteenth
century. The Eastern Abenakis were a small but fierce
people. "The terror they inspired among the English
colonies and the Iroquois is a most amazing thing," wrote
Father Joseph-Anselme Maurault in his *Histoire des
Abenakis* (1866). Eastern Abenakis, Micmacs and Malecites were originally based along the rivers and coastal
regions of what is now Maine and the Maritime Provinces.
They wore distinctive conical headwear and hooded
cloaks, often beautifully embroidered and sewn with
shells. The Abenaki, sworn enemies of the English,
eventually retreated to the Jesuit missions on the Saint-
François, Bécancour, and Mississquoi rivers in New
France. From a rare set of watercolours found in the
collection of the Abbé Louis-Stanislas Malo (1801–1884).
C51 42500, Collection Philéas Gagnon, Bibliothèque de
la Ville de Montréal. Photo: Robert Rohonczy.

us Christians, wouldn't have missed."

"How right you are, my boy," replied the scholar. "There's another question to resolve. Is it better to take aim with one eye or two? Well, I'll deal with that once I've shown you that the invention of oars . . ."

"Never mind, Captain," interrupted Joncas. "There's no point proving the age of these delightful instruments of torture. Since the Devil invented them to drive Christians mad, he must have been in a hurry to let them in on this invaluable discovery!" Monsieur Couillard burst out laughing at the sailor's artful dig, and promptly set course for Berthier Bay.

Berthier or Bellechasse Bay, as it is indiscriminately called, lies in the parish of Saint-Valier at its southwest end, and in the parish of Berthier at its northeast and southerly extremities. At high tide it becomes a stretch of water four miles round. The southwest end, where travellers land, runs for about thirty arpents in a straight line from a bluff, crowned by a magnificent maple grove at the entrance to the bay, to the little Bellechasse River emptying into the southernmost part of this splendid shoreline.

The tide was in, and the twilight solitude was broken only by the gentle lap of water on the sandy shore, the twittering of the horned larks and sandpipers that literally covered the beach, and the last songs of birds in the lofty stand of trees above. Three wigwams[5] stood on the highest part of the river bank. A few Indian children played beneath the leafy maple boughs while an old Indian, the image of the Roman god Terminus, sat silently smoking at the door of his modest dwelling, apparently oblivious of the strangers and their approaching craft. This typically picturesque Canadian scene was lit by the last rays of the sun as it sank behind the Laurentian mountains on the far side of the river.[6]

"It's my old friend Katoueh!" exclaimed Monsieur Couillard. "He's recognized me, but he's afraid to lower his dignity as a chieftain." (The Abenakis never made the first move.)

Monsieur Couillard leapt onto the shore and went up to the chieftain. "Your brother Paleface has come to ask for shelter this night in his brother Redskin's dwelling," said he.

"My brother Paleface is welcome," replied the old chief, offering him his hand. "He is now master

in the wigwam of his brother Katoueh, and everything here is his."

After a brief exchange, Monsieur Couillard
noticed that while his friend Katoueh had a generous heart, his larder offered the prospect of a most
meagre supper. The Indians are frugal with gun-
powder and often starve themselves rather than use
it up. Thinking this the case, the captain asked
Lebrun to take a gun and kill some small game.

"Stop, my brother!" called the Indian. "When
Katoueh asks his friend Couillard for shelter in his
great wigwam, Couillard says to him, 'Be seated,
my brother, and eat.' Does Katoueh bring supper
to his friend the Paleface?" And so saying, he took
a gun and left his guests.

"This aboriginal's hospitality is touching," said
Monsieur Couillard.

"I don't want to be a nuisance, Captain, but what
kind of animal is an aboriginal?" asked Joncas.

"My son," replied the scholar, "it's very true that
Man is an animal that prides himself on being
intelligent, although that biting critic Boileau
assures us that Man is the stupidest beast in
creation. Leave that aside for the moment, however,
and I'll get back to it later. Actually, you can use

the word 'animal' in speaking of Man, but always with a qualifying adjective of some kind — something you seem to have overlooked, no doubt through sheer absentmindedness. But to answer your question — you've read in Roman history about a people in Italy who were called aboriginals. You also know that the French word *aborigène* is a derivative of the Latin *aborigenes*, meaning native in origin or first inhabitants. My friend Katoueh belongs to this race of men and is therefore an aboriginal or native of Canada.

"But to get back to my point, this Indian's hospitality is indeed touching. Here he is, surrounded by game, and yet he'd probably go without food rather than use up his ammunition, since his powder horn — that's the common name, although powder *flash* is of course the correct expression — looks nearly empty to me.

"My children, I've been entertained by the rich, even in the châteaux of France and elsewhere, but I've always thought that only the poor man is truly hospitable. Seven times out of ten, the rich man is probably indebted to his guest for relieving his boredom, brightening his solitude, and giving him a chance to show off his grand possessions and his wealth. On the other hand, the poor man or one of modest means does without when exercising this noble virtue — which reminds me of a little legend that my sainted mother, now in heaven, used to tell."

A POOR COTTAGE

There was once a family of poor peasants consisting of father, mother, and six young children. They lived in a little thatched cottage on the edge of a Normandy forest. Let us enter this miserable hut. It was eight o'clock in the evening on a dark November night. The wind had been wuthering and the rain falling in torrents for a week, as though the waterfalls of heaven had opened and were threatening Earth with a second Flood. The parents and two of the children, aged ten and twelve, watched by the hearth where a dwindling fagot burned, despite wind and water swirling down the chimney. Occasional puffs of smoke left the watchers in total darkness. The four youngest children lay sleeping on piles of filthy rags and straw.

Antoine-Gaspard Couillard de l'Épinay (1787–1847), de
Gaspé's childhood friend, was the son of the seigneur of
Rivière-du-Sud whom the author used as a model for the
"Captain Couillard" of "Woman of the Foxes." The Saint-
Jean Port-Joli seigneurie was a short ride from the
Rivière-du-Sud (Saint-Thomas de Montmagny) fief.
Couillards and de Gaspé had been friends for generations.
Antoine-Gaspard became a physician and legislative coun-
cillor, but fell on hard times after investing too heavily
in the restoration of the family manor. Pastel attributed
to Dulongpré, A.67.102.D. Musée du Québec.

"What misery and heartache poor people have to bear before they die," said the woodcutter sadly. "It makes me lose heart!"

"You've never talked like this before, my man," said the woman. "Have you lost all faith in God and Our Lady — and you such a good Christian?"

"No indeed," replied the husband. "Without that faith to sustain me, without my love for my family, I'd have died of heartbreak long ago. I've never complained about my suffering before God or man. It's *your* misery, dear wife and children, that tears at my heart. This evening there was only a quarter of a loaf of bread left in the hutch, and the four youngest wept with hunger. We gave each of them a small piece, and now they're asleep. But you — you're going without food to dry the tears of poor innocents too young to understand our poverty. It's enough to make a man tear his hair in despair!"

There was a moment of silence within the hut, made more solemn by the raging elements outside and the sobs of mother and children. Then the woodcutter spoke.

"You're right, my dear wife, I've failed in my duty. This is the hour of prayer. Let us pray to the good Lord with fervour and trust, and beg his forgiveness for me in this moment of weakness.''

This act of Christian piety was barely done when a knock on the door startled the family. "Come in,'' said the peasant. The door of the hut opened to admit an aged woman bent double, walking with the help of a long cane. The family hurried to help her off with a dripping old cape that barely covered her shoulders, then sat her down beside the hearth and threw another fagot on the fire.

"I'm hungry,'' said the beggar-woman, once she had warmed herself. "Give me some supper, for the love of God.''

"We're very poor, my good mother,'' replied the peasant. "We've nothing but bread, but I offer you that with all my heart.'' And so saying, he gave her the little bit of bread that remained in the hutch. While the old woman devoured this meagre fare, the children gazed at her tearfully.

"I've had nothing to eat for two days,'' said the old woman, once she had downed the last mouthful. "Another bit of bread for the love of Our Lady!''

"We have no more,'' said the woodcutter. "But wait, good mother — I'll run over to my neighbour's house not half a league from here. He's rich and has plenty of everything. He knows I'm honest and hardworking, and he won't refuse me a loaf of bread."

"He'll be poorer than you tomorrow," said the old woman with assurance. "I've just come from his house, and not only did he refuse me the shelter of his roof this terrible night: he even denied me the paltry scrap of bread one gives the poor. But hark!"

The raging wind fell silent as if at the behest of some powerful genie, and a bright fire blazed up on the hearth. The beating of wings was heard, as though a huge bird with a twenty-foot wingspan had passed over the forest.

"It's the ministering angel of God's justice," said the old woman solemnly, "going his nocturnal round in the kingdom of Saint Louis, the friend and father of the poor on earth and in heaven!"

The family was seized with terror at this pronouncement, and all fell face down on the earthen floor. The old woman rose from her seat, opened the door of the hut, and stretched her hand toward the dwelling of the pitiless rich man. "Behold the justice of the Lord passeth over!" she cried. An immense bolt of lightning lit up the sky and a dreadful clap of thunder shook the forest as torrents of flame heralded the merciless nabob's ruin.

"Have pity! Have pity on him!" cried the wood-cutter and his wife.

"The justice of the Almighty is inflexible," replied the old woman with authority. "This man has always refused the poor the shelter of his roof and the crumbs from his table. The hand of God has struck justly!" The beldam said nothing for a moment, then added, "The hutch from which you took the last bit of bread for the poor beggar-woman will fill up as fast as you empty it, and when you are rich, you will build a shelter for suffering humanity in place of this hovel." And with these words she disappeared.

The arrival of Katoueh with a bag full of small game put an end to a long and scholarly discourse in which the erudite Monsieur Couillard cited numerous hospitable traits among the Hebrews, Greeks, and Romans, not forgetting the generosity of King Evander to pious Aeneas.

Supper over, Monsieur Couillard seated himself on the sand in front of his host's wigwam and smoked a pipe as he talked of war and hunting with the old Indian. A piercing shriek made him look

up to see a young Indian girl of eleven or twelve
being pursued by other children, one of whom
carried a burning brand. The unfortunate child ran
to the captain for safety, and he saw that her eye
was a welter of blood.

Monsieur Couillard chased off the black imps.
The old chief said not a word, but kept on smoking
as though he had seen nothing.

"Why do you let your children play such cruel
games?" asked Monsieur Couillard.

"It's a slave!" retorted the Indian, shrugging and
pointing scornfully at the child.

"Merciful God, a slave!" cried Monsieur
Couillard, "doomed to eat the others' scraps when
they've had their fill, fighting over the leavings with
her masters' dogs — and she barely twelve years
old! Doomed to sleep when her tormentors are tired
of torturing her, to wear their discarded rags in the
cold! To be denied the warmth of her masters'
wigwam unless the other children don't care for the
cruel pleasure of seeing her grovel in the snow,
paralysed with cold. A child barely twelve years old!
She looks as though she had a strong constitution
and is in for a long and painful martyrdom."

And as he soliloquized, the excellent man tore a

Although relatively modern, this sensitive ink sketch of
the Rue Couillard in Quebec City gives an accurate idea
of the huddled intimacy of the old Quebec streets. It was
here, wrote de Gaspé, "in the street that bears his name,"
that "the excellent Monsieur Couillard died in my arms"
in 1808. "Rue Couillard à Québec," ink on paper drawing
by Simone Hudon. 84.42.26. Musée du Québec. Photo:
Patrick Altman.

handkerchief and dipped it in cold water to make a compress, applying it to the half-gouged eye of the unhappy slave.

"My brother Katoueh is a great hunter. He treks long distances through the forest in pursuit of moose and caribou, and this child is too young and weak to follow him."

"If the slave cannot reach the wigwam by nightfall," replied the Indian, "she will stay in the forest to be eaten by wolves, just as her dogs of brothers, the Iroquois, ate the hearts of their Abenaki prisoners."

Monsieur Couillard was too well versed in the Indians' vengeful nature to suggest buying the girl after hearing these cruel words. Instead he said to the old chief, "Couillard has always been the Redskins' friend. He has shared the hardships of the hunt and the dangers of war with them. A hundred times the forest has trembled beneath the feet of French and Abenaki warriors marching together against the English and their allies, the Foxes. The hatchet of Katoueh and the sword of Couillard are still red with the blood of their foes!^{G} Warriors are brothers and give presents to each other."

"My brother has spoken well and truly," said the old chief.

"Your brother needs a young girl to amuse and take care of his son, who is but three years old. My brother Katoueh will please his friend greatly by giving him this slave."

"If the Iroquois girl belonged to Katoueh, he would say to his Paleface friend, 'The slave is yours, as is everything in his wigwam,' " asserted the old chief. He waved a hand toward the second wigwam. "But she is the slave of his son, the Panther, who spared the young squaw to serve his wife and amuse his children."

"Good God!" exclaimed Monsieur Couillard. "His son spared her for his children's amusement! Why didn't he burn her alive to satisfy his vengeance, as he probably did with the rest of her family! Why didn't he inflict the same terrible torments! She would now sleep where all the tortures of her butchers could not trouble her! The Panther spared her to amuse his children! Thus the tiger drags live prey into his den so that his young can learn to tear the palpitating flesh from his victims!" Then he ventured, "Does my brother Katoueh think the Panther will agree to sell his slave?"

"The son of Katoueh loves silver, but he loves vengeance more," said the old man. "Before he killed the young squaw's mother at the stake, he told her, 'I will spare your daughter, but she will be more unhappy than the dogs in my wigwam.' And the mother cried, 'Kill her! Kill her!' "

Monsieur Couillard heaved a sigh that seemed almost a moan. "Couillard has promised his wife a slave to care for her *baboujine*," he said. "He loves his good wife and would like to please her. Katoueh is a father who knows the right words to touch his son's heart. Let him speak to his son if he loves his friend the Paleface, and Couillard will thank him."

The Indian smoked silently for several minutes, then answered, "Let my brother look to the mountains of the north, and he will see one that towers above all others. The Panther is more proud and vain than this high mountain. Palefaces have the supple tongue of that serpent Black-Robe has told us about, who with fine words flattered the vanity of the first woman, our grandmother, and made her eat the apple that doomed all her children. Let my brother vaunt the exploits of the young warrior, and as a reward for such bravery let him give the warrior his fine hunting gun and powder horn with their silver mountings. The Panther, shamed at having nothing to offer in return, will be proud and happy to give him the slave."

We shall see with what success Monsieur Couillard followed the counsels of old Katoueh.

The captain's gun was a valuable arm that came from his late father, and like every brave hunter he was greatly attached to it. He felt the sacrifice keenly, and would have preferred to pay twice its worth in gold. But this was an act of charity. Without a moment's hesitation, he picked up the gun and walked over to the wigwam of the young Indian, who sat stolidly smoking his pipe, seemingly oblivious to the captain's approach.

"Your brother Paleface didn't wish to leave Bellechasse Bay without smoking a pipe with the son of his old friend Katoueh," remarked Captain Couillard.

"My brother Frenchman is welcome," the young man responded, removing the *calumet* from his mouth and waving it gracefully at a seat on the fallen log where he was sitting.

"Great Onontio[H] loves his Redskin allies," announced Captain Couillard. "He has told his French officers, 'When you meet one of their great warriors,

thank him on behalf of their father Onontio.' The
Panther is a great warrior, and his brother Paleface
thanks him in the name of great Onontio for the
services rendered to his brothers the French."

"The Panther is still very young," replied the
Indian. "Only six English and Iroquois scalps hang
from his belt, and he has burned but three of his
enemies at the stake. As yet his hatchet is stained
by just a few drops of blood, for his enemies flee
before him as the deer when the forest panther
roars."

"The Panther is a great warrior!" exclaimed
Monsieur Couillard. "He deserves to carry fine
weapons, for he is the terror of his enemies and
those of the French!" And so saying, he presented
him with his silver-mounted gun and powder horn.

"The Paleface has a generous heart!" cried the
young Indian, unable to suppress the sudden blush
that suffused his face, despite his habitual stoicism.
He handled the weapons admiringly, squinting
down the barrel of the gun, then added dejectedly,
"The Frenchman's friend has nothing to offer in
return today, but the Panther is a great hunter and
will very soon give him a hooded beaver coat that
the Great Onontio himself would be proud to wear.[7]

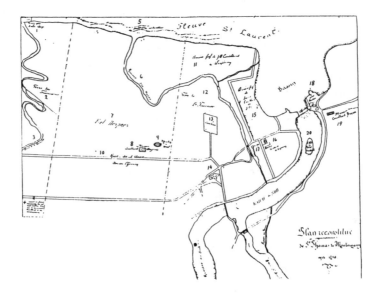

This early unidentified map was reproduced in the
valuable *Histoire des seigneurs de la Rivière-du-Sud*
(1912) by Abbé Azarie Couillard Després. The Couillard
de l'Épinay manor house is shown to the left of the Rivière
du Sud (no. 16). The earlier manor house described in
de Gaspé's piece would have been closer to the Saint
Lawrence shore. Before bridges were built, inhabitants
apparently had to ford the Rivière-du-Sud and the Bras
Saint-Nicholas (probably at lower right, where small
bridges are shown on this map) when skirting the bay on
horseback.

"The Panther's heart is as great as it is brave,"
responded Captain Couillard, "and his brother
Paleface thanks him for his rich gift. But let my
brother heed the words of his friend. Couillard has
a small boy of three who is so naughty that he hits,
bites, and scratches the women who look after him,
and it is only by paying them much silver that your
brother persuades them to stay with his son. The
Panther has a young slave. Let him give her to his
friend the Frenchman to amuse and serve his
baboujine, and the Frenchman will thank him and
accept nothing more."

"My brother Paleface has said in his pride,
'Couillard is rich, with great wigwams, land, and
herds. The Panther is poor and needs his pelts, so
I shall accept only his slave — a thing he values
less than his dog,' " retorted the Indian. "The
Panther will keep his slave."

"The Panther has boasted of his great heart,"
countered Monsieur Couillard, "yet he refuses his
friend a worthless slave and promises him skins of
beaver that swim in the lakes and rivers of the
forest!" And with this he made as if to leave.

The young Indian's eyes flashed as bright as a
steel blade. His instinctive reaction was to hand

back the gun and powder horn, but the pride of being able to adorn himself with them was too strong. "When the Panther refused to give his friend the slave, he thought the Paleface too scornful of the Redskin to accept a valuable gift. But since my brother wishes to have the young squaw, let her follow him. The Frenchman will see that the Panther has a generous heart and is a great hunter who knows the haunts of the beaver, hidden beneath the earth like field mice." The Indian drew himself up haughtily. "Couillard will find the word of a poor Abenaki well worth that of a rich Frenchman."

The excellent Monsieur Couillard waited impatiently for the outgoing tide so that he could carry the unfortunate child home, there to receive the care her pitiable condition and mutilated eye demanded. The young Indian girl soon won her masters' confidence. Obliging, gentle, and affectionate, she developed a tender and maternal devotion for the lovable child who was hers to amuse. She called him her "son" as soon as she learned to prattle in French. The depth of her love may be gauged from the fact that fifty years later, on learning that her son (as she still called him) was

gravely ill at Quebec, she died of a broken heart —
but of that, more later.

Monsieur and Madame Couillard, seeing how the
young Indian girl loved their son and made up little
games to amuse him, gave him into her care as to
a trusted maidservant. One day, however, the
strength of their confidence was severely tried. In
those days the seigneurial manor house stood on
the crest of a bluff overlooking the bay — a
splendid stretch of water that, at high tide, lapped
the foot of the cliff beneath the very windows of
the house.

Madame Couillard entered her drawing room one
day to see a spectacle that filled her with terror.
There, swimming across the bay, was the young
Indian girl with the child on her shoulders. The
mother gave an agonized shriek that brought her
husband running.[1] When he saw what had frightened her, he begged his wife to remain silent lest
she expose the child to the gravest danger.

For a while the young girl played like a dolphin
in the warm waters of the Saint Lawrence, then
landed the youngster on the far shore of the bay,
where she amused him with stones and shells at the
water's edge. Monsieur Couillard did his best to

water's edge. Monsieur Couillard did his best to calm his wife, telling her that their son ran no risk with such an expert swimmer. On the contrary, the real danger lay in frightening the girl, as she was very timid. Finding it impossible to calm his wife, he offered to go to the far shore of the bay, on the express condition that if the young Indian swam back with the child during his absence, his wife must not cry out for fear of startling the girl. He leapt on his horse and set off, but the way was long and he was forced to ford the Rivière-du-Sud some ten arpents off, and cross a second stream call Le Bras, after which he had to cover a further twenty arpents before reaching the beach where his son was playing. In the event, the Indian girl had brought the child back safe and sound before he had gone barely half way. Madame Couillard finally realized that her son ran no risk, for she used to tell how the child, who had been of a naturally delicate constitution, owed his health to the cold baths La Grosse gave him in the Saint Lawrence.

Poor Grosse! She would frequently tell us in her patois, as she looked across the fine reach of the Saint-Thomas bay at high tide, "Cross bay many times with my son on back, va! But not now. Me six-foot Seigneur Couillard, now a man in his prime.

In early October of 1808 I was at Saint-Thomas en route for Quebec. It was about two in the afternoon, and we were drinking coffee after our meal when La Grosse came into the room shouting, "A letter from my son! A letter from my son!" It was indeed a letter from Monsieur Couillard, on his way home after a three-week trip to Montreal. He wrote his wife from Quebec to say that a slight indisposition prevented him from coming to the seigneury for several days, and asked her to join him in the city.

Madame Couillard[J] was not particularly worried. "Your glutton of a father has probably dined too well with the priests and other friends in the District of Montreal, old classmates who trotted him around like a fatted calf," she said to her son.[K] "Without me to keep an eye on what he eats, the way I do here, he's probably gorged himself on his beloved pears and grapes, despite all his promises before leaving." She seemed perfectly unconcerned, but when La Grosse cried out, "My son is going to die! My son is going to die!" Madame Couillard burst into tears.

My friend, young Couillard, hurried to his

mother's side. "It's all La Grosse's fault. She's frightened you."

The reproach silenced the poor Indian woman, who leaned her head on her right shoulder and sobbed at length, tears streaming from her dull, half-closed eye. The good woman's forebodings had not been wrong. She died of anxiety and a broken heart at Saint-Thomas, repeating incessantly, "My son is going to die!" About three days later, the excellent Monsieur Couillard expired in my arms in Quebec City, in the street that bears his name.[L] He was very fond of the gentle Indian, and we had been careful not to tell him of her death.

Thus ended two very different lives — master and slave, one the *parfait gentilhomme*, remarkably handsome and learned, the other a poor Indian woman of limited intelligence, ugly, disfigured, and yet each resembling the other in the most precious qualities of heart and soul. They left this earth to meet in heaven, there to receive in equal measure the rewards God grants to virtue.

"Big Louis"

TRANSLATOR'S ADVICE TO THE READER

With consummate but seemingly casual artistry, de Gaspé gives us a series of complex messages in the telling of the Legend of Indian Lorette.

His avowed aim is to record an item of oral history of the remnant of the Huron confederacy that settled at the Jesuit mission of Jeune Lorette, a few miles inland from Quebec City, after the Huron diaspora. This is a legend told with wit, charm and irony. De Gaspé the author projects himself as the easy-going narrator, seeker of tales of old, in a chance encounter with a pensive Huron. Big Louis epitomizes the dilemma of his tribe — the sense of the Hurons' past greatness contrasted with their present plight. He encapsulates the confrontation of two cultures, with brandy and Christianity as symbolic catalysts.

At another level, de Gaspé portrays the thoughtless teasing of even such a sensitive observer as his narrator/self. He lets us hear the colloquial familiarity of the white man's talk compared to the formal phrases of Big Louis. As the two match wits, very human characters emerge from behind the masks of Canadian *gentilhomme* and Noble Savage.

Deepest of all is the author's kindred feeling for a fallen nation in a society where time is sweeping forward as he writes, where railways and industry and progress, the watchwords of the nineteenth century, are relegating both the narrator, last seigneur of Saint-Jean Port-Joli, and his subject, the brave of a fading tribe, to historical footnotes.

The pride of being a full-blooded Indian lay close to the hearts of the dwindling tribesmen, as this story shows. Zacharie Vincent, the Huron artist of Jeune Lorette whose self-portrait is on the cover of this book, styled himself as the last of the full-blooded Hurons.

BIG LOUIS
AND THE LEGEND
OF INDIAN LORETTE[1]

Some forty years ago, everyone in Quebec knew Ohiarekwen,[2] a Huron Indian nicknamed Big Louis. He was a tall man who always walked with shoulders held high, his superb bearing that of a Roman emperor. This born philosopher had never studied at any of our schools, but was nevertheless a formidable logician. He knew that his tribe, now virtually wiped out, had once been a great and powerful nation which had ruled immense stretches of forest, lake, and river. Furthermore, he was aware that the Palefaces had seized these vast possessions, cheating the Indians of even a fief called Saint-Gabriel,[A] as the Hurons had lost the title deeds. And since the Indian knew nothing of the white man's sense of fair play when stripping the weak of their possessions, he naturally enough

A Huron man and woman of the mid eighteenth century. The Hurons had established a farming and trading economy that widened into an empire once they became middlemen between the furtrapping northern Algonkians and the beaver-hungry French. Huronia fell before the onslaught of the white man's diseases and the determined Iroquois foe. By the end of the seventeenth century, a small remnant of Huron Christians had found refuge at the Jesuit mission of Jeune or Indian Lorette, north of Quebec City. From a rare set of watercolours found in the collection of the Abbé Louis-Stanislas Malo (1801–1884). C51 42500, Collection Philéas Gagnon, Bibliothèque de la Ville de Montréal. Photo: Robert Rohonczy.

concluded that they merely acted according to the right of might. On the basis of this premise Big Louis thought he, too, could legally and in good conscience exact a small tribute from time to time — tribute in the form of a little brandy from the counters of the pale-faced female citizens of Quebec and its environs, their natural protectors being absent. He kept himself plentifully supplied in this way, which shows how right I am in asserting that this natural philosopher was also a logician to be reckoned with.

It was about five in the afternoon of a fine June day, around the year 1816, that I came to Saint Ambroise in search of a night's hospitality from the curé, my old friend, Monsieur Bédard, at one time a director of the Little Seminary of Quebec. I was on my way to Lake Saint Charles for a fishing and hunting expedition on the morrow. Monsieur Bédard had been away on missions among the Indians of the Gulf of Saint Lawrence, and I hadn't seen him since his return. But the worthy priest being absent and only expected late in the evening, I pushed on to the Indian village of Lorette, a little way from the presbytery of Saint-Ambroise. Dusk was falling as I walked along the pretty Saint

Charles River that runs by the village, when, a little way above the falls, I beheld the face of a man reflected in the clear waters flowing at his feet. As I drew near I recognized Ohiarekwen, back bowed, arms folded, and chin resting on his chest. Big Louis was sober and pensive.

"Good day, my brother," said I.

But the Huron kept silent, and it was only after a second or third challenge that he muttered a few words in the Indian dialect.

"Aren't you speaking French this evening?" I asked.

"And you," he retorted, giving me back my familiar *tu*, "are you speaking Huron?"

"No," said I shortly.

"Yet it is a beautiful language!" observed the Indian.

"What good would the Huron language be to me?" I countered. "There are twenty Indians at most in your village who can speak it now, and in thirty years there won't be a single one left."

"Have you come here to taunt me with the extinction of my race?" cried the Huron. "Go away!" And he resumed his ruminative stance.

"In thirty years," said I, "you'll all have good

French blood in your veins."

The Indian drew himself up proudly and exclaimed, "In thirty years the Huron blood that
coursed in the veins of my ancestors, as pure as the
clear waters of this cataract, will be as murky as the
stagnant waters of the swamp where frogs paddle!"

I felt all the bitterness of the sarcasm I had
brought upon myself, and a sudden blush suffused
my face. Ohiarekwen had spoken the truth: when
Indian blood ran unsullied in the veins of the
Huron, the Redskins were free of the hideous vices
transmitted by the Palefaces. As he so rightly said,
the proud Huron, once the terror of all the natives
of North America, will vanish. The pure blood that
made the Hurons a race of heroes and dauntless
hunters will resemble the muddy waters of the
swamp.

I was on the point of retiring, thoroughly embarrassed by Big Louis' rude lesson. Still, as I was
rather anxious to learn something about a pet
subject of mine, I said to him, "Let there be peace
between us, my brother. I'm sorry to have given
you pain, and I ask your pardon. Let us think of it
no more."

"But I *do* think of it," retorted the Huron. "I

am on my own ground here. Go away, and trouble my rest no further." And he fell back into his former pensive attitude.

I saw the Indian was deaf to all my arguments, but knowing of one that would surely make him more sociable, I drew from the pocket of my smock the little flask of brandy which was the companion of every hunter of the time — and probably still is, temperance cards notwithstanding.[B]

"Let's have a drink and make peace," said I.

The Huron made no answer at first. But the gurgle of the liquid as I poured it into a small tumbler and the even more persuasive smell of alcohol made him straighten up, and he swallowed nearly half a cup of brandy at one go.

"Your drink is good, Gaspé," said he, handing me back the tumbler.

Surly bear, said I to myself, I knew I could loosen your tongue.

"Now my brother," I resumed aloud, "let's have a friendly chat. Is it true the Hurons of Lorette believe their village will neither grow nor shrink because each night a huge serpent swims in this river from which you drink?"

"Who told you that tale?" replied the Huron

sharply, departing from the cold reserve usual to men of his race.

"Someone who ought to know as well as you: Vincent-Ferrier Sasennio,[3] who studied at the Quebec Seminary and was a boarder with me for several years."

"Sasennio would have done better to read his Latin books, since he wanted to be a priest, rather than jabbering of things he knew nothing about." Big Louis bowed his head again, remaining sullen and silent for a long time despite my pressing questions.

"*Va-t-en*," he said at length. "I don't like you. Five years ago I was at your home, sober and well-spoken, and I said to you, 'Gaspé, Canadian gentlemen like beaver meat during Lent, and Louis is a great hunter!'

" 'True,' you said, 'and if you bring me beaver, I will pay you generously.'

" 'There's no need of that,' I replied, 'but you see, my brother, the hunter can't live in the forest without powder and lead, and he also needs flour to make *sagamité*.[c] Lend me five *piastres* and I will repay you in beaver meat.' You laughed in my face and shouted, aping the Indian manner, '*Hoa!*

An Algonkian man and woman of the mid eighteenth century, from a rare set of watercolours found in the collection of the Abbé Louis-Stanislas Malo (1801–1884). For many years a missionary at Carleton on the Baie des Chaleurs, the abbé worked among the Micmacs of Ristigouche and collected curiosities of the region. He was curé of Bécancour from 1850 to 1884. C51 42499, Collection Philéas Gagnon, Bibliothèque de la Ville de Montréal. Photo: Robert Rohonczy.

You'll drink my money, Louis, and I certainly won't
get fat on the beaver meat *you* bring me!' "[4]

The Huron was evidently very thirsty and deliberately picking a quarrel in order to drink another
tumbler of my brandy. He was too clever to be
unaware of my keen interest in the legend I'd
mentioned, but with the natural deviousness of the
Indian, he went roundabout to gain his end.

"Come now, Louis, let's forget about that beaver
business and be at peace with one another. I'll give
you another drink to ratify the articles of peace as
follows: first, you'll tell me the story of the great
serpent without leaving anything out, and second,
you won't be thirsty until the story is told."

"It is well. Give now," said the Huron brusquely.

I was pretty sure Big Louis had mental reserva-
tions about our treaty, but since I held the key to
the cellar I wasn't unduly concerned.

Ohiarekwen swallowed another tumbler of
brandy and pursed his lips. "Your flask is empty?"
he inquired.

"Wrong, *mon vieux*," I replied. "It's hardly been
touched. When I'm off to the wars I always carry
a healthy supply of good ammunition."

"But," said the Indian, as sharp-witted as ever

and a thought striking him, "if you give me all your brandy, you'll have none left."

"Very true, Louis. Your logic is irrefutable. But don't worry, I'll get my flask refilled by my friend, the curé of Saint-Ambroise. Now tell me the story of the great serpent."

The Huron, reassured on a subject so close to his heart, began his tale as follows.

The Legend of the Great Serpent[D]

"The Hurons were not always the handful of men you see in this village. Their warriors were as numerous as the stars of heaven on a fine night. In other times they made all the nations of North America tremble, from the Great Lakes to the Lower Saint Lawrence. If a Huron camped beside a lake or river, what foe was brave enough to trouble its waters? What enemy hunter dared come within a month's march of his village! When a great Huron chief struck the stake with his hatchet, the trees shook as they do in great storms and their leaves covered the earth for miles around, as though a terrible hurricane had passed through the forest. See," said Ohiarekwen sadly, stretching his arm toward his village. "See what little is left us of so much greatness and glory!"[E]

The Huron's head dropped upon his breast, and for a long time I silently contemplated his reflection in the watery mirror. An artist would have taken him as a model for the statue of affliction.

"Let us leave these painful memories, my brother," said I. "I know the history of your nation, its exploits in war, its greatness and misfortunes. Pray continue with the legend of the great serpent."

"Not long after my tribe left Sillery to come and live on this land, an old Huron, a holy man named Haouroukaeh[5] was returning from the hunt. The night was dark, and the old Huron, being very tired, lay down to sleep beside this river. The French call it the Saint Charles, but the Huron name for it is Oriawenrak,[F] which means river of trout. He fell asleep about an arpent farther down from where we stand now. In the heat of summer, an Indian sleeps just as well under a tree as in a house or cabin, if not better.

"As he slept, the old man had a dream. A beautiful woman dressed in scarlet silk appeared to him, her garnet-red eyes shining like stars.

" 'Haouroukaeh!' she called, her voice as sweet as the nestlings' chirp. 'Haouroukaeh! Before the new leaves bud on the trees of this forest, you will sleep forever.'

" 'Thank you,' replied the Huron in his dream. What blood remained in the veins of old Haouroukaeh, after spilling so much in wars against his enemies and those of the French, ran only drop by drop. His body weighed heavily upon his legs, and his one desire was to rest.

" 'I love you,' said the beautiful woman. 'You are a good Christian, the example of your village, and I will open the gates of heaven for you.'

"Haouroukaeh awoke, but the beautiful woman had disappeared. The next day the old man recounted his dream to the missionary, and the priest told him that Our Lady of Lorette, patron saint of the village, had appeared to him. The old man was overjoyed and told his friends, 'I'll soon go to my heavenly rest. The Blessed Virgin has promised it.'

"After the death of Haouroukaeh several old

men, hoping for pleasant dreams, went and slept beneath the tree where he had seen Our Lady of Lorette, but the Blessed Virgin had no wish to send them visions.

"There have always been wicked people among Palefaces as among Redskins," commented Ohia-rekwen, waxing philosophic, "and it will be so after our time."

"True, my brother," said I. "Such a profound remark shows your knowledge of the human heart, but it has nothing to do with the story of the great serpent."

"You will see that it has," retorted the Huron. "If the white men had not sold the Indians rum, Otsitsot[6], the thieving wolverine whom the whites called Carcajou, would not have visited the great serpent upon us. Otsitsot was a young Huron who would sell his very blanket for firewater, the old people's name for rum. He scoffed at the good Christians who slept beneath Haouroukaeh's tree. 'If I knew Our Lady of Lorette would show me a big bottle of firewater, I'd go and lie under the tree of pleasant dreams myself.'

" 'You speak evil, my brother, and evil will befall you,' the good Christians told him.

The Falls of Lorette on the Saint Charles River, a popular
subject for paintings and lithographs. This version of the
scene was painted in 1854 by Cornelius Krieghoff.
A.49.101.P. Musée du Québec.

Otsitsot only laughed at them, and that very evening found him beneath Haouroukaeh's tree. The night was dark, and he lit a pipe while waiting for sleep. As he lay there, pondering his misfortunes, he heard a sound far to the north, as though the mountain had trembled, followed by a noise like that of a heavy body forcing its way through the forest, crushing trees and bushes in its path. When it passed through our village, the earth shook as it does when the soldiers drag a big canon through the streets of Quebec. A massive form plunged into the river a few feet from Carcajou, and all was silent.[7] For a moment he was blinded by a great flash of light on the river. Then he saw that the light streamed from the eyes of a great serpent, its head lifted some ten feet above the water. The reptile shook its long, horse-like mane, sending out showers of sparks as though from a blazing fir and making its skin of silvery scales shine like little plates of golden mail beneath a bright noon sun. The serpent opened a huge mouth bristling with teeth like bayonets. In a thunderous voice that shook both shores, it cried, 'I detest the Huron race, but I like you, Carcajou the Wolverine. I wish to be your friend and make you prosper.'

" 'Thank you for your preference, my brother,' said Otsitsot through his chattering teeth, 'but couldn't you lower your voice a little? Otherwise it will burst my eardrums and crack my skull.'

" 'I am the little manitou worshipped by the Hurons of old,' retorted the serpent. 'When I am angry, my voice shakes the mountains and churns up the waters of lakes and rivers. But I will soften it, since I like you.' And the manitou's voice became as sweet as the trill of a nightingale.

" 'Black-Robe tells us the little manitou of our fathers was the Christians' devil. Is it true?' asked Carcajou, who instead of our good Lady of Lorette found himself conversing with an alarming neighbour.

" 'I'm surprised you say that,' replied the manitou, 'as I know you laugh at Black-Robe. But listen, my son: the little manitou is as wicked as the Christian devil to his foes, and as gentle as the newborn hare to his friends. I like you, you see, so let us have a quiet talk.'

" 'You frighten me,' replied Carcajou. 'I'm only a man, and it's difficult to have a quiet talk with such a terrifying serpent.'

" 'Oh, that's nothing!' exclaimed the serpent. 'I'll

change you into a lizard, a toad, a grass snake, or a bullfrog. Take your pick.'

" 'Much obliged,' replied Carcajou, 'but I'd rather stay the way I am. Couldn't *you* take some less horrifying form?'

" 'Let my friend's wish be my command,' said the serpent. 'My son, I can take the shape of a polar bear, a wolf, a panther, or a rattlesnake that will charm your ears like the sound of the *chichicouè* [8] — or even a man, if you prefer.'

" 'The last will suit me,' declared Carcajou.

"Scarcely had the words left his mouth than the serpent disappeared and Carcajou found himself face to face with a little old man, some three feet tall, with burning, tiger-cat eyes.

" 'Now,' said the manitou, 'mark my words carefully and profit by them. You are a lazy good-for-nothing, but you will be able to sleep or stroll about all day long with a purse full of money in your coat.'

" 'Good!' exclaimed Carcajou.

" 'You are proud and vain. I will cover you with silk, fine scarlet wool, and silver arm bands like a great chief on a visit to Onontio.'

" 'Good!' replied Carcajou again.

Huron chief Zacharie Vincent of Jeune Lorette painted this portrait of himself and his son in the early nineteenth century. 47.156. Musée du Québec. Photo: Patrick Altman.

" 'You are a drunkard, and in your tobacco pouch you will always find a bottle of firewater that is never empty.'

" '*Hoa!*' cried Carcajou. 'You are a good manitou who takes care of your friends.'

At this point in his tale, my interlocutor pursed his lips and spat two or three times in the Oria-wenrak, either as a mark of burning thirst, or perhaps out of scorn for the water running at our feet. However, when he saw that I studiously ignored this reminder of his dessicated state, he muttered through clenched teeth, "The little man-itou was clever. He knew that once an Indian has tasted firewater, he's always thirsty. The little manitou was generous and gave Carcajou something to quench his thirst when he needed it."

Since I was bent on proving to the Huron that I was as clever and generous as the little manitou, I poured him another tumbler of brandy. Ohiarekwen wet his whistle and continued his legend.

" 'The Great Chief refuses to let you marry his daughter, whom you love, because you are poor, lazy, a drunkard, and a rake. But he'll give her to you once you're rich, otherwise I'll wring his neck.'

" 'Good!' exclaimed Otsitsot, who took a somewhat cavalier view of his future father-in-law's neck.

" 'Black-Robe wants the village chiefs to throw you out, but I'll play him so many bad tricks that he'll leave you alone. I'll send weasels to throttle his hens, and rats and mice to eat his meat and flour or tear holes in his clothes, books, and papers. Every night I'll bedevil his house with such a witches' sabbath of caterwauling tomcats from twenty leagues around, that he'll be unable to sleep and will leave your village.'

" 'Good!' said Carcajou — 'although if he doesn't sleep at night, he'll sleep during the day. Wouldn't it be better to wring his neck?'

" 'That's my business, not yours,' retorted the manitou angrily. 'I'll change myself into an invisible wolf, and then you'll see what a dreadful din all the village dogs make, howling all day long around Black-Robe's house!'

" 'Good!' exclaimed Carcajou. 'But what must I do to obtain these boons?'

" 'A mere nothing, my son. Renounce the Christian faith and pray to the little manitou, as did the Hurons of old.'

" 'But there is something that bothers me, my father,' said Otsitsot. 'When I die, where will I sleep the first night?'

" 'In my paradise, my son.'

" 'Can one drink firewater in your paradise?'

" 'What a question!' cried the manitou. 'There
are so many liquor swillers in my paradise that I'm
obliged to keep them dead drunk from morning to
night, and from night to morning, otherwise they'd
make a fearful racket!'

" 'What a wonderful time they must have!'
remarked Carcajou.[9] 'I too would like to enter your
paradise and worship you, my father.'

" 'Very well,' said the manitou, 'but mark my
words, if you return to the Christian faith I'll have
my revenge on you and all your race. To begin with
I'll wring your neck. I'll swim in the Oriawenrak
every day, and your village will never get bigger or
smaller.' The manitou spat in the river. 'In a
hundred years the proportion of Huron to French
blood running in your veins will be no more than
my spittle mingled with the waters of the Oriawenrak.'

"With these words, the little old man disappeared. The great serpent lifted its head for an
instant above the water, shooting forth flames, then
vanished in the river."

A pensive Huron wears trade or treaty silver armbands
and medallion in this portrait by Coke Smyth (c. 1840).
McCord Museum of Canadian History, McGill University.

"What did Carcajou do then?" I asked, seeing Ohiarekwen[10] bow his head once more.

"He drank when he was thirsty," retorted the Huron gruffly.

I wish the manitou would wring *your* neck, thought I. You mean to empty my flask without finishing your legend, but we'll see about that!

"Listen to me, Louis. A Huron brave is a man of his word, and therefore I've relied on yours. But since you refuse to stand by our agreement, good evening to you, and may the devil quench your thirst if he's one of your friends!"

"Stop! Stop! my brother," called the Huron. "My heart is sore at the thought of it all, you understand, and it makes me sad."

"I understand, Louis. You want to drown your sorrows and I'd gladly believe the remedy would work. But a Huron brave must rise above these troubles. If you're a man of your word, tell me what happened to Carcajou, who has no doubt been in the devil's clutches for many a year."

The Indian drew himself up proudly. "Ohiarekwen is as true to his promise as the tide from the great lake that flows up the Saint Lawrence each day. But as for Carcajou, the old ones disagreed about his fate, some saying yes, the devil got him, others no. He left the village the very night he spent with the manitou and only returned much later. By this time he was rich, and he gave a feast lasting eight days. The rum ran like the waters of the Oriawenrak in the village. Ah! those were the days! The young people amused themselves at Carcajou's expense, and didn't worry about where the money came from. But the old people's tongues wagged. Some said he'd found a treasure, others that he'd sold his soul to the devil, and since he was often absent for long periods, some thought he was fishing with two lines and had become a spy for both French and English, who were always at war in those days.

"After thoroughly enjoying himself for years, Otsitsot fell ill and asked for Aharatenha, the village doctor.

"You know Aharatenha, my brother?" the Huron asked me. "The one the Canadians call Coska?"

"Of course I know Coska," I retorted. "A clever, well-spoken man — a native doctor, as he himself says when tending the Canadians. But surely he wasn't the man Carcajou called for?"

"No, no," said Louis. "What a foolish thing for a lawyer to say, my brother. You see, all the

Aharatenhas knew good medicine, and this was perhaps the great-great-grandfather of the one you know.

"Well, when Aharatenha came with his bag full of healing herbs, he looked into the eyes of Otsitsot, sat down beside his bed, and muttered something through his teeth.

" 'What are you saying, my brother?' asked the sick man.

" 'I am saying,' said the doctor, 'get your snow-shoes ready, for you have a long trail to cover.'

" 'But Aharatenha,' answered Otsitsot faintly, 'you can see very well I'm much too weak to walk on snowshoes!'

" 'Since you don't understand me, my brother, I'll have to speak more plainly,' snapped the doctor. 'You may see the sun set this evening, but you'll not see it rise tomorrow morning.'

" 'You know good medicine, Aharatenha. Give me some to drink, and if you cure me, I'll give you a great deal of money!'

" 'If you gave me a pile of money as big as the northern mountains, I still couldn't do a thing to save your life. The firewater is burning your stomach, and if I made you drink the whole Oriawenrak, it wouldn't quench the fire that's devouring you any more than a little goblet of water could put out a bucketful of the pitch we use to caulk our bark canoes. You'd get nothing but flames.'

" '*Hoa!*' wailed Carcajou, hiding his head beneath his blanket.

" 'Now listen to me,' said Aharatenha. 'You have always lived like a dog, and if you don't want to roast in hell once you're dead, on a brazier that all the snows of Canada and all the water in the great lake will never put out, send as fast as you can for Black-Robe.'

"At that very moment, a little old man pushed open the door of the house and began shouting, 'Hurry up, Otsitsot, send for Black-Robe!' And he fell to laughing in such a mocking, diabolical manner that everyone present shook with fear.

" 'I'm choking!' cried Carcajou. 'Somebody's strangling me! Quick! Get Black-Robe!'

Someone ran to get the missionary, but he was away from home. By the time he returned, Carcajou was as cold as a bullfrog in Lake Saint Charles. The priest recounted how a little old man had come and told him to go to Quebec as quickly as possible, for his brother had fallen suddenly ill and wanted to see him before dying. The old people believed the devil had played a trick, for when the priest got to Quebec he found his brother perfectly healthy."

"Louis, I was right in telling you the devil would finally get that dog of a Carcajou in his clutches."

"What do you know about it?" responded the Huron slowly. "It's none of your business, nor mine. Perhaps he had a good time before dying."

Hearing Ohiarekwen express such charitable Christian sentiments, I thought he must have forgotten the second article of our treaty, and accordingly I bade him good evening. He promptly reminded me of it, however, and I was obliged to pour him one for the road.

"General Wolfe's Statue"

Speculating on historical details of old Quebec was a favourite pastime among the elderly citizens of the city in the mid nineteenth century, and de Gaspé was no exception. Modern readers may wonder why this statue of General Wolfe should have been a subject of such keen interest.

The colourful statue, which may be seen today in the library of the Literary and Historical Society of Quebec on the Rue Stanislas in Quebec City, was a familiar sight on Rue Saint-Jean for nearly a century. Carved in the commanding spirit of a figure on a bowsprit, its site came to be called "Wolfe's Corner" by generations of Quebec citizens, French and English alike.

Its appeal was such that, according to C.-B. Casgrain in a paper read before the Royal Society of Canada, "In 1838–39, some playful *middies* of the Royal Navy took down the statue in a youthful freak, and gave it a sea trip to Calcutta on a man-of-war, whence it came back with a broken arm." After reposing for a time in what is now the Garrison Club, "it was restored and replaced in its niche."

The aging statue was restored and presented to the Quebec Literary and Historical Society in 1898 by the Bell Telephone Company, then owner of the building. A second General Wolfe by the wood-carver Jobin took the place of the first. It braved the rigours of Quebec winters until February 1964, when a flurry of local press articles remarked on the disappearance of the Quebec landmark. Had the General been kidnapped once again? Was the removal of the British hero the result of a threatening phone call? It was being cleaned, said a noncommittal spokesman for the owner of the building, Esmond Léonard. *Le Soleil* revealed that there were two statues, and reviewed the history of the original. Shortly afterward, the spruced-up second statue went on view in the museum of the Royal 22nd Regiment — Canada's legendary "Van Doos" — in the Quebec Citadel. It became the property of the museum in 1977, a legacy under the late Monsieur Léonard's will.

GENERAL WOLFE'S STATUE[1]

I was staying downriver with my son-in-law, Seigneur Fraser,[A] at   Rivière-du-Loup, when I read in
the *Journal du Québec* of September 19 last the
following article:

"A reader writes from the District of Trois-
Rivières as follows:

" 'I have just read an extract from the *Mémoires
de P. A. de Gaspé*, esquire, in the *Echo du Cabinet.*
In it I find the account of his scuffles with Ives
Cholet,[B] but he has neglected to mention that the
city of Quebec is indebted to this sculptor for the
statue of General Wolfe that adorns the corner of
the Rue du Palais and the Rue Saint-Jean.' "

Although this omission is a very minor sin, I felt
it deserved attention nonetheless. I was then anxious for this same paper to publish a statement
explaining that, until the very day, I had no idea

Joseph Légaré (1797–1855), one of Canada's first native-born landscape painters of note, gave full reign to Romantic imagination in this painting of Wolfe's statue in a woodland setting, with a carefully posed Indian for company. The fluid stance of the figure as well as the raised right arm (rather than the left) resemble the work now in the Museum of the Royal 22nd Regiment in the Quebec Citadel rather than the original. This second statue replaced the first after the latter was donated to the Literary and Historical Society of Quebec in 1898. A.55.109.P. Musée du Québec. Photo: Patrick Altman.

that General Wolfe's statue was the work of Ives Cholet. For a reason which the reader will perhaps appreciate, I preferred to wait until returning to Quebec. It seemed to me the history of this statue from days of old might interest the present generation, and that I would be more likely to find worthwhile information on the subject once back in the city. However, poor Ives Cholet and his statue — for there *is* a statue — had already slipped my mind when my attention was again caught by the following article, published in the same paper on September 22.

"Our correspondent from the District of Trois-Rivières, whose words on Ives Cholet and General Wolfe's statue we quoted the other day, has written us on the 20th concerning the same subject:

" 'You referred to my little note about Ives Cholet and General Wolfe's statue, which adorns the corner of the Rue Saint-Jean and the Rue du Palais. You may wish to complete this note by adding that Cholet and his brothers, carpenters and sculptors, had a shop in the Rue Saint-Louis. They did some work for an English innkeeper named Hipps who wanted a statue of General Wolfe for a sign. The officers of the 15th regiment were garrisoned in

Quebec at the time, and they supplied the brothers with a likeness of Wolfe in a commanding pose. Cholet worked as best he could under their direction, and the combined result of their instructions and his labour was the statue in question. People used to say it bore a fair likeness, not to General Wolfe, but to portraits of this glorious leader that were once circulated.' "C

While morally certain that the statue of General Wolfe had not been carved by the Ives Cholet whom I knew, this second note was so precise that it shook my confidence, although I was still not convinced. How could I really believe that the members of the Cholet family, with whom I was familiar for some twenty years, would have said nothing about a statue that we had spoken of a hundred times, and that would have been a source of pride. True, Ives was a taciturn fellow, but his brother Hyacinth was a chatterbox and something of a braggart. Is it likely he would have held his tongue on such a subject? I boarded for nearly five years with his three sisters, the Widow Corbin, Catiche (Catherine), and Charlotte Cholet. They used to take immense pride in showing off two mahogany-framed mirrors, one carved by Ives and the other by Hyacinthe. Surely they would have mentioned Wolfe's statue in this connection?

I was in a hurry to return to Quebec and clear up this mystery. If any one could tell me, I knew it would be Assistant Commissary General Thompson,[D] born in Quebec City and its oldest living citizen. I was not wrong to wait, for here is his note — an extract from a journal kept by his father, a veteran of General Wolfe's army who died in Quebec in the year 1831 at the patriarchal age of ninety-nine.[E]

"We had a loyal fellow in Quebec, one George Phipps (Hips), a butcher, who own'd that house at the corner of Palace and John Streets, still called 'Wolfe's Corner,' and it happened to have a niche, probably intended for the figure of some saint;[2] he was very anxious to fill it up, and he thought he could have nothing better than the statue of *General Wolfe*; but he did not know how to set about getting one. At last he finds out two French sculptors, who were brothers, of the name of Chaulette,[F] and he asked me if I thought I could direct them how to make the likeness of the General in wood. I said I would, at all events, have no objection to undertake it, and accordingly they, the

Over 200 years old, the much-restored statue of General
Wolfe is reminiscent of a ship's figurehead as it gazes
benignly over the heads of visitors to the library of the
Literary and Historical Society of Quebec. A local landmark for over 100 years, it originally stood in a niche at
the corner of the Rue Saint-Jean and Rue du Palais. In
1898 it was presented to the Society, and another statue
was commissioned to take its place. An engraving of the
statue in its niche can be seen in the Museum of the Royal
22nd Regiment in the Quebec Citadel. Photo: W.B.
Edwards Inc., by kind permission of the Literary and
Historical Society of Quebec.

Chaulettes, tried several sketches, but they made a poor job of it after all.

"The front face is no likeness at all, and the profile is all they could hit upon, and which is good. The body gives a poor idea of the General, who was tall and straight as a rush, so that, after my best endeavours to describe his person (and I knew it well), and for which purpose I attended every day at their workshop. . . . I say we made a poor General Wolfe of it."[G]

Well, I thought to myself, I must indeed be a naturally cussed octagenarian to spurn such convincing evidence as this. Yet I shook my head despite this sagacious reflection. My memory was not playing me false, I felt sure. How could I forget such an important detail when I remember the most insignificant things about my childhood and youth? With this in mind, I asked my venerable friend, Assistant Commissary General Thompson, whether he knew the same Cholet family I had known.

"Certainly," said he. "The two brothers were carpenters."

"Do you believe these two carpenters carved General Wolfe's statue?" I asked.

"Given their age, I don't think so," he replied.

"My father often told me that Phipps had put up this statue before the Catholic cathedral was rebuilt. It had been burned in the siege of 1759. Phipps was a butcher by trade, and I must say to his shame that he appropriated the church ruins as a pen for his livestock."

Mr. Thompson, one of the most reputable men I know, seemed pained at making this admission. But for me it shed a gleam of light.

Now, thought I after this conversation, I'll simply find out exactly when the Quebec cathedral was rebuilt, then get extracts of my Cholet brothers' baptismal certificates, and the mystery of who carved the statue will be solved. I put the proposition to my eminent relative and friend, the Abbé Casgrain,[H] and two days later the indefatigable abbé sent me the information I desired.

"The cathedral was completely rebuilt between 1746 and 1748," he wrote, "but was burned again in 1759 during the siege of Quebec. Once the parishioners had returned to the city, services were held in the Ursulines' church until December 4, 1764, and then in the seminary chapel rebuilt after the siege. The cathedral was rebuilt between 1768 and 1771, and dedicated on April 14, 1771."

Let us look now at the Cholet family genealogy, which I also owe to the Abbé Casgrain's kindness.

"The first Cholet to come to Canada was Pierre Cholet, shipwright, son of Jacques Cholet and Marie Blanchard of the parish of Saint-George [sic] on the Ile d'Oléron in the diocese of Xaintes.¹ On February 4, 1743, he married Marie-Catherine Pelot, *dite* Laflèche. They had issue:

"Pierre, born April 26, 1743, deceased September 12 of the same year.

"Timothée, born October 77, 1744.

"Louis-François, born March 25, 1746, deceased January 16, 1748.

"Marie-Catherine, born October 19, 1747.

"Marguerite, born March 25, 1749.

"Pierre, born October 20, 1750.

"Louis, born September 13, 1751, died the 19th of the same month, 1751.

"Ignace, born October 20, 1752.

"Jean, born December 20, 1754.

"Louise-Charles [sic], born April 25, 1756.

"Dominique, born January 22, 1758, died January 23, 1758.

"Ives, born April 8, 1761."

These two authentic extracts show that, even

Possibly a portrait of Sergeant James Thompson (1733–1830), last surviving veteran of the Battle of the Plains of Abraham. A military engineer by profession, James Thompson was a well-known figure in Quebec. He had helped repulse the attacking Americans outside the walls of Quebec City on December 31, 1775, and for many years kept the sword of Richard Montgomery, the slain American commander, as a relic. For most of his active career, Thompson kept a comprehensive journal which was subsequently donated to the Literary and Historical Society of Quebec. This journal is now housed in the Quebec Archives. From the A.J.B. Milborne Collection, Public Archives of Canada, PA-148846.

supposing Wolfe's statue had not been carved until the parish church was consecrated in 1771, Ives Cholet could not be the sculptor, since he was barely ten years old at the time. If we accept Mr. Thompson's version, he would have been barely five years old. So here I am, absolved of all blame for omitting this detail about Ives Cholet.

Hyacinthe Cholet, whom I mentioned earlier, looked much younger than his brother Ives. He often told me how he and the urchins of Quebec used to play at soldiers while the Americans were besieging the city in 1775. "We were divided into two camps — the English and American armies," he used to say. "The snowball fights were tremendous, and we made as much noise as the armies that really were besieging and defending Quebec." Hyacinthe's baptismal certificate is missing from the registers, but this is merely further proof that he was a very young child in 1771, and so the honour of working on General Wolfe's statue can't revert to him, either.[3]

One of the Cholet brothers was killed in a brawl on the Beauport parish feast day, but the family never spoke of him. His foe split his skull with a bottle. I suppose it was a painful subject and a sad memory for them. However, my own family often described the unfortunate young man's lamentable end, adding that out of regard for the murderer's sister and aged mother, the Cholet family never laid any formal charge. But innocent blood cried to heaven for vengeance and the hand of God weighed heavily on the murderer. The avenging furies entered D_____'s soul, and with them the thirst for bloodshed. He was sentenced in Montreal to a long prison term for a second assault, having fired a pistol pointblank at a man whom he suspected of wanting to arrest him for debt. Far from from coming to his senses, he emerged more bloodthirsty than ever after serving his term. D_____ then entered the service of a North West trader, I think it was, and murdered his master. He was brought back to Quebec, condemned to death for this second murder, and executed in Montreal. My friend Major Lafleur, who seems to be a walking encyclopedia of the old days, yesterday showed me the house in Quebec where the mother and sister of D_____ lived until the heartbroken women betook themselves to the exile of New Orleans.

It's not clear to me which of the Cholets was murdered by D_____. According to Quebec parish registers, it must have been either Pierre, born in 1750, or Jean, born in 1754. I have not seen the burial certificates.

It was on All Souls' Day of the year 1794 that I went to board with the Cholet sisters. We gathered for evening prayers. Old Catiche (Catherine) recited the usual prayers and the rosary for All Souls, then added, "Let us pray for the soul of poor Ignace." Who was Ignace, I asked? "One of our brothers. He went off travelling some twenty years ago," she replied, using an expression common among the populace. "The last we heard of him, he'd died in a shipwreck."

The next summer, a somewhat tipsy sailor came into the house just as dusk was falling. He leaned back against the door and started talking English. No one understood a word, apart from the *goddams* with which he liberally peppered his conversation. The poor old spinsters had only me for company.

"Run and get Hyacinthe," they said, taking fright.

I tried to leave, but the sailor shoved me back.

"Hove to, cabinboy!" said he in French, pointing to the second-storey window of the room we were in, "or I'll toss you over the bulwarks."

Although the women were a little comforted at hearing him speak their tongue, they took his threat seriously and begged him not to harm the child. "What do you want?" they asked him.

"What do I want? Thunder and lightning! Why, to kiss you both, even though you're somewhat weathered by years of rough seas!"

"You're not very polite for a Frenchman," retorted Catiche, who was nudging fifty.

"Well, blow me down! It seems you don't take kindly to being told your rigging's been battered by the waves! But no hard feelings, mind. I've come to give you news of a jolly fellow you used to call your brother Ignace, twenty years agone."

"What!" shrieked the two sisters. "Poor Ignace is still alive? And us praying for him and having masses said for the repose of his soul!"

"Masses and prayers won't do him no good at this point, m'lovelies, since he's not much better a fellow today than he was when he bid you *adieux* these twenty years past — unless you can credit them to those you'll have said when the bo'sun makes him walk the plank in the wide Atlantic with a thirty-pound cannonball tied to his feet."

"Sit down, Master Sailor, and tell us about poor

Ignace," said Charlotte.

"May a shark eat me raw if these two nitwits don't recognize me! Come on, come kiss Ignace, send for Hyacinthe, Ives, and Marguerite (the Widow Corbin) if they're not down in Davy Jones' locker by now."

Soon the whole family had gathered to celebrate with an improvised supper at the Widow Corbin's home. Ignace, who was a ships's carpenter, didn't return to his vessel until next morning.

Although Ignace Cholet had been at sea for twenty years, he wasn't a regular sailor. As a ship's carpenter he enjoyed certain privileges, one of the most important being that he was safe from the warships' press-gangs, a danger for all sailors. This was the only time I ever saw him, for it was vacation time, and when I returned to Quebec he had gone. His family never saw hide nor hair of him again.

This, then, is the only Cholet brother known to me — albeit he passed like a shadow in my childhood memories — who might have worked on the statue of General Wolfe. He was born in 1752 and would have been nineteen when the statue was carved, although if we accept Mr. Thompson's version, Ignace would have been only fifteen or sixteen. The statue is certainly the work of my Cholet family, nevertheless, for it was the only one of that name in Quebec. All the Canadians knew one another in those days. With only one parish church, it could hardly have been otherwise.

But to return to my story, how was it that the Cholet family never mentioned a statue carved by one of their brothers? I find it a complete mystery, although the reader may not care one way or the other. As for my old friend Ives, I ask forgiveness of his shade if I am guilty of an oversight — but in that case how can we account for his being only ten when the statue was carved?

The statue of General Wolfe is the work of two Cholet brothers — of that I have no doubt. The explanation may be that the brother who was so barbarously murdered worked on the statue. Might the family not have shrunk from the thought of linking him with a work that evoked such bitter memories?

Notes and Annotations

NOTES TO THE INTRODUCTION

A Luc Lacourcière, "L'Enjeu des *Anciens Canadiens,*" *Les Cahiers des dix* (1967) 22: 223–254.

B Pierre-Georges Roy, *La Famille Aubert de Gaspé* (Lévis: J.E. Mercier, 1907), p. 174.

C Lacourcière, p. 245–246.

D J.-B.-A. Ferland, *Cours d'histoire du Canada*, vol. 1 (Quebec: Augustin Côté, 1861), pp. 97, 100, as cited in Serge Gagnon, *Quebec and its Historians: 1840–1920*, trans. Yves Brunelle (Montreal: Harvest House, 1982), p. 58.

Yellow-Wolf, Malecite Chieftain of Old

FOOTNOTES TO THE FIRST EDITION

1. God of war.

2. The Indians used the expression "scouting" [*aller à la découverte*] for going on the warpath. With both Indians and Canadians of old, war involved surprise and ambush.

3. *Sic.* [Original editor's note.]

4. In the author's youth, the Indians went in such terror of the smallpox that Canadian women, who when alone feared visiting Indians, often shouted, "We have the smallpox here!" and the Indians would take to their heels. This cruel malady took a terrible toll among them, and it was rare for an infected Indian to survive.

Yellow-Wolf, Malecite Chieftain of Old

TRANSLATOR'S ANNOTATIONS

[A.] The once-migratory Malecites (or Maliseets) are an Amerindian people closely related to the Algonkian-speaking Micmacs, now mainly living in southern New Brunswick. At one time their hunting territory reached to the Saint Lawrence River opposite Tadoussac. They were members of the Abenaki confederacy and therefore allied with the French against the Iroquois confederacy, which sided with the English in the bloody fur trade wars. See Jacques Rousseau and George W. Brown, "The Indians of Northeastern North America," in *Readings in Canadian History: Pre-Confederation*, 2d ed. (Toronto: Holt, Rinehart and Winston of Canada Limited, 1986), p. 4.

[B.] The de Gaspé manor house near Saint-Jean Port-Joli stood among shore meadows on the south bank of the Saint Lawrence River, below Quebec City. The back or north side of the house overlooked fields running down to the river and the beach where Yellow-Wolf pitched his tent. The south or front side faced inland toward the nearby road, on the far side of which rose a steep, rocky bluff or cape.

[C.] It is not easy for modern readers to understand in context the documented cruelty of many Amerindian groups toward captives. In principle, the brave sufferer gained inestimable honour in the afterworld and therefore welcomed and even incited torture, much as the early Christians welcomed martyrdom. The coward, by contrast, brought dishonour to his name and family. The Malecites, including the women, were as ferocious as their enemies toward captives, according to Captain William Pote (1745) who found himself in this unenviable position. Another captive, John Gyles, recounted how "my unfortunate brother [and] . . . another Englishman . . . were both tortured at a stake by fire for some time; then their noses and ears were cut off, and they [were] made to eat them. After this they were burnt to death at the stake." Wilson D. Wallis and Ruth Sawtell Wallis, *The Malecite Indians of New Brunswick* (Ottawa: Dept. of Northern Affairs and Natural Resources, 1957), p. 9.

D. De Gaspé inserts the word "skirts" in brackets to define the word *matchiotes.*

Woman of the Foxes

FOOTNOTES TO THE FIRST EDITION

1. The Iroquois.

2. Monsieur Jean-Baptiste Couillard [b. 1729], seigneur of Saint-Thomas and Saint-Pierre, was killed by the English on September 14, 1759, as was Monsieur Joseph Couillard, ecclesiastic [a cousin], and both were buried in the church of Saint-Thomas, September 28, 1759. (*Note by the Abbé Tanguay.*) [Tanguay's *Dictionnaire généalogique* gives September 22, 1759, as the date of burial.]

3. Known equally as Berthier or Bellechasse Bay.

4. I never knew this Monsieur Couillard, and some readers may feel I have assigned him a rather arbitrary rôle. However I did know his son, also Jean-Baptiste [d. 1808], and I can vouch for having painted *him* to the life. Although

very scholarly, he was anything but a pedant. At the same time he thought, with a certain childlike naivete, that all the world was as knowledgeable as himself. When I was barely eleven, he held forth to me on the abstract sciences and subjects of advanced philosophy, unmindful of my father's expostulations.

"Couillard, it's quite obvious the child doesn't know what you're talking about!" said my father, hitching me up on his shoulders.

"He understands me perfectly well, *cher ami*," replied Monsieur Couillard, looking at me with an air of angelic sweetness unlike any other I ever saw. "Isn't that so, Philippe — you understand me?"

I bobbed my head like a jack-in-the-box, unwilling to hurt his feelings and perhaps inspired by a touch of vanity.

"I knew Philippe understood me, *cher ami!*" cried Couillard, looking at my father.

If a farmer expressed to Monsieur Couillard his fear that the full August moon would harm the field peas, the vegetables, and whatnot, the "Jean-Baptiste," as they call farmers in Canada, would be treated to a forty-five-minute dissertation on astronomy. Only after travelling through the entire zodiac had the farmer any chance of escaping. It is because I consider Captain Couillard's character — that of the unintentional pedant, if I may express it thus — so unique that I describe him here. It is far from my intention to mock the memory of a *gentilhomme* possessed of all the qualities and virtues that honour the human race.

5. Civilized man needs a lot of time to build a house, but the primitive Indian needs scarcely an hour. A four-seater

birch-bark canoe was almost always sufficient to carry an Indian family, which rarely consisted of more than four members — father, mother, and one or two children. There was never any surplus baggage, either, for all was reduced the bare necessities. A gun, a powder horn, a pouch of lead, a small kettle, a dog about the size of a fox, and a roll of birchbark made up the cargo. A pole seven or eight feet long was stuck in the ground, and a fine wigwam was soon constructed to provide shelter for the whole family.

⁶· The magnificent maple grove that now crowns the western bluff of Berthier Bay must have stretched right to the Bellechasse River in other times. This pretty river empties into the southern end of the small bay, after gushing forth, much to the spectator's surprise, from the middle of a little wood containing many different species of trees and shrubs.

This fine domain has been in my family for about seventy years. My late maternal uncle, Xavier-Roch de Lanaudière, (deputy adjutant-general of militia) and co-seigneur of Saint-Valier, struck by the beauty of the place, bought the land and built a *pied-à-terre* toward the middle of the bay shore, on a mound about a hundred feet back from the river. His two sisters inherited it after his death and built an addition to the little house, later ceding the domain to their nephew, the late Mr. John Young, who also built a considerable addition onto this charming "cottage."

This fine property now belongs to my son-in-law, the Honourable Charles Alleyn, sheriff of the District of Quebec, who bought it in order to keep it in the family. And despite the size of the cottage, it is still too small for his hospitable Irish heart. I have spent delightful evenings seated around a small fire on the shore, chatting with him and his wife, while their children played on the sandy beach, their cries of joy being — in the words of a great poet — so shrill that they seemed to be in physical pain.

7. The price of a beaver coat in my childhood was 50 louis.

Woman of the Foxes

TRANSLATOR'S ANNOTATIONS

A. André Marie Chénier (1762–1794), a French writer born in Constantinople, was active in the early days of the Revolution, but turned against its excesses and was later guillotined. His *Poèmes, Élégies, Idylles* first appeared in 1819.

B. Amerindian slaves were not an unusual phenomenon in New France at this time. Slavery was so customary among the Indians themselves, according to historian Marcel Trudel, citing Lohantan (*Voyages*, letter of May 26, 1688), that the terms for "prisoner" and "slave" were synonymous. The Pawnee tribes of the Nebraska region were a popular target for the supply of slaves by Amerindian middlemen. In 1709 the ownership and trading of blacks and Pawnees was legalized in New France, and the French word for Pawnee — *panis* — came to mean an Amerindian slave, although various civil registers show that about a third came from other tribes. Trudel found a total of 2,472 Amerindian slaves recorded, over two-thirds during the French régime.

The Foxes, an Iroquoian tribe originally found on the western shore of Lake Michigan, began appearing as slaves following hostilities between the Iroquois and the French in 1716 and 1730. The Abenakis, allies of the French, were in the habit of raiding English colonies and capturing Indian and black slaves whom they usually sold in Montreal.

A number of owners freed their slaves, although where long association and ties of affection existed, slaves were not always willing to be freed. Lisette, the mulatto slave purchased by de Gaspé's grandfather Philippe-Ignace around 1787, indignantly rejected her liberty: "She didn't give *that* for her emancipation, said she, snapping her fingers, for she had as much right to stay in the house where she was brought up as her master and all his family."

The *panisse* of this tale, baptized Marie-Geneviève Couillard, was probably one of the last Amerindians to die a slave. Marcel Trudel, *L'Esclavage au Canada française: Histoire et conditions de l'esclavage* (Quebec: Presses de l'Université de Laval, 1960), pp. 6, 41, 60, 73, 312, 313, 318, 329. Philippe-Joseph Aubert de Gaspé, *Les Anciens Canadiens* (1863; Montreal: Librairie Beauchemin Ltée, 1913), p. 248.

^{C.} Abbé Cyprien Tanguay (1819–1902), priest, archivist, statistician, was the author of a number of works, including the valuable *Dictionnaire généalogique des familles canadiennes.* (Lejeune, *Dictionnaire générale du Canada*, II, 695.)

^{D.} Saint-Thomas de Montmagny, known in early times as Pointe à la Caille, now Montmagny. Located a few miles below Quebec on the South Shore of the Saint Lawrence

River, it lay within the seigneurie of Rivière-du-Sud.

ᴱ· Captain Jean-Baptiste Couillard de l'Épinay (1729–1759) was *seigneur primitif* (principal seigneur among co-seigneurs) of the fief of Rivière-du-Sud, and a captain of militia. We may consider this tale as being loosely based on fact, since the author himself notes that he is using the character traits of Captain Couillard's son, whom he knew well, in portraying the father (see author's note 4 above).

For the record, however, the historical Captain Couillard was only 17 in 1746, around the time of the first episode. Possibly the actual purchase of the slave occured after 1754, as the story refers to the captain's "late" father's gun and powder horn. A more appropriate figure would have been the captain's father, Louis Couillard de l'Épinay (1694–1754), seigneur of Saint-Thomas and Saint-Pierre. He would have been about 52 at the time, his own father was dead, and he had a small son of six, details that are more in keeping with the episode.

Couillards and de Gaspés were friends and South Shore neighbours for generations. Captain Jean-Baptiste Couillard was a family hero who fought at the Plains of Abraham and was killed the following day (September 14, 1759) in a skirmish with a party of 60 English soldiers, while returning to Saint-Thomas to defend his home. The British reportedly ravaged everything in Saint-Thomas except the church. Burial services for the mutilated bodies of Couillard and his friends were held a week later.

The young widow, Marie-Geneviève Alliés (b. 1739, m. 1755) took over the management of the seigneurie with the help of her father, the notary André Alliés, who then came to live at the manor house with his wife and remained there until his death. No doubt, as custom and circumstances dictated, such family members as André-Thomas Couillard (b. 1738), a young priest and brother of the slain seigneur, made their home at the manor as well.

Madame Couillard had given birth to the couple's only child (three others had died at birth) two months before her husband's death. This child was the Jean-Baptiste Couillard de l'Épinay (1759–1808) described in note 4, father of the author's lifelong friend, Dr. Antoine-Gaspard Couillard.

Abbé Azarie Couillard Després, *La Première Famille française au Canada, ses alliés et ses descendants* (Montreal: Imprimerie de l'École Catholique des Sourds-Muets, Mile-End, 1906), p. 297, and *Histoire des seigneurs de la Rivière-du-Sud et de leurs alliés* (Saint-Hyacinthe: Imprimerie de "La Tribune," 1912), pp. 278, 283, 321, 343. Pierre-Georges Roy, *Bulletin des recherches historiques*, 24 (1918), pp. 372–374. Abbé Cyprien Tanguay, *Dictionnaire généalogique des familles canadiennes depuis la fondation de la colonie jusqu'à nos jours*, vol. 3 (Montreal: Eusèbe Senécal & Fils, 1887), pp. 162–165.

F. "Canot" (*Divers*, p. 12). This generally meant "canoe" before the middle of the nineteenth century, according to J.M. Lemoine. However, de Gaspé describes the craft in this tale as having sails, oars and a tiller, and we can assume he had in mind the type of small rowboat with sail of the French régime shown in such early illustrations as "View of the town of Trois-Rivières in Canada . . . ." (anon., 1721), Edward E. Ayer Collection, the Newberry Library, Chicago.

Numerous drawings and prints show birchbark canoes as a common form of being ferried about in the days before bridges crossed the Saint Lawrence, and de Gaspé gives an amusing anecdote on the subject in his notes to chapter 1 of *Les Anciens Canadiens*. *Records of Our History: Taking Root, Canada from 1700 to 1760* ed. André Vachon (Ottawa: Public Archives Canada, 1985), p. 62. J.M. Le Moine, *The Chronicles of the St. Lawrence* (Montreal: Dawson Bros., 1880), 344, 345.

G. "Even as Christians, the Abenakis retained their war-like habits and natural ferocity," wrote historian Thomas-M. Charland. Father Joseph-Anselme Maurault, whose lengthy *Histoire des Abenakis* appeared in 1866, remarked the "the terror they inspired among the English colonies and the Iroquois is a most amazing thing" for a people "who never numbered more than 3,000." The Abenakis originally came from the region of the Kennebec and Penobscot Rivers in Maine. At their own request, Jesuit missions were established among them between 1646 and 1660. Their early relations with the English were soured by the latter's refusal to come to their aid against the Iroquois. The Abenaki eventually retreated to the protection of the Saint-François, Bécancour, and Mississquoi River missions, vowing implacable vengeance against the English. They became the firm allies of the French. The famous Deerfield massacre was but one of the many raids in which they were involved, usually with the official backing or participation of the French. The English repaid the attackers with such expeditions as Major Roger's bloody raid on the Saint-François mission in 1759. Prisoners (Indian, black, or white) were often sold, sometimes in return for a government bounty, or to Canadians who used them as domestic servants. The Abenakis hunted beaver for the fur trade, but otherwise had a fairly fragile economy based on hunting, fishing, gathering and some agriculture. Thomas-M. Charland, *Histoire des Abénakis d'Odanak (1635–1937)* (Montreal: Les Éditions du Lévrier, 1964), pp. 11–13, 51–52, 49, 53, 54, 58–60. Joseph-Anselme Maurault, *Histoire des Abenakis, depuis 1605 jusqu'à nos jours* (Sorel: Imprimé à l'atélier typographique de la Gazette de Sorel, 1866), p. 229.

H. "Onontio" (Great Mountain) was originally the Indian name for Charles Huault, Sieur de Montmagny (1583?-1653), governor of New France from 1636 to 1648. The name continued to be used for governors of New France. *Dictionary of Canadian Biography*, 1:372–374.

I. As Captain Couillard was killed in 1759, the man in this anecdote was possibly Madame Couillard's father or her late husband's younger brother, André-Thomas, whose general presence could be inferred from his signature on the Indian slave's baptismal certificate.

J. This Madame Couillard was Marie-Angélique Chaussegros de Léry (1756–1841), wife of Jean-Baptiste Couillard de l'Épinay, 1759–1808. *Bulletin des recherches historiques*, 40 (1934): 594–595.

K. The Honourable Antoine-Gaspard Couillard de l'Épinay (1787–1847), physician and legislative councillor. *Bulletin des recherches historiques*, 50 (1955): 139.

L. In his notes to chapters 5 and 6 of *Les Anciens Canadiens*, de Gaspé recounts further anecdotes about Seigneur Couillard and gives an account of his last illness.

For the historical record, he died in December 1808, nearly three months (not "about three days") after the death of La Grosse. He fell ill upon returning from Montreal, and remained in a boarding house in Quebec, too sick to be moved to Saint-Thomas. *Les Anciens Canadiens.* pp. 314–320.

Big Louis and the Legend of Indian Lorette

FOOTNOTES TO THE FIRST EDITION

1. Published in *Le Foyer canadien.*(Publisher's note.) ["Le Village indien de la Jeune Lorette (Tradition)," Vol. 4, (1866) p. 536–551.]

2. [Ohiarek8en in the original French.] The figure 8 is pronounced as "ou" in the Huron language. Ohiarek8en means snake. [For ease of reading, an anglicized spelling is used here. *Trans.*]

3. Sasennio was an adopted Iroquois name. [See de Gaspé's memoirs, *A Man of Sentiment*, p. 178, where "Big Vincent" is described as being the best runner in the seminary, and some six years older than the author.]

4. At the time, I was unaware that Ohiarekwen repaid those who advanced him money with scrupulous exactitude, hence my refusal.

5. The author is not positive as to the name of this Indian.

6. The word Otsitsot [for wolverine] means evildoer in Huron. If one credits accounts of North American aboriginals and Canadian hunters of yesteryear, the Otsitsot well

merited its name. All agreed in attributing to it a spirit of malevolence and almost diabolical mischief. It not only uncovered and destroyed the snares of the Indian hunters of old, but had apparently guessed the mechanical secret of firearms. When hunters laid aside their guns in the forest, the Otsitsot would open the flintlock pans and fill them with snow, or most often with excrement. [To this day, wolverines (really giant weasels) "are notoriously adept at working traplines." The French name, Carcajou or wolverine, was a synonym for a wily thief in popular French-Canadian parlance. *Wild Animals of North America* (Washington, D.C.: National Geographic Society, 1987), p. 259, *Glossaire du parler français au Canada* (1930; repr. Quebec: Presses de l'Université Laval, 1968), p. 173.]

7. The tradition of the Great Serpent is still alive among the Indians of Jeune Lorette. Paul Tahourhenché (Daybreak) recently told me that next morning the people of his tribe followed the trail left by the serpent as it passed through their village in the night. They lost it among the pebblestones of the Saint Charles River, about an arpent below their church. The furrow left by the serpent was as big as the trail of a huge pine dragged over the ground. "But," added Paul, "I never heard tell that the village must stay the same size because the serpent swam in the Oriawenrak."

Something always remains of childhood impressions, which makes me think that Paul was sensitive about an admission that was humiliating to his tribe, for he added, "It is true that my village stayed the same size for a long time, but within the last ten years it has grown." Paul

Tahourhenché might also have added that it is thanks to his talent, perseverance, and industry that his village is prospering and increasing at a remarkable rate. This Huron prince, while working for the good of his tribe, has built a fine, independent fortune for himself as well. What I admire about him is that he recalls with pride the Huron blood in his veins.

8. The sound of the angry rattlesnake somewhat resembles the *chichicouè*, an instrument used by the Indians to beat time when they danced.

9. Carcajou's remark reminds me of a little interchange I overheard between two confirmed drunkards who met in the Lower Town marketplace.

"Where've you been?"

"To a wedding."

"Did you have a good time?"

"*Ah, mon cher!* Three days dead drunk, passed out — *non compos mentis.*"

"You must have had a *really* good time!"

10. Ohiarek8en [Ohiarekwen] means serpent in the Huron language, and by sheer coincidence it was the Serpent [Big Louis] who recounted this legend to me.

Big Louis and the Legend of Indian Lorette

TRANSLATOR'S ANNOTATIONS

A. Possibly the fief of Saint Gabriel in the District of Quebec, a sizeable inland seigneurial holding in the area of Jeune Lorette, extending into the hinterland and including part of the Saint Charles River. See Louise Dechêne's map, "The Seigneuries," *The Historical Atlas of Canada*, 1: plate 51, fief listed as no. 17 in the District of Quebec.

In plate 47, "Native Resettlement, 1635–1800" of the same work, Bruce G. Trigger writes "In 1650 and 1651, following their defeat by the Iroquois, 600 Huron Christians came as refugees to Quebec, where their descendents still live." They had eventually migrated from Sillery to Nouvelle Lorette (about eight miles inland from Quebec City, also referred to as Jeune Lorette or Indian Lorette), a Jesuit mission, by 1697. A hunting territory of forty arpents in the neighbourhood was set aside for their use. *The Historical Atlas of Canada* (Toronto: University of Toronto Press, 1987). See also Trigger, *The Children of Aataentsic* (Montreal: McGill-Queen's Press, 1976), pp. 818–820.

B. "The first symbols of temperance placed in the hands of members [of the Société de tempérance founded in Lower Canada by Father Charles Chiniquy] were printed cards showing the name of the member, the date of his pledge, and the signature of the parish priest." Stanislas Lemay Hugolin, *Bibliographie des ouvrages concernant la tempérance* (Quebec: Imprimerie de "l'Événement," 1910), p. 20, quoting the Abbé Mailloux in "L'Ivrognerie, etc.," p. 110.

C. *Sagamité* was a porridge of hulled corn and sometimes meat, a common food among North American Indians.

D. This legend was retold by folklorist Marius Barbeau in substantially the same terms, as recounted to him by the old Huron of Jeune Lorette, Prudent Sioui. See "The Tree of Dreams," *Quebec: Where Ancient France Lingers* (Quebec: Librairie Garneau, 1936), pp. 128–144. The legend possibly had its origin in a natural phenomenon, similar to the severe earthquake that occurred in February 1663, the effects of which are still visible at Les Éboulements on the North Shore, a few miles downriver from Quebec City. The Charlevoix area is noted for the most severe earthquakes in eastern Canada.

E. The four tribes of the Huron Confederacy (Bear, Rock, Cord, and Deer, an Iroquoian agricultural people speaking the same language as their foes, the Iroquois) numbered an estimated 30,000 when the French first began to colonize North America. First the Recollets, then the Jesuits penetrated Huronia — the latter leaving to posterity the epic *Jesuit Relations.* The Hurons had already established a farming and trading economy that widened to an empire once they became middlemen between the furtrapping northern Algonkian tribes and the beaver-hungry French. Huronia, centred in the Lake Simcoe-Georgian Bay area, was relentlessly destroyed by its Iroquois trading competitors from the south, who sought furs for the Dutch and English market. Even before this, however, the Huron's once-numerous population had been reduced to some 12,000 by smallpox and measles. Bruce G. Trigger, "The French Presence in Huronia: The Structure of Franco-Huron Relations in the First half of the Seventeenth Century," *The Canadian Historical Review,* 49 (1968): 107–141. Rousseau, Jacques, and George W. Brown, "The Indians of Northeastern North America", *Dictionary of Canadian Biography, Vol. 1 (1000–1700)* (University of Toronto Press, 1966), pp. 5–12.

F. Ohiaren8ak in *Divers,* 124.

General Wolfe's Statue

FOOTNOTES TO THE FIRST EDITION

[1.] Published in *Le Foyer canadien*. (Publisher's note). ["Le Statue de Général Wolfe," vol. 4 (1866), pp. 513–523.]

[2.] This niche was occupied by the statue of Saint Jean-Baptiste. It was placed immediately above the door within easy reach. Tradition has it that for this reason the citizens feared it might be removed and profaned after the fall of Quebec, and so it was taken to the Hôpital-Général, where it is still.

[3.] The following burial certificate, which I owe to the kindness of the Abbé Tanguay, shows beyond all doubt that Hyacinthe Cholet was only eight years old when Wolfe's statue was carved:

"Register [of the parish] of Saint-Nicolas, December 23, 1820, burial of Hyacinthe Cholet, carpenter, husband of Josephte Blondin, aged 57 years, etc."

I was in fact under the impression that he had died in this parish after 1818, at the home of his wife's son, Monsieur André Bezeau.

General Wolfe's Statue

TRANSLATOR'S ANNOTATIONS

[A.] In 1857, William Fraser married Wilhelmine-Anaïs Aubert de Gaspé (b. 1834), the author's twelfth child. Fraser was co-seigneur of Rivière-du-Loup. Pierre-Georges Roy, *Le Famille Aubert de Gaspé* (Lévis: Printed by J.E. Mercier, 1907), p. 170.

B. See *A Man of Sentiment: The Memoirs of Philippe-Joseph Aubert de Gaspé (1786–1871)*, pp. 130–153. The Cholet family name is given as Cholette in the memoirs, and Chaulette by James Thompson in the journal extract referred to in note G.

C. In a paper by P.-B. Casgrain read before the Royal Society of Canada in 1904, the existence of such a picture was discussed, as was the wooden statue of General Wolfe. Casgrain felt the statue was carved around 1779 or 1780, just prior to its installation in the niche on Wolfe's Corner, while de Gaspé's considers it to have been done before 1771, based on a remark by James Thompson.

Casgrain describes how one George Hips, thought to have come to Quebec with Wolfe's army, had a butcher shop until 1774 on the Rue Saint Jean near Wolfe's Corner. He became a burgess of the city, acquired the house with the empty niche on April 20, 1780 and installed the statue then, or possibly earlier. He died in the spring of 1781, and the house was sold by "judicial sale . . . without reservation . . . save . . . the statue of General Wolfe [as Hips had expressly stated in a notarial deed]." Thus began a tradition that lasted until the early 1900s, when C.F. Sise of Montreal, president of "the Bell Company" which then owned the building, presented it to the Literary and Historical Society of Quebec for safekeeping, and there "it has found a proper shelter and a final rest in the library" on the Rue Stanislas, where visitors may still see it in 1990. The original building was acquired in 1846 by "Messrs. François Évanturel and Isaac Dorion, two brothers-in-law." Along with an adjacent building, it was torn down and replaced with "new buildings fronting the whole lots," still standing today. Dorion reinstalled the statue in a specially constructed third-storey niche on the same corner as before. Interestingly enough, during demolition Dorion found "a coloured engraving (14.3 x 10 ins.), corresponding exactly to the coloured statue, and as if intended to accompany it. This peculiar relic went afterwards to the late Honourable Frs. Évanturel, co-proprietor, and is now in the possession of his son, Colonel Evanturel, of this city, who has gathered from his father much interesting information about the effigy of General Wolfe.

"The origin and authenticity of this remarkable picture and engraving is apparent by the following engraved inscription thereon:

"From an original picture in the possession of Hery. Smith, Esq. —— Rich. Houston, Fecit.

MAJOR GENERAL JAMES WOLFE.

"*Commander* in *Chief* of His *Majesty's* Forces, on the Expedition against Quebec.

"Printed for J. Bowles & Son, in Cornhill, Eliz. Bakewell & Parker, opposite Birchin Lane, in Cornhill, J. Bowles, in St. Paul's Churchyard and Robert Sayer, at the Golden Back, in Fleet Street."

P.-B. Casgrain, "The Monument to Wolfe on the Plains of Abraham, and the Old Statue at 'Wolfe's Corner,' " offprint from *Transactions of the Royal Society of Canada*, second series (1904–1905), 10:2, pp. 215–222.

D. Assistant Commissary General James Thompson, a son of the Plains of Abraham veteran and military engineer, Sergeant James Thompson, was a member of the informal

"Club des Anciens" in Quebec City, and like de Gaspé, took a keen interest in unearthing, discussing, and recording historical details of olden-day Quebec.

E. "Mr. James Thompson, Sr., [1733–1830] was sergeant in the 78th (Fraser Highlanders), and served under Wolfe at Louisbourg and Quebec. He knew the General perfectly well, and used to speak of his kindness to all his men, and to him in particular, addressing them all in private as *'Brother soldier.'* When the Highlanders were disbanded, Mr. Thompson remained in Quebec, where he was employed in conducting divers military works. . . . Mr. Thompson lived on the opposite side of the street [from the Cholet brothers], at the south-east corner of Parlor and St. Louis Streets; the workshop of the sculptors being situate where Mr. Campbell's stables are now erected, 45–47 St. Louis Street." P.-B. Casgrain, "The Monument to Wolfe," p. 219, n. 1 and 3.

In 1828, "as last survivor of the battle on the Plains of Abraham," he was asked to help lay the foundation stone of the Wolfe and Montcalm monument in the garden of the Château Saint Louis. *Dictionary of Canadian Biography*, 6:769.

F. "Thomas-Hyacinthe & Ives, carpenters, sons of Pierre Chaulette, shipwright. . . . They were merely wood-carvers, not sculptors of statuary. P.-B. Casgrain, "The Monument to Wolfe," p. 219, n. 2.

G. As quoted from "*Thompson MSS.*, vol. 1, p. 4" by P.-B. Casgrain in "The Monument to Wolfe," pp. 219–220. Formerly in the archives of the Literary and Historical Society of Quebec, "The Journal of Sergeant James Thompson, 1758–1830" is presently housed in the Quebec Archives on the campus of Laval University in Quebec City.

H. The Abbé Henri-Raymond Casgrain (1831–1904) was a well-known historian, essayist, and biographer who encouraged and advised his kinsman, de Gaspé, in the latter's late blossoming literary career.

I. That is, Saintes. The Ile d'Oléron lies opposite La Rochelle, the Atlantic port that was the embarkation point for many French settlers bound for the New World.

Appendix

The following anecdote from de Gaspé's notes to chapter 6 of *Les Anciens Canadiens* is translated here for the first time. The reader, having been introduced to the Couillard household in "Woman of the Foxes," may enjoy this small bonus.

Several people have asked me whether my old pastor wasn't typical of a former curé of Saint-Thomas, who also baptized, married and buried three generations of parishioners. He was indeed the model that I had in mind when writing "Le Débâcle." I knew the respectable Monsieur Verreault well from my childhood until his death. He was a priest of tireless zeal, but as indulgent for others as he was hard on himself. He was a sociable man, and when in company dropped the stiff behaviour required of a priest in the course of his duties. On such occasions he became lively and amiable, giving himself up enthusiastically to the delights of conversation. However, the saintly man's good-hearted tolerance of society was sorely tried one day when supping with the local seigneur.

I have already said in an earlier note that Seigneur Couillard, father of my friend Doctor Couillard who was so well-known in the District of Quebec, was something of a pedant. He spoke Latin, English, and German as easily as his mother tongue. His memory was so prodigious that he would no doubt have been a distinguished linguist in

Europe, where he would have been able to study the languages of various foreign countries.

A regiment of German troops was stationed in Saint-Thomas. Monsieur Couillard got to know the officers, and within three months spoke German as well as they. He enjoyed using the language, and when his new friends departed was in despair at having no one to converse with in German.

On the very day of the aforementioned supper, he learned that a German doctor had arrived the previous evening and was planning to settle in Saint-Thomas. What luck! He recalled the pleasant times spent a few years earlier in the company of Doctor Oliva. This physician had married the seigneur's first cousin, and was distinguished as much for his wide literary learning as for his professional skill. No doubt all German doctors must be just like him. The seigneur called on the stranger forthwith, and was greeted with the greatest friendliness. They conversed in jaw-breaking German for two hours, and in the end Monsieur Couillard invited his new acquaintance for supper that same evening.

We were about to sit down to table when the new doctor arrived, half seas over as the English say — in other words, half drunk. The only French the unfortunate man appeared to have learned was a lexicon of all the oaths of Canadian guttersnipes, which he proceeded to recite with merciless gusto. The poor priest, seated between my mother and the mistress of the house, was unable to contain himself.

"*Dites donc un peu!*" he kept crying (this was a favourite phrase of his). "Gracious me, ladies! The good

Lord finds a man like that offensive!"

We were all appalled. Madame Couillard glared at her erudite husband, her baleful glance clearly saying, "Where did you pick up this animal?" Monsieur Couillard strove to turn the conversation entirely to German. This may have spared the curé's saintly ears, but the devil had his due all the same. Judging by the grimaces of Monsieur Couillard, a very pious man, the doctor must have sworn just as much in German as he had in French.

At last the seigneur did what he should have done in the first place: he whispered in a servant's ear, and in a few minutes we heard a vehicle stop in front of the manor door. In came a farm boy, looking rather flustered, to announce that he'd come to fetch the doctor for a dying woman. The Aesculapius made the most touching farewells. Being now completely drunk, he tearfully shook the hand of his generous host, clinging like a limpet for at least five minutes.

The venerable priest, greatly relieved to see this tiresome guest depart, cried, "Gracious me, my friends, how the good Lord is offended by that man!" Thereupon he recovered his good humour and abandoned the *schlinderlitche* to his unhappy fate.

Needless to say, as of that day all intercourse ceased between the good doctor and the polite society of the parish for the remainder of his stay.

A Selected List of Works Consulted

Aubert de Gaspé, Philippe-Joseph. *Les Anciens Canadiens*, 1863; Montreal: Librairie Beauchemin Ltée, 1913.

Aubert de Gaspé, Philippe-Joseph. *A Man of Sentiment: The Memoirs of Philippe-Joseph Aubert de Gaspé (1786–1871)*. Translated from the French by Jane Brierley. Montreal: Véhicule Press, 1988.

Barbeau, Marius. *Quebec: Where Ancient France Lingers*. Quebec: Librairie Garneau, 1936.

Beaudet, Abbé Louis. *Québec: Ses monuments anciens et modernes, ou Vade Mecum des citoyens et des touristes*. 1890; Quebec: La Société historique de Québec, 1973.

Casgrain, P.-B. "The Monument to Wolfe on the Plains of Abraham, and the Old Statue at 'Wolfe's Corner.' " offprint from *Transactions of the Royal Society of Canada*, second series (1904–1905). Ottawa: J. Hope & Sons, 1904, 10:2, 213–222.

Charland, Thomas-M. *Histoire des Abénakis d'Odanak (1635–1937)*. Montreal: Les Éditions du Lévrier, 1964.

Couillard Després, Abbé Azarie. *La Première Famille française au Canada, ses alliés et ses descendants*. Montreal: Imprimerie de l'École Catholique des Sourds-Muets, Mile-End, 1906.

Couillard Després, Abbé Azarie. *Histoire des seigneurs de la Rivière-du-Sud et de leurs alliés*. Saint-Hyacinthe: Imprimerie de "La Tribune," 1912.

Serge Gagnon. *Quebec and its Historians: 1840–1920*, trans.

Yves Brunelle. Montreal: Harvest House, 1982.

Klinck, Carl F., gen. ed. *Literary History of Canada: Canadian Literature in English*, 2d ed., vol. 1. Toronto: University of Toronto Press, 1976.

Lacourcière, Luc. "L'Enjeu des *Anciens Canadiens*," *Les Cahiers des dix* (1967) 22: 223–254.

Le Moine, J.M. *The Chronicles of the St. Lawrence.* Montreal: Dawson Bros., 1880.

Lemoine, J.M. *The Explorations of Jonathan Oldbuck, F.G.S.Q. in Eastern Latitudes. Quebec: L.J. Demers & Frère, 1889.*

Macpherson, Mrs. Daniel. *Old Memories: Amusing and Historical: A Sequel to Reminiscences of Old Quebec.* Montreal: Printed for the Author, 1890.

Maurault, Joseph Anselme. *Histoire des Abenakis, depuis 1605 jusqu'à nos jours.* Sorel: Imprimé à l'atélier typographique de la Gazette de Sorel, 1866).

Rousseau, Jacques, and George W. Brown, "The Indians of Northeastern North America," *Dictionary of Canadian Biography, Vol. 1 (1000–1700).* University of Toronto Press, 1966, pp. 5–12.

Roy, Pierre-Georges. *Bulletin des recherches historiques*, 24 (1918), 40 (1934) and 509 (1955).

Roy, Pierre-Georges. *La Famille Aubert de Gaspé.* Lévis: J.E. Mercier, 1907.

Tanguay, Abbé Cyprien. *Dictionnaire généalogique des familles canadiennes depuis la fondation de la colonie jusqu'à nos jours*, vol. 3. Montreal: Eusèbe Senécal & Fils, 1887.

Thibault, Claude. *L'Art du Québec au lendemain de la*

Conquête (1760–1790). Quebec: Musée du Québec, 1977.

Trigger, Bruce G. *The Children of Aataentsic* (Montreal: McGill-Queen's Press, 1976).

Trigger, Bruce G. "The French Presence in Huronia: The Structure of Franco-Huron Relations in the First half of the Seventeenth Century," *The Canadian Historical Review*, 49 (1968): 107–141.

Trudel, Marcel. *L'Esclavage au Canada française: Histoire et conditions de l'esclavage*. Quebec: Presses de l'Université de Laval, 1960.

Vachon, André, with Victorin Chabot and André Desrosier. *Taking Root: Canada from 1700 to 1760*. Ottawa: Public Archives of Canada, 1985.

Wallis, Wilson D. and Ruth Sawtell Wallis. *The Malecite Indians of New Brunswick*. Ottawa: Dept. of Northern Affairs and Natural Resources, 1957.

Index